THE COMPLETE IDIOT'S GUIDE®

Music
Dictionary

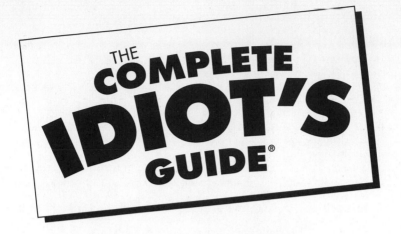

Music Dictionary

by Dr. Stanford Felix

ALPHA

A member of Penguin Group (USA) Inc.

ALPHA BOOKS

Published by the Penguin Group

Penguin Group (USA) Inc., 375 Hudson Street, New York, New York 10014, USA

Penguin Group (Canada), 90 Eglinton Avenue East, Suite 700, Toronto, Ontario M4P 2Y3, Canada (a division of Pearson Penguin Canada Inc.)

Penguin Books Ltd., 80 Strand, London WC2R 0RL, England

Penguin Ireland, 25 St. Stephen's Green, Dublin 2, Ireland (a division of Penguin Books Ltd.)

Penguin Group (Australia), 250 Camberwell Road, Camberwell, Victoria 3124, Australia (a division of Pearson Australia Group Pty. Ltd.)

Penguin Books India Pvt. Ltd., 11 Community Centre, Panchsheel Park, New Delhi—110 017, India

Penguin Group (NZ), 67 Apollo Drive, Rosedale, North Shore, Auckland 1311, New Zealand (a division of Pearson New Zealand Ltd.)

Penguin Books (South Africa) (Pty.) Ltd., 24 Sturdee Avenue, Rosebank, Johannesburg 2196, South Africa

Penguin Books Ltd., Registered Offices: 80 Strand, London WC2R 0RL, England

International Standard Book Number: 978-1-59257-997-6
Library of Congress Catalog Card Number: 2009943481

12 11 10   8 7 6 5 4 3 2 1

Interpretation of the printing code: The rightmost number of the first series of numbers is the year of the book's printing; the rightmost number of the second series of numbers is the number of the book's printing. For example, a printing code of 10-1 shows that the first printing occurred in 2010.

Printed in the United States of America

Note: This publication contains the opinions and ideas of its author. It is intended to provide helpful and informative material on the subject matter covered. It is sold with the understanding that the author and publisher are not engaged in rendering professional services in the book. If the reader requires personal assistance or advice, a competent professional should be consulted.

The author and publisher specifically disclaim any responsibility for any liability, loss, or risk, personal or otherwise, which is incurred as a consequence, directly or indirectly, of the use and application of any of the contents of this book.

Most Alpha books are available at special quantity discounts for bulk purchases for sales promotions, premiums, fund-raising, or educational use. Special books, or book excerpts, can also be created to fit specific needs.

For details, write: Special Markets, Alpha Books, 375 Hudson Street, New York, NY 10014.

Publisher: *Marie Butler-Knight*
Associate Publisher: *Mike Sanders*
Senior Managing Editor: *Billy Fields*
Acquisitions Editors: *Karyn Gerhard, Tom Stevens*
Senior Development Editor: *Phil Kitchel*

Production Editor: *Kayla Dugger*
Copy Editor: *Lisanne Jensen*
Cover Designer: *Rebecca Batchelor*
Book Designer: *Trina Wurst*
Layout: *Ayanna Lacey*
Proofreader: *John Etchison*

Dedicated to the memory of Dr. Jeffrey Hodapp (1957–2009), an extraordinary friend, colleague, and musician.

Contents

Introduction

Dictionaries have always been a main source of inspiration and discovery for me. I would find the word I was looking for and then maybe see a picture on the side and start looking at that, then see another interesting word, and soon I'd learned a lot more than I had intended to. You can't do that with online dictionaries. You only get the word you want (in the middle of a lot of pop-up ads). So when I started writing this dictionary, I wanted to give the beginning and intermediate musician an easily accessible source for only the most interesting and necessary music terms they would need.

How to Use This Dictionary

It's easy to find the term or symbol you are looking for in this dictionary. Why look through a lot of musical terms that are irrelevant to your needs? Most people don't have time to flip through a thick dictionary that's full of terms only doctoral music students need to know. Believe me, I've gone that route, and it's not necessary to know the name of some archaic medieval instrument or an obscure treatise from the renaissance period. Only the most commonly used terms are covered, and I will often abbreviate the country from which the term originated and for which a translation is given. (For example, It. = Italian, G. = German, F. = French, and L. = Latin.) Most importantly, I will use definitions that are clear and to the point.

What makes this dictionary easier to use than others is the "meaning within a meaning" style I have opted to use for many of the words. In most dictionaries, a definition of a term uses more unfamiliar words than the actual term (there is definitely a lot of jargon in music). Although this is hard to avoid, I often define what those definitions actually mean—in layman's terms, and in the same paragraph. You want a dictionary that makes things easier, not harder.

From A to Z

I think you'll find this dictionary is very user-friendly. I've included only the most used and relevant classical, jazz, and rock and music theory terms; musical notation definitions; instrumental names and descriptions; and the most famous performers, composers, and bands. If you want to see who else is playing the same kind of music you are, and the names of a few of their songs, I've included many names of different kinds of musical styles and genres, performers who play them, and titles of some of the most famous songs from these styles so you can check it out for yourself. I even give you a lot of jazz and rock slang that will catch you up on the "language" of being a musician.

The Visual Index

My favorite part is the Visual Index in Appendix B, which names a musical note or symbol you would find in a written piece of music and tells you where in the dictionary to find the definition and its usage. So now, when you see a symbol or note in a piece of music, you can just look it up in the Visual Index. Very handy.

And More!

Online guitar, piano, instrumental, and theory lessons are helpful in getting you started playing, so I've actually included a number of online and book-based instructional sites in the resource section of this dictionary.

Although I think of music as the best vocation there is, there is also a lot of work involved in getting as good as you can be. I hope you find this dictionary helpful in making your musical ambitions more fruitful.

Acknowledgments

I would like to acknowledge the wonderful support of my editor Karyn Gerhard and literary agent Marilyn Allen. Also thanks to Dr. Jeffrey Hodapp for his invaluable contribution. Most of all, I would like to thank my wonderful wife, Antonia, for all her love and support. Her eye for detail and encouraging words were a great help.

Trademarks

All terms mentioned in this book that are known to be or are suspected of being trademarks or service marks have been appropriately capitalized. Alpha Books and Penguin Group (USA) Inc. cannot attest to the accuracy of this information. Use of a term in this book should not be regarded as affecting the validity of any trademark or service mark.

A Pitch name for the sixth step in the C-Major scale. The sixth white note above the piano's middle C.

a cappella A musical term indicating there is no accompaniment used to back up a solo line or choral piece.

A section The part of a song in which the main melody first appears.

a tempo If the tempo of the song being performed has changed, "a tempo" indicates to the performer a return to the established tempo.

A440 Also called "concert A," the A above middle C on the keyboard. This is the audio frequency used to tune musical instruments, established by the American Standards Association in 1936.

AABA form A song structure often used in popular music that follows this specific format: A, first verse (main melody); A, second verse (same or different words put to the same music); B, the chorus of the song (different melody than A); and A, third verse (repeats the original melody).

ABBA   Pop band from Sweden formed in 1972. ABBA uses the first letter from the four members' names (Agnetha, Björn, Benny, and Anni-Frid). They have sold more than 370 million records around the world and are considered one of world's best-selling musical groups.

Abduction from the Seraglio   German opera composed in three acts by Wolfgang Amadeus Mozart, with libretto by Christoph Bretzner. Produced in 1782 in Vienna, the setting is Turkey in the sixteenth century.

absolute music   Music representing or describing nothing in particular. It uses no text and has no reference to images or stories. The opposite of *program music.*

absolute pitch   A person's ability to exactly identify the rate of vibration of a certain pitch, using no reference to other sounded pitches in the musical scale, and give it a name. Although it is no indication of musical talent, it is more often found in people with some musical experience.

abstract music   *See* absolute music.

AC/DC   A hard rock/heavy metal band from Sydney, Australia, which formed in 1973 and put out their first album, *High Voltage,* in 1975. Nominated for one American Music Award, five Grammy Awards, and one MTV Video Music Award, one of AC/DC's most famous songs was "Highway to Hell."

academy   The name used throughout history for artistic societies and musical organizations.

accelerando (It., accelerated)   A notation in the music for the performer to play faster.

accent   An emphasized chord or note.

accentuation   The proper use of accents, especially in music with text.

acciaccatura   An ornamental note that is played at the same time as the principle note a half or whole step above. This "crushed" sound adds dissonance to the harmony.

accidental   A musical sign used to chromatically alter or cancel individual notes. The symbols are ♯, sharp; ♭, flat; ♯♯, double sharp; ♭♭, double flat; and ♮, natural.

accompaniment   The musical background to a solo line. For example, a solo vocalist with orchestra or piano or a flute soloist with guitar accompaniment.

accordion   Musical instrument consisting of two rectangular end pieces connected with a folding bellows. Modern instruments have a keyboard on the right side to play the melody and buttons on the left side to play bass notes and chords. Inside, it has valves called pallets that open when the keys are pressed, causing air to flow across brass or steel reeds and produce the sound within the body. Sometimes called a *squeezebox* and related to the English made *concertina*. The earliest instruments were made in 1822.

acid jazz   A genre of jazz that combines electronic dance music, funk, and hip-hop. Developed in the United Kingdom in the 1980s and '90s, acid jazz is considered a revival of sorts of jazz funk and jazz fusion and is used by bands such as Jamiroquai and Incognito.

acid rock   Also called psychedelic rock, it is the music most associated with the San Francisco Bay area and hippie scene of the late 1960s and early 1970s. Acid rock was mostly defined by its ability to enhance the LSD and drug experience. Bands famous for this type of music include Jefferson Airplane and the Grateful Dead and artists such as Jimi Hendrix and Janis Joplin.

Acis and Galatea   An Italian dramatic cantata written by G. F. Handel around 1720, with a story based on the Greek myth.

acoustic bass   Developed in the early 1960s by Ernie Ball to be played with acoustic guitars. Similar to the guitarron used in mariachi bands, it has four strings and a deep, hollow wooden body.

acoustic guitar   Made with a hollow wooden body and 6 or 12 strings. When the strings are strummed or picked, the sound is increased by the soundboard and hollow cavity after the vibration from the bridge makes it vibrate. There are many variations of guitars that use either nylon or steel strings. May be amplified by either piezo or magnetic pickups or by a microphone.

acoustic instrument   A musical instrument that is amplified by natural means or handcrafted to a shape that will intensify the original vibration, such as an acoustic guitar.

acoustics   Science that includes the production, effects, and transmission of audible sound.

action   Mechanism on a musical instrument that transmits the motion of the hands or feet to the part of the instrument that produces the sound, such as the key mechanism on a piano.

ad libitum (ad lib)   A direction in the score that gives the performer the choice of changing tempo, omitting a part, or creating a part of the song with an invention of his or her own.

adagio   A slow tempo designation set between the faster tempo of andante and the slower tempo of largo. Also used as the name for the slow second movement in a symphony or sonata.

Adams, John (b. 1947)   An American Pulitzer Prize–winning composer who wrote largely in the minimalistic style (steady beat, simple musical material, and much repetition). Famous compositions include the operas *Nixon in China* (1987) and *Doctor Atomic* (2005) and the choral piece *On the Transmigration of Souls* (2002), written to honor the victims of the September 11, 2001, World Trade Center attacks.

"Adeste, Fideles"   Also known today as the Christmas song "O Come, All Ye Faithful." Published in 1750 with words and music by John F. Wade.

Adieux, Les   Also called the *Farewell Sonata*. Written for piano, opus 81A, in E-flat, by Beethoven in 1809.

aeolian mode   The ninth of 12 musical church modes. Known today as a diatonic scale.

aerophone   A musical instrument that makes sound by the use of air. Woodwind and brass instruments are all aerophones.

aerophor   A device invented in 1912 by Bernhard Samuel that provides additional air to the player of a wind instrument when he or she cannot hold a tone long enough or play a long legato line without breathing in the middle. The object is a small bellows operated by the player's foot that supplies the air through a mouthpiece at the end of a tube.

Aerosmith   An American rock band that launched in Boston in 1970. Using a blues-rock hybrid sound, Aerosmith was regarded as one of the best and most popular rock bands in the 1970s. After a falling-out in 1979, the group got back together again in 1984 and regained their popularity through the 2000s. Some of their most famous songs include "Walk This Way," "Sweet Emotion," "Janie's Got a Gun," and the Oscar-nominated hit "I Don't Want to Miss a Thing" from the film *Armageddon*.

aesthetics of music   Originating from the Greek word *aisthesis*, or "feeling, sensation," the study of how music affects the human intellect and senses.

Africaine, L' (F., *The African Woman*)   Opera written in five acts by Giacomo Meyerbeer, with libretto by Eugène Scribe. First produced and performed in Paris in 1865, L'Africaine is set in Lisbon and Madagascar at the end of the fifteenth century.

agitato   Italian musical term indicating agitation or excitement.

AGMA (American Guild of Musical Artists)   An American labor union that represents the women and men involved in the creation of opera, choral works, and dance. Its sister union is the Actors' Equity Association. Anyone performing in major American dance or opera companies must have an AGMA contract.

aguinaldo   Religious Spanish folk song sung throughout Latin America.

Aïda   Italian opera written in four acts by Giuseppe Verdi, with libretto by Antonio Ghislanzoni. Produced in Cairo in 1871 for the opening celebration of the Suez Canal, the setting is Egypt during the time of the pharaohs.

al finé (It., to the end)   Indicates repeating the composition from the beginning (da capo sign) or somewhere in the middle (dal segno sign) to the end (finé).

D.C. al Fine

Albert Herring   Comic opera written in three acts by Benjamin Britten, with libretto by Eric Crozier. Produced in East Sussex, England, at the Glyndebourne Festival Opera in 1947 and set in nineteenth-century England.

alberti bass   Broken-chorded accompaniment played in the pianist's left hand. Named after Domenico Alberti (1710–1740).

album   A collection of music to be distributed to the public. Originally called a "record album" and distributed on 78–RPM (revolutions per minute) phonograph records in the early twentieth century, albums have used different formats over the years: 78–RPM and 33⅓–RPM vinyl, reel-to-reel magnetic tape, cassette tape, 8-track tape, CD, DVD audio, MP3, and AAC music files and streaming audio.

aleatory music   Sometimes called "chance" or "dice" music, the composer incorporates elements of unpredictability and chance in the composition and/or its performance by giving the performer certain liberties of interpretation. John Cage's *Music of Changes* (1951) is an example of this type of composition.

Alexander technique   Formulated by Frederick Matthias Alexander (1869–1955), this method studies body coordination and is helpful in improving muscle flexibility and posture and helps eliminate or reduce habits that cause muscle tension. The seminal text is *The Use of the Self* (1984) by F. M. Alexander and Wilfred Barlow.

alla breve   An Italian musical tempo marking that indicates the half note instead of the quarter note gets counted as one beat. The key signature would then be 2/2 instead of 4/4. *See* cut time.

allegretto   A musical tempo between andante (moderate speed) and allegro (fast speed).

allegro   Tempo marking indicating a fast speed.

alleluia   An elaborate chant used in the Proper of the Mass.

Alpert, Herb (b. 1935)   An American trumpet player and leader of the group "Herb Alpert and the Tijuana Brass." His group won 8 Grammy Awards, 15 gold albums (more than 500,000 copies sold), and 14 platinum albums (more than 1,000,000 copies sold). Two of these hits were "A Taste of Honey" and "Tijuana Taxi." "Spanish Flea" and "Whipped Cream" were both used on TV's *The Dating Game*.

Also Sprach Zarathustra   Written by Richard Strauss, a symphonic poem, opus 30, written in 1896. Famous for being the title song in Stanley Kubrick's movie *2001: A Space Odyssey*.

alternative rock   Developed in the 1980s, "alt-rock" grew from the independent British and American punk rock and New Wave music scenes, with subgenres such as gothic rock, indie pop, and grunge. Popular alternative groups include the Cure, R.E.M., and Nirvana.

altissimo (It., very high)   Indicates the highest range of a wood-wind instrument.

alto   Choral term for mezzo-soprano, the lowest female voice next to contralto. Also used to indicate a certain size of instrument, such as the alto saxophone.

alto clef   A clef designed with two curves that meet in the middle on the third line of the staff, which is the note C. Used especially in notating music for the viola.

Amahl and the Night Visitors   Opera composed in one act by Gian Carlo Menotti to his own libretto. The first opera commissioned for television, it was produced in New York City on NBC on Christmas Eve 1951. Set during the birth of Jesus in Bethlehem.

ambient music   Musical compositions of an atmospheric or un-obtrusive quality. Often used in airports and restaurants to create a pleasant or peaceful "ambiance" for the people present.

Amelia Goes to the Ball   English opera in one act composed by Gian Carlo Menotti with his own libretto. Produced in Philadelphia in 1937, it is set in Milan in 1910.

American Bandstand   A television show hosted by Dick Clark from 1957 to 1990 featuring teenagers dancing to the latest Top 40 hits. Many of the top bands of the day appeared or began their careers on the show.

American Guild of Organists   National professional organization founded in 1896 to serve the organ and choral fields.

amplification   When a sound source is made stronger or louder artificially (with an electrical PA system using a microphone, amplifier, and speakers) or with a natural structure, such as a cave.

amplitude   Also called intensity or loudness, one of the four properties of musical tone, the others being frequency (pitch), timbre (tone color), and duration.

anacrusis   A pickup note or pickup measure that begins the song with a lead-up to the first measure.

analysis   The study of music theory and composition techniques such as structure, form, harmony, melody, style, phrasing, and orchestration. Analysis plays an important part in musical instruction.

andante   Tempo marking in music that indicates the performer should play the piece at a moderate speed.

Anderson, Marian (1897–1993)   An American mezzo-soprano, she was the first African American to sing at the Metropolitan Opera House in New York City. She spent most of her career singing recitals and concerts in the United States and Europe and was an important figure in the battle against racial injustice, breaking down many color barriers in the arts.

Andrea Chénier   French opera in four acts written by Umberto Giordano, with libretto by Luigi Illica. First produced in 1896 in Milan; the story is set during the French Revolution.

Anglican Church Music   Sacred music composed for choirs and congregations of the Church of England.

anonymous   The designation for an unknown composer.

anthem   An English choral piece composed with religious text from the Bible and used in the worship services of Protestant churches. Also, a song used by a group of people to celebrate a common cause or country, such as a national anthem.

Anthony and Cleopatra   English opera in three acts written by Samuel Barber, with libretto by Franco Zeffirelli. Composed for the opening of the new Metropolitan Opera House in New York City in September 1966. The work is set in Alexandria and Rome in the first century B.C.E.

anticipation   When one or more tones in an upcoming chord is sounded early, creating a temporary dissonance. The opposite of suspension.

antiphon   A sung response to a psalm (a text from the Old Testament) in a Catholic mass or vespers religious service. There are more than 1,000 Gregorian chant antiphons.

antiphonal   When two or more choruses alternate singing. Often used to give an echo effect or emphasize the text. Also called *polychoral*.

anvil   A percussion instrument made of a small steel bar that is struck by a metal or hard wooden mallet.

Anything Goes   Broadway musical produced on November 21, 1934, at the Alvin Theatre in New York City. Music and lyrics by Cole Porter and book (story) written by P. G. Wodehouse, Guy Bolton, Russell Crouse, and Howard Lindsay. Much of the setting takes place aboard a luxury liner on its way from New York City to Southampton, England. Some of the more popular tunes include "I Get a Kick Out of You," "Easy to Love," "It's De-Lovely," and "Anything Goes."

Apollo Club   Amateur male singing organization in America. Some of the most ambitious Apollo clubs are found in Boston, Brooklyn, Chicago, Cincinnati, and St. Louis.

Appalachian Spring   An orchestral suite and ballet music written by Aaron Copland and premiering in 1944. It was commissioned by dancer and choreographer Martha Graham. Since its first performance, it has been used in hundreds of TV and radio commercials and movies. Part of the suite, the Shaker song "Simple Gifts," is one of America's most recognized melodies.

"Appassionata, Sonata"   The popular name given to a piano sonata, opus 57, in F minor, written by Ludwig van Beethoven in 1805.

appoggiatura   An ornamental note that anticipates the following note from the lower or upper second. Sometimes called a grace note.

arabesque   A whimsical title for songs that are more informal or casual. The term was used by composers such as Robert Schumann (1810–1856) and Claude Debussy (1862–1918).

architectural acoustics   Used for the construction of concert halls, opera houses, and recording studios to help optimize their acoustical properties (resonance, reflection, and echo).

Argento, Dominick (b. 1927)   A leading American composer of 14 lyric operas, including *Postcards from Morocco*, *The Masque of Angels*, *Casanova's Homecoming*, and *The Aspern Papers*. He is also known for his choral music and his song cycle *From the Diary of Virginia Woolf*, which won the Pulitzer Prize for Music in 1975.

aria   An expressive melody usually associated but not necessarily performed by a singer. Usually associated with a solo voice composition (song) used in opera, oratorios, cantatas, and concerts with an orchestral or keyboard accompaniment.

Ariadne auf Naxos   German opera composed in one act and a prologue by Richard Strauss, with libretto by Hugo von Hofmannsthal. First produced in Stuttgart, Germany, in 1912, the opera setting is Vienna in the eighteenth century and Naxos in Ancient Greece.

arietta   Shorter than an aria (operatic song) and with less-elaborate notation.

arioso   A lyrical and expressive recitative (sung speech) used primarily in opera that features the qualities of both a recitative and an aria.

Armstrong, Louis (1901–1971)   Nicknamed Satchmo, he was one of the most influential American jazz musicians of the twentieth century. Armstrong was known not only for his cornet and trumpet playing but also for his raspy singing voice, scat singing (improvising on nonsense words), and stage presence (which included his facial expressions and signature handkerchief). Born in New Orleans to a very poor African American family, he grew up working in dance halls where he crafted his individual performing technique and style. He was awarded a posthumous Grammy Lifetime Achievement Award in 1972 and had 11 of his recordings entered in the Grammy Hall of Fame in 1973. Three of these songs were "St. Louis Blues," "Hello Dolly," and "What a Wonderful World."

arpeggiated chord   *See* arpeggio.

arpeggio   The notes of a chord played one after another, either from the top downward or from the bottom upward . Often played on a piano or harp. Also called an *arpeggiated chord*.

arrangement   The product of changing an existing melody or piece of music by adding different compositional techniques such as modulations, transitions, or new thematic material to give the piece musical variety.

arranger   An individual who takes a composition meant for one instrument or medium and changes it to work for another instrument or medium.

art music   Music originating from the classical music tradition that requires more effort by the listener to appreciate than popular music.

art rock   A form of rock music written to appeal more intellectually or musically and more for listening than for dancing. Art rock usually uses more piano or keyboard than guitar, consists of a longer structure with several different themes, and often tells a story with its lyrics. Examples include the rock opera *Tommy*, by the Who, and *Hamburger Concerto*, by the British rock group Focus.

art song   A song usually written for piano and voice by a trained composer, compared to writers of folk or popular songs.

articulation   The clarity used to indicate aspects of a musical composition, such as phrasing, breathing, attack, and legato or staccato. Used in conjunction with phrasing to express the musicality and emotion of a piece.

ASCAP   American Society of Composers, Authors, and Publishers. A society founded by Victor Herbert in 1914 to protect performing rights and copyrights.

assai   An Italian musical description indicating "much" or "very."

Astaire, Fred (1899–1987)   Broadway dancer, singer, and actor. His stage and film career spanned 76 years and 31 film musicals.

atonal   An absence of tonality in a musical composition, as in the serial and 12-tone compositions composed by Arnold Schoenberg.

attacca (It., attack)   Starting a musical phrase with promptness and intent resulting in a precise entry of the music being played.

audiophile   A person whose hobby is listening to recorded music at the highest level of fidelity using the highest-quality audio components. Magazines such as *Hi-Fi World* and *Stereophile* are publications catering to the interests of the audiophile.

audition   A scheduled performance in which a performer is given a hearing by judges or potential employers who measure their talents and abilities and either reward or dismiss the auditionee.

augmented interval   One of the five types of intervals (distance between two pitches) in a diatonic scale (seven-note musical scale consisting of five whole steps and two half steps). The five intervals include diminished, minor, perfect, major, and augmented. In the key of C, the augmented intervals are C–D♯ (3 half steps), C–E♯ (5 half steps), C–F♯ (6 half steps), C–G♯ (8 half steps), C–A♯ (10 half steps), C–B♯ (12 half steps), and C–C♯ (13 half steps).

aulos   Ancient Greece's most important woodwind instrument. Similar to a modern-day oboe with a double reed and from 4 to 15 holes.

autoharp   Often used in folk music, the autoharp is a member of the zither family. It most commonly has 36 or 37 strings and is strummed with a finger or pick while the other hand pushes chord bars attached to dampers that, when depressed, mute all strings except those of the preferred chord.

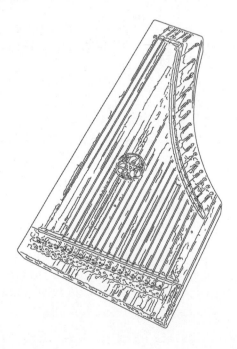

A

avant-garde jazz A combination of avant-garde music and jazz, distinguished by a musical structure with improvisation played over it. Musicians such as Charlie Parker, Miles Davis, and John Coltrane all played this form of jazz.

Ave Maria Latin for "Hail Mary," this traditional Catholic prayer has been set to music by many composers—two of the most famous being Franz Schubert and Charles Gounod.

axe A jazz term for a saxophone or other musical instrument.

B 1. Pitch name for the seventh step in a C-Major scale. 2. The white key below C on the piano.

B section The second section of a composition in which the music sharply contrasts with the first section in melody, harmony, and sometimes rhythm.

B-minor Mass One of Johann Sebastian Bach's masterpieces composed for orchestra, chorus, and soloists and considered one of the greatest achievements of classical music.

Babbitt, Milton (b. 1916) American composer who is a pioneer in electronic and serial music. He studied with Roger Sessions in the late 1930s and was on the music faculty at both Princeton University and the Julliard School. He composed what were considered the earliest examples of total serialism. *See* serial music.

Bach, Carl Philipp Emanuel (1714–1788) German composer and the second son of Johann Sebastian Bach and Maria Barbara Bach. He followed in his father's footsteps and became one of the most influential composers of his time, being an essential influence in the transition between two different musical periods, baroque (1685–1750) and classical (1750–1820).

Bach, Johann Sebastian (1685–1750)   One of the most famous composers of all time, his orchestral, choir, and solo instrument works defined all aspects of music in the baroque period (1600–1750). Although he was not well known as a composer during his lifetime, his music was revived in the early nineteenth century—and he is now considered one of the world's greatest musicians. During his lifetime, he was well known throughout Europe as a highly respected organist. He came from a long line of musicians and learned how to play violin and harpsichord from his father, organ from his uncle, and clavichord from his oldest brother, with whom he lived from age 10 after his mother and father died. Bach married twice and had 20 children in all, with 9 living to adulthood and 5 of them going on to have musical careers.

Bacharach, Burt (b. 1928)   American pianist and composer of popular music. He wrote 70 Top-40 hits in his career and performed with many of the great singers of the second half of the twentieth century. Some of his most famous songs are "What the World Needs Now Is Love," "What's New Pussycat?" "Alfie," "Do You Know the Way to San Jose?", and "Raindrops Keep Fallin' on My Head."

backbeat   A rhythmic style used in rock and roll that places a sharp, percussive effect on the second and fourth beats of a 4/4 measure. Along with the rock rhythmic layer, it forms the foundation of rock rhythm.

bagatelle   A short, light piece written for piano.

bagpipe   An instrument usually associated with Scotland and made of a windbag connected to two reed vibrators, with one being used as a drone (one note or chord continually sounded throughout the entire piece) and the other for the melody. The performer blows into a pipe containing finger holes and intermittently pumps a small pair of bellows under his or her arm to fill the bag with air.

balalaika A Russian string instrument with a triangle-shaped body and three strings.

ballad A narrative popular song that tells a romantic and sometimes tragic story. Usually written in common meter (a poetic rhythm), a ballad rhymes on the ends of the second and fourth lines. Today, the term ballad is often applied to any kind of slow popular song.

Ballad of Baby Doe, The American opera in two acts composed by Douglas Moore, with libretto by John Latouche. Premiered in Colorado with the Central City Opera Company in 1956. The story takes place in both Colorado and Washington, D.C.

ballet Classical dance performed with a dancing troupe and accompanied by music without singing or narration. Ballets are written for dance performance alone and also as part of other works, such as opera and musical theater. Famous ballet music includes the *Nutcracker Suite* and *Swan Lake* by Pyotr Ilyich Tchaikovsky (1840–1893) and *Rodeo* by Aaron Copland (1900–1990). Rogers and Hammerstein's *Carousel* is one of several classic American musicals that contains a ballet.

band Any group of instrumentalists who collaborates to play music.

banjo A string instrument with five to nine strings and a body with a long neck. With or without frets, the banjo has a one-headed drum stretched over a round, hollow body. Often used in country, bluegrass, and folk music. Popular examples of the banjo sound are found in the theme songs from the TV show *The Beverly Hillbillies* and the movie *Deliverance*.

bar Also called a measure, a bar is a unit of musical time containing a set amount of beats separated by vertical bar lines.

bar line The vertical line on a staff of music that separates the composition into measures (bars). Different types of bar lines mean different things: a double bar means that a new section follows, a thick and thin bar with two dots beside them indicates repeating the section, and a thin and thick bar with no dots signifies the end of the piece.

barbershop quartet A group of four male or female vocalists who sing four-part harmony a cappella (without accompaniment) to tunes made popular in the late nineteenth and early twentieth centuries.

Barbiere di Siviglia, Il (It., *The Barber of Seville*) Italian opera composed in two acts by Gioachino Rossini, with libretto by Cesare Sterbini. The opera was produced in St. Petersburg, Russia, in 1782 and is set in Seville, Spain, in the eighteenth century. It is one of the most popular of the comic operas.

baritone   The male voice type between tenor and bass. The range of the baritone voice is from two Fs below middle C to the first G above middle C. Types include dramatic baritone, Helden baritone, lyric baritone, and bass-baritone. The term also applies to instruments such as the baritone horn and baritone saxophone.

baritone clef   A musical symbol that indicates the placement of notes on a staff. One of three F-clefs, it is rarely used in modern notation.

baritone horn   Often simply called the baritone, it is a member of the brass family of instruments. It's commonly confused with the euphonium, although it has a smaller bore, tighter wrap, and smaller bell. Throughout the twentieth century, it was the more prevalent of the two in American school bands but is now being replaced by the euphonium. Like the euphonium, the baritone horn is pitched in B♭ and has three valves.

baritone saxophone   A single-reed woodwind instrument tuned in the key of E♭ like its smaller brother, the alto saxophone. The "bari sax" is the lowest of the saxophones used today (the bass saxophone being fairly obsolete), with the tenor, alto, and soprano saxophones pitched progressively higher. Used in symphonic and jazz bands.

baroque period   The musical era between the renaissance and classical periods, running from approximately 1600 to 1750 (the death of Johann Sebastian Bach). The common use of chromaticism, dynamic rhythms, expressive melodies, improvisation, ornamentation, and a repeated bass line emphasized the musical characteristics of the baroque period. Some of the important baroque composers, from earliest to latest, include Claudio Monteverdi (1567–1643), Arcangelo Corelli (1653–1713), Antonio Vivaldi (1678–1741), Johann Sebastian Bach (1685–1750), and George Frideric Handel (1685–1759).

Bartók, Béla (1881–1945)   Hungarian composer and pianist. He and Franz Liszt (1811–1886) are regarded as Hungary's greatest composers. His music was inspired by the modes, themes, and rhythmic patterns of Hungary and later of other nationalities, which made him the father of musical nationalism. He believed that folk music could appear in serious music to enrich it and should in no case be atonal. He and his friend Zóltan Kodály (1882–1967) can be said to have started the field of ethnomusicology, the study of ethnic and local music.

Bartók pizzicato   A strong pizzicato technique used by Hungarian composer Béla Bartók in some, but not all, of his compositions. Used on any of the bowed string family, it allows the string to slap against the fingerboard for more of an effect than an actual tone.

Basie, William "Count" (1904–1984)   American composer and jazz pianist. Known as Count Basie, he was one of the most vital jazz bandleaders of all time. He led the Count Basie Orchestra for nearly 50 years and, as an African American, was instrumental in breaking down race barriers by recording with singers such as Frank Sinatra, Tony Bennett, and Bing Crosby.

bass   1. The lowest male voice type. There are four types of basses: the bass-baritone, basso contante, basso profundo, and basso buffo. Approximate vocal range extends from two Cs below middle C to the F just above middle C. 2. The lowest and largest musical instruments, including the string bass and bass clarinet. 3. In musical composition, the lowest note, which determines the harmonic structure of the piece.

bass clef   In music notation, the most common staff used for bass and baritone voice, low brass, woodwind, and string instruments. Also, the staff used for the left hand in keyboard music.

bass-baritone   Male singer's vocal range between bass and baritone, consisting of vocal colors and timbre characteristic of both.

basso continuo   A bass accompaniment that runs through an entire composition in works from the late Renaissance, baroque, and early classical periods. Also called "throughbass" or "thoroughbass," it is often played by lower strings, organ, or harpsichord and is the basis for the harmonies in the piece.

bassoon   A double-reed woodwind instrument played most prominently in orchestras and chamber music groups. Its long, u-shaped tube contains holes and attached keys and measures approximately 4 feet long. Music for the bassoon is written in the tenor and bass registers and is known for its agility, tone color, and wide, 4-octave range. Famous examples of bassoon solos appear in Rimsky-Korsakov's *Scheherazade* and the opening melody in Stravinsky's *The Rite of Spring*.

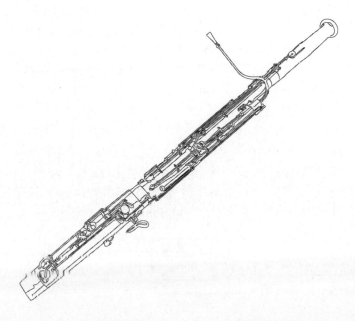

baton   A stick used by musical ensemble conductors to conduct a musical performance. Made of fiberglass or wood with a wooden or cork hand grip. Baton lengths vary from 10 to 24 inches.

Bayreuth Festival   A yearly event devoted to the operas of Richard Wagner (1813–1883), which the composer himself launched in 1876. Wagner designed the theatre in which the festival is held, and fans from around the world flock to attend performances of *Parsifal, Das Rheingold* (G., *The Rhine Gold*), and his other operas.

Beach, Amy (1867–1944)   The first critically successful female American composer and pianist. She composed large works such as the *Mass in E Flat Major* in 1892 and *Gaelic Symphony* in 1896. A child prodigy, she had only one year of musical training and was otherwise self-taught.

Beach Boys, The   American rock band formed in 1961 and popular for their lyrics about Southern California youth and their love of surfing and cars. The group's signature close vocal harmonies and innovative style earned them 36 Top-40 hits and 56 Hot-100 hits. Tallying album and singles sales, *Billboard* magazine ranked the Beach Boys as the number-one selling American band in history. In 2001, they received a Grammy Lifetime Achievement Award, and in 2004 *Rolling Stone* magazine ranked them 12 on their 100 Greatest Artists of All Time list. Their hit songs include "Surfin' USA," "Wouldn't It Be Nice," and "God Only Knows" (the theme song for HBO's hit series *Big Love*).

beam   A musical notation made of a thick line that connects a series of eighth notes or musical notes of a shorter value (using multiple beams).

Beatles, The   British pop and rock band that started in Liverpool, England, in 1960. The most commercially successful band in the history of pop music, the Beatles have sold more than one billion records. The band consisted of Paul McCartney (vocals, bass guitar, and songwriter), John Lennon (vocals, rhythm guitar, and songwriter), George Harrison (vocals, lead guitar, and songwriter), and Ringo Starr (vocals, drums, and songwriter).

More albums by the Beatles were sold in the United States than by any other band. They released more than 40 number-one albums, singles, and EPs (extended play) and were ranked 1 in *Rolling Stone* magazine's 2004 list of the 100 Greatest Artists of All Time. Although their musical style originally incorporated 1950s rock and roll and skiffle (a type of folk music), the group later used several musical genres—from psychedelic rock to Tin Pan Alley. Nicknamed "The Lads from Liverpool" and "The Fab Four," their long hairstyles, clothes, and music created a frenzy called Beatlemania among teenagers. Their most famous tunes include "A Hard Day's Night," "I Want to Hold Your Hand," and "Hey Jude." The Beatles broke up on April 10, 1970, but all went on to have successful solo careers.

bebop   A jazz form identified by improvisation and a fast tempo. Developed in the early 1940s, it arose from the earlier jazz style of swing and was made popular by musicians such as saxophonist Charlie Parker and trumpeter Dizzy Gillespie. Bebop was emotionally and structurally more complex than swing and used more intricate melodies, a rhythm section that played underlying harmonies and strict rhythms, and improvised solos using the chords of the tune. This type of jazz is usually played by small groups and meant more for listening than dancing.

Bee Gees, The   A trio of brothers (Barry, Maurice, and Robin—the Brothers Gibb) from Australia whose singing won them nine Grammy Awards, five American Music Awards, and one World Music Award in their 40 years of music recording. They have sold more than 200 million records, which makes them one of the top-selling music acts ever. Some of their more famous songs include "How Deep Is Your Love"; "Islands in the Stream," recorded by Dolly Parton and Kenny Rogers; and "Chain Reaction," recorded by Diana Ross. Their soundtracks for the movies *Saturday Night Fever* and *Stayin' Alive* helped bring them great commercial success.

Beethoven, Ludwig van (1770–1827)   German composer and pianist who remains one of the most influential composers of all time. Beethoven was an important transitional figure between the classical (1750–1820) and romantic (1820–1900) periods. As the musical heir of Mozart and Haydn, he used new forms and techniques to create tension and excitement through the use of dissonance and syncopation. His most popular works are his nine symphonies, including the fifth, which features that famous opening four-note phrase. His 32 piano sonatas, including the well-known "Moonlight," experiment with compositional techniques he later used in his symphonies and string quartets. He also composed vocal music, including two masses and *Fidelio*, his only opera.

bel   Named after Alexander Graham Bell, a measurement of sound intensity equaling 10 decibels (db), the smallest increment of loudness change that the human ear can detect. Twelve bels is so loud that it can cause pain.

bel canto (It., beautiful singing)   An eighteenth-century Italian vocal technique that is still taught in many music schools around the world. The technique emphasizes smooth movement between vocal registers, purity of tone, excellent vowel formation, good posture, and the need for vocal exercises and practice to build the voice.

Belafonte, Harry (b. 1927)   American singer and actor of Jamaican descent who was one of the most popular singers of the 1950s and '60s. His record *Calypso* from 1956 was the first LP to sell more than one million copies, which earned him the title "King of Calypso." Belafonte went on to receive two Grammy awards, six gold records, an Emmy Award (he was the first African American man to do so), a National Medal of Arts Award, and a Grammy Lifetime Achievement Award.

bell   1. The opening from which the sound comes out of a wind instrument, such as a trumpet or trombone. 2. A hollow, metal vessel or percussion instrument sounded by a metal clapper inside. Bells have been used in church towers since the sixth century.

bell tree   Member of the percussion family. A vertical rod with inverted metal bowls arranged and nested in order, the top bells being largest down to the smallest bells at the bottom. Used in orchestras for a glissando effect when stroked, from top to bottom, with a mallet or triangle beater.

bellows   A device that produces a stream of air when put under pressure. Bellows are used in pipe organs, bagpipes, and accordions.

belly   Another name for the soundboard of a piano or the upper plate found in the resonant box of some string instruments.

belt or **belting**   A vocal technique used by pop or musical theater singers in which the singer drives the chest voice into the high part of the voice; essentially, a controlled yell.

Benson, George (b. 1943)   Two-time Grammy Award–winning American pop and R&B singer and jazz guitarist. Since recording his first album in 1964, he has made more than 67 albums and still performs in more than 100 shows a year. He has recorded three platinum and two gold albums, and his hits include "This Masquerade" and "Give Me the Night."

bent pitch   Effect used in jazz and the blues when the third, fifth, and seventh tones of the scale are slightly dropped. Also called a blue note or a bent note.

Berg, Alban (1885–1935)   Austrian composer, member of the Second Viennese School, and student of Arnold Schoenberg, Berg combined atonality effectively with the nineteenth-century Romantic tradition. He adopted the 12-tone system, which he used in his most well-known instrumental piece, *Violin Concerto*. He is also famous for his two operas, *Wozzeck* and *Lulu*.

Berlin, Irving (1888–1989)   One of the greatest American song writers of the twentieth century. Both a composer and a lyricist, his compositions number nearly 1,000 songs, including "White Christmas," "Alexander's Ragtime Band," "Cheek to Cheek," and "There's No Business Like Show Business."

Berlioz, Hector (1803–1869)   French composer, conductor, and music critic of the romantic period, best known for his important contribution to modern orchestral instrumentation. His most famous work is the *Symphonie fantastique*, and his *Treatise on Instrumentation* is an important technical study of musical instruments and their different aspects, such as tone quality and range.

Bernoulli effect   Named after eighteenth-century mathematician Daniel Bernoulli, this physics principle deals with resistance, velocity, and the pressure of moving air. When we sing, it accounts for the vibration of the vocal chords.

Bernstein, Elmer (1922–2004)   American film score composer who, after 50 years writing for television, Broadway musicals, and movies, was awarded 14 Academy Awards, 1 Emmy, and 2 Golden Globes. Some of his most famous film scores were *The Ten Commandments* (1956), *The Great Escape* (1963), *True Grit* (1969), *National Lampoon's Animal House* (1978), *Airplane* (1980), *My Left Foot* (1989), and *Wild Wild West* (1999).

Bernstein, Leonard (1918–1990)   American composer, conductor, pianist, and teacher recognized as one of the leading musicians of the twentieth century. He was equally adept at composing for the concert hall and Broadway. During his nearly 50 years of conducting, he was music director of the New York Philharmonic and other major orchestras and festivals. His many awards and honors included a Tony Award, 11 Emmy Awards, and a Lifetime Achievement Grammy Award. Bernstein's Young People's Concerts, televised programs with the New York Philharmonic from 1958–1972, are among his most outstanding achievements, teaching an entire generation of children the joy of classical music. As a composer of Broadway, opera and film, symphony orchestras, choral works, and small ensembles, Bernstein captured the sound of urban America using simple and complex forms and styles. He is most remembered for his Broadway hits *West Side Story*, *On the Town*, and *Candide*.

Berry, Chuck (b. 1926)   American guitarist, songwriter, and singer, Chuck Berry is the most influential pioneer of rock and roll music—shaping and developing its instrumental structure and voice. He was one of the first musicians to be inducted into the Rock and Roll Hall of Fame, and *Rolling Stone* magazine ranked him 5 on its 100 Greatest Artists of All Time list and 6 on its 100 Greatest Guitarists of All Time list. His famous songs include "Rock and Roll Music," "Johnny B. Goode," and "Maybellene."

bewegt   A German term meaning to play "with movement," in an agitated and rushed manner.

big band   A large musical ensemble made up of 12 to 25 jazz musicians. Featuring trumpet, saxophone, trombone, and rhythm sections, the big band became popular in the Swing Era of the 1930s and '40s and is also known as a stage band, dance band, jazz band, or jazz ensemble. Some of the more popular big-band leaders of the Swing Era include Glenn Miller, Duke Ellington, Tommy Dorscy, and Benny Goodman.

big beat   Musical style developed in the mid-1990s that commonly uses loops and patterns that are synthesizer-generated and used in techno and other electronic dance music. There are usually between 90 and 140 compressed and distorted breakbeats (the rhythmic foundation for hip-hop tunes) per minute in a big beat piece. This music may also include loops taken from 1960s and '70s rock, pop, jazz, and funk songs. Bands that use this style include Propellerheads, Fatboy Slim, and the Chemical Brothers.

Billboard   Weekly American magazine dedicated to tracking the most popular songs and albums in the music industry.

Billy Budd   English opera composed in four acts by British composer Benjamin Britten and libretto written by E. M. Forster and Eric Crozier. First produced in London in 1951, the story is taken from the short novel by Herman Melville and takes place aboard the ship HMS *Indomitable* in 1797.

binary form   The structure of a musical composition in which two sections, A and B, complement each other, are close to equal duration, and are repeated. This form was popular in the baroque period and was associated with choreographed dance.

Bingen, Hildegard of (1098–1179)   German composer, visionary, philosopher, scientist, and poet. She wrote liturgical songs, the first surviving morality play (medieval drama with a moral theme), and *Ordo Virtulum*, one of the first liturgical dramas. Her sacred medieval music became popular to modern audiences largely through the recordings of the professional female quartet Anonymous 4.

bird's eye   Also called a fermata, a musical notation that directs the performer to hold a certain note or chord for a length of time determined by the performer or conductor. *See also* fermata.

⌒

bitonality   The use of two or more different keys at the same time in a composition. In a bitonal piece for piano, for example, the left hand may be playing in F minor while the right hand plays in C Major. Used by twentieth-century composers such as Darius Milhaud and Charles Ives.

Bizet, Georges (1838–1875)   French composer well known for being a virtuoso pianist during the romantic period and the composer of the opera *Carmen*.

black gospel   *See* gospel music.

Black Sabbath   A British rock band from Birmingham, England, formed in 1968 and featuring Ozzy Osbourne on lead vocals. Earned the title "Greatest Metal Band of All Time" from MTV and helped define the style of heavy metal with their 1970 album, *Paranoid*.

blind octaves   A piano technique used by virtuosic performers in which both hands alternate rapidly, with the thumbs and little fingers playing octaves on a trill or scale.

block chord   A musical chord in which all the notes are played at once instead of one at a time (arpeggiated or broken chord) below the melody line. Usually played on a strong beat or in rhythm with the melody, block chords in succession make up a composition technique called chorale-style chording.

block harmony   A composition style in which similar or identical chords are played in succession. This trait was a characteristic of Claude Debussy's piano music.

blow   Jazz slang for when a performer is playing to the limits of his physical or creative ability.

blue note   Effect used in jazz and the blues when the third, fifth, and seventh tones of the scale are slightly dropped. Also called a bent pitch.

Blue Note   1. Famous jazz club founded in Greenwich Village in New York City and now a chain of jazz club/restaurants located around the world. 2. Jazz record label started in 1939 and now owned by the EMI Group.

bluegrass   A type of country music with roots in both blues and jazz. Inspired particularly by Scottish and Irish immigrants to the Appalachian Mountains of the southeastern United States, bluegrass uses acoustic string instruments such as guitar, banjo, mandolin, violin (fiddle), and upright bass (bass violin). Types of bluegrass include bluegrass gospel, progressive bluegrass, and neo-traditional bluegrass. The Foggy Mountain Boys and Earl Scruggs are popular examples of bluegrass performers.

blues   A type of music developing from African American spirituals, shouts, chants, and work songs of the nineteenth century. Based on the three-chord blues progression (minor thirds and sevenths are common) in the most common 12-bar, 4/4 time pattern, the lyrics are often about someone's problems or depressed feelings (they have "the blues"). This style of music has had a great influence on all popular music from the 1960s to the present, including rock, jazz, bluegrass, and rhythm and blues.

blues poetry   Poetry influenced by, or written for, blues music.

blues progression   A chord progression used in popular music, jazz, and blues. The "12-bar blues" is a basic popular blues progression that uses the I IV V chords in any key.

blues scale   In jazz theory, a major scale with lowered third, fifth, and seventh notes used in the improvisation and composition of jazz. This Western scale was influenced by African scales.

bocal   The curved, tapered metal mouthpiece used between the double reed of the bassoon, oboe d'amore, and English horn.

Bocelli, Andrea (b. 1958)   Italian tenor who has sung and recorded 20 classical, pop, and opera albums and sold more than 65 million albums around the world. Blind since an early age, Bocelli sang and accompanied himself on piano in bars until being discovered by Italian rock star Zucchero and Italian superstar tenor Luciano Pavarotti in 1992. Some of his most famous songs include "Time to Say Goodbye," "Vivo per lei," and "The Prayer."

Bohème, La (It., *The Bohemians*)   Italian opera composed in four acts by Giacomo Puccini, with libretto by Giuseppe Giacosa and Luigi Illica. The world premiere took place in Turin, Italy, in 1896, and according to *Opera America* magazine it is the second most-performed opera in the United States. The story takes place in the Latin quarter of Paris in 1830.

Böhm system   Invented by Theobald Böhm around 1830, a method of cutting the appropriate acoustical position and hole size in a woodwind instrument to fit the finger spread of the average hand.

bolero   A Spanish dance in moderately slow 3/4 meter, originating in the late eighteenth century. Accompanied by singers, guitars, and castanets and usually using a triplet on the second beat of each measure. The popular Cuban version, developed in the late nineteenth century, uses the same name but has a 2/4 meter.

bomb   A term from the bop period to describe a drum accent in music; a drummer would keep time on the cymbals and "drop bombs" with the bass or snare drum.

Bon Jovi   American rock band from New Jersey started in 1983 featuring lead singer/guitarist Jon Bon Jovi, guitarist Richie Sambora, keyboardist David Bryan, and drummer Tico Torres. Bon Jovi has sold more than 120 million albums and is one of the world's biggest-selling touring bands. Two of its most famous songs are "Always" and "Livin' on a Prayer."

Bono (b. 1960)   Stage name for Paul David Hewson, an Irish musician and singer who is the lead vocalist for the rock band U2. He was nominated for a Golden Globe (for Best Original Song, "The

Hands That Built America," from the movie *Gangs of New York*),
Academy Award, Grammy, and the Nobel Peace Prize and was
named *Time* magazine's Person of the Year in 2005.

boogie-woogie   Developed in Chicago in the early 1920s, this
type of piano blues was revived and became popular again in the
late 1930s. The style is characterized by the use of a 12-measure
blues progression, using an ostinato (repeated rhythmic pattern)
bass figure in the left hand and the free-flowing right hand playing
the melody and improvisation.

boombox   A portable stereo system that originally contained a
radio and cassette recorder and later a CD player. Because of its
size and volume, the portable boombox was steadily replaced by
more portable devices such as the Walkman and iPod.

bop   *See* bebop.

borrowed chord   A chord in a parallel minor or parallel major
key that a composer integrates into an established chord, using
accidentals if necessary.

bossa nova (Sp., new trend)   A style of music developed by young
musicians in Rio de Janeiro, Brazil, from 1958–1963. This Latin
beat evolved from the samba and was used in a number of popular
jazz tunes of the day. Stan Getz was a well-known performer of
bossa nova. It's still popular in its original form and in new incar-
nations called TecnoBossa or BossaElectric in the lounge bars of
Asia and Europe.

Boulanger, Nadia (1887–1979)   French composer, music professor, and conductor. One of the most influential teachers of composition during the twentieth century. A short list of the famous
composers she taught includes Leonard Bernstein, Aaron Copland,
Philip Glass, Gian Carlo Menotti, Quincy Jones, Ned Rorem,
Roger Sessions, and Virgil Thompson. She was also the first
woman to conduct the Boston Symphony Orchestra and New York
Philharmonic, among others.

bow A device used to play string instruments. Made of a special wood (good modern bows are generally made of Brazilian pernambuco wood) with horsehair strung between each end, the bow is drawn across the instrument's strings, causing vibration that makes musical sound. Other parts of the bow include the frog (the near end that adjusts the horsehair), often made of ebony, ivory, and tortoiseshell; the grip, with a wrap made of wire or silk; the tip plate, made of metal, ivory, or bone; and the thumb cushion, made with snakeskin or leather.

bowing The action and technique of using the bow to play a string instrument. There are many different manners of bowing, but the most common four are sautillé, détaché, staccato, and spiccato.

brace In written music, a bracket that connects two or more of the staves of the score together.

bracket *See* brace.

Brahms, Johannes (1833–1897) German pianist and leading composer of the romantic period. His highly complex and disciplined style of composition is found in works for piano, symphony orchestra, chamber ensembles, voice, and choir. In addition to his symphonies, his *German Requiem* is one of his most well-known works.

Brandenburg Concertos   Six of the finest and most famous instrumental works written during the baroque period, composed by Johann Sebastian Bach in 1721 for a nobleman from Brandenburg-Schwedt in Germany.

brass band   Group consisting of 24 or 25 brass instrument players. They were once popular in the United States and have a long tradition in England. Often, the band is organized around a community or city's industry with annual competitions being held. Occasionally, the brass band has a percussion section of two or three players.

brass instruments   Musical instruments made of brass or other metal that utilize a cup-shaped mouthpiece. The most common brass instruments used today (from lower to higher pitches) are the tuba, baritone or euphonium, trombone, French horn, and trumpet. These are played in orchestras, concert bands, brass bands, jazz bands, and ensembles of all types.

bravura   Italian term pertaining to a brilliant, virtuoso passage of music or musical technique.

break   The time period in which the instrumentalists stop or take a "breather" in a piece while the percussion plays a short interlude. In jazz, a solo break occurs when the rest of the band drops out while a soloist plays by him– or herself.

breakbeat   An electronic drumbeat in a syncopated 4/4 pattern. Used in funk, techno, hip-hop, and acid house music, it is often mixed with digital effects such as reverb or pitch shifting.

breath mark   A musical notation symbol indicating a slight pause used to take a breath. Also used to indicate a bow lift for string players. Used at the end of a musical phrase and placed above the staff.

,

bridge   1. The wooden support on a string instrument across which the strings are stretched. 2. A transitional passage that connects two sections of a composition; also called the B section, channel, or release.

Brigadoon Broadway musical with music by Fredrick Loewe and book (story line) and lyrics by Alan Jay Lerner. The show opened at the Ziegfeld Theater in New York City in 1947 and ran for 581 performances. In the fantasylike story, two American tourists stumble upon a Scottish village that only appears every 100 years.

brio, con Italian term that directs the performer to play "with fire" or "vigor."

British Invasion The period from 1964 to 1966 when pop and rock-and-roll bands from the United Kingdom became popular in the United States, including the Beatles, the Rolling Stones, the Kinks, and the Who.

Britten, Benjamin (1913–1976) English composer, conductor, and pianist. He is most famous for his operas, including *The Rape of Lucretia*, *Albert Herring*, *Billy Budd*, and *The Turn of the Screw* and the orchestral piece *The Young Person's Guide to the Orchestra* written in 1946.

broadcasting The transmission of radio and television or video signals through the atmosphere or cable to an audience.

Broadway musical A musical (play with spoken dialogue, songs, chorus, and orchestra) that is performed in any of the 40 theaters in New York City's theater district surrounding Broadway.

broken chord A musical chord in which each note is played individually instead of simultaneously. *See* arpeggio.

broken time A style of jazz where the bass and drums use unusual or irregular syncopation so that the steady beat is not obvious.

Brown, James (1933–2006) Nicknamed "The Godfather of Soul," James Brown was one of the most influential American pop music entertainers of the twentieth century. A singer, dancer, songwriter, and bandleader, he earned many prestigious music industry awards during his 50-year career, including a Grammy Lifetime Achievement Award. He was one of the first artists to be inducted into the Rock and Roll Hall of Fame, and *Rolling Stone* magazine ranked him 7 on its 100 Greatest Artists of All Time list. He made guest appearances in films such as *The Blues Brothers*, *Rocky IV*, and

The Tuxedo and recorded hits such as "Papa's Got a Brand New Bag," "Please, Please, Please," and "Get Up (I Feel Like Being a) Sex Machine."

Bruckner, Anton (1824–1896)   Austrian composer whose complex polyphony, harmonic language, and lengthy musical ideas were written into his motets, masses, and symphonies.

bubblegum pop   A form of pop music characterized by catchy melodies with sing-along choruses, popular from 1967–1972. The themes were usually about love and frequently referenced sweet foods such as honey, candy, and jelly. Focused on singles rather than albums, the major hit-makers were groups such as the Partridge Family, the Jackson 5, the Banana Splits, and the Archies.

buffo   Comic voice type in opera, such as a basso buffo.

bugle   Military trumpet without valves used to signal military personnel to attention, dinner, lights out, and other commands. Also used to give commands in battle and played at military funerals.

Burleigh, Harry T. (1866–1949)   African American baritone singer, classical composer, arranger, and music editor instrumental in making black music, especially spirituals, more available to trained musicians and the public in general. He composed more than 200 American art songs and broke down many color barriers with his singing and compositions.

burlesque   "Low-brow" variety show using funny dialogue and songs that are sung to familiar melodies. Striptease is a major component of this attraction.

Buxtehude, Dietrich (1637–1707)   Renowned baroque German Danish composer and organist who was a major influence on composers Johann Sebastian Bach and Heinrich Schütz. His organ works are an important part of the organ repertoire.

Bye Bye Birdie   Tony Award–winning musical written by Charles Strouse with lyrics by Lee Adams and book (storyline) by Michael Stewart. Premiered on Broadway in 1960. The show is a spoof on 1958 American society and inspired by Elvis Presley and his 1957 draft into the army.

Byrd, William (1540–1623)   English composer of both religious and secular vocal and keyboard music. His enormous output of more than 470 compositions made him one of the most famous Renaissance composers.

C Pitch name for the first step of a C-Major scale. First white key in a C-Major scale on the piano keyboard.

C86 A cassette compilation released in 1986, of new bands from independent labels, released by the British magazine *New Music Express*.

cacophony The use of a meaningless, harsh mixture of chords or sounds such as cars honking, hoots, whistles, and screams.

cadence A progression of two chords or a rhythmic pattern used to create a sense of finality at the end of a phrase, section, or composition.

cadenza A technically virtuosic passage inserted at the end of a composition to give the performer a chance to show off his or her mastery of the instrument.

Cage, John (1912–1992) Leading American composer of post World War II avant-garde style, aleatory (chance), and electronic music. He used common musical instruments in nonstandard ways, such as works for prepared piano (piano strings are altered to create an unusual sound). His teachers included Arnold Schoenberg and Henry Cowell. John Cage is best known for his composition "4'33"" in 1952, in which all three movements (lasting 4 minutes and 33 seconds) are performed without playing a single note, using the environment and the sounds of the audience as source material for the experience.

cakewalk   A type of music and dance originating in the southern United States among slaves, who won a prize—sometimes cake—for being the best dancers.

Cakewalk   A music-sequencing software originally created for DOS (operating system on a PC), originating with version 1.0 in 1987.

call and response   Known as antiphony in classical music, a type of music in which a second performer directly responds to a first performer's initial phrase. Used in the verse-chorus musical form of popular, folk, and Christian congregational music and African American–based musical forms such as jazz, blues, and gospel.

Calloway, Cab (1907–1994)   American bandleader, jazz singer, and actor known for his scat singing (improvised vocal patterns with random syllables and vowels) and leading one of the most popular black big bands from the early 1930s to late 1940s. He won a Grammy for his jazz single "Minnie the Moocher" and appeared in 13 feature films and many shorter films.

calypso   A ballad sung in Trinidad that uses a mix of English, French, and African words and few melodic patterns over a repetitious and very syncopated drum rhythm. A type of Caribbean folk music. Popular singer Harry Belafonte made this type of song famous in 1956 with his record *Calypso*, which was the first LP to sell more than a million copies.

canon   A musical composition in which a melody is exactly imitated one or more times (also called a round; for example, "Row, Row, Row Your Boat") or in which the melody is repeated with a variation.

cantabile   An Italian musical term meaning "songlike" or "singable"; used to indicate how the instrumental performer is to interpret part or all of the music.

cantata A religious (or secular) vocal form, with instrumental accompaniment, developed in the baroque period (1600–1750). A cantata uses elements similar to opera and oratorio (which originated at the same time), such as arias, duets, recitatives, and choruses. Johann Sebastian Bach is the most famous composer to write in this genre.

canticle Derived from the Latin word for "song," a canticle is a hymn written to Biblical text other than the Book of Psalms.

cantor The vocal soloist who sings the chant in Roman Catholic liturgy and leads the congregation and choir in singing in Protestant and Jewish services.

cantus firmus The melody used in Gregorian chant (oldest notated music) that was later the basis of polyphonic music (composition that uses more than two independent melodic lines).

capriccio A piece of music composed with a free form.

Capriccio 1. The title of a chamber piece written for chamber ensemble and piano (left hand) in 1926 by Leoš Janáček. 2. The title of a German opera composed by Richard Strauss in 1942.

Carey, Mariah (b. 1970) American singer, songwriter, producer, and actress. She was the most successful recording artist in the United States in the 1990s, according to *Billboard* magazine. She has received 5 Grammy Awards, sold more than 200 million albums around the world, and as a solo artist sold 18 number-one singles in the United States, second after the Beatles. A few of her hit singles include "Vision of Love," "Dream Lover," and "I'll Be There."

carillon Bells that are hung in a tower or church and played by a keyboard. Originally consisting of 4 bells, the modern carillon has 30 to 50 bells.

Carlos, Wendy (b. 1939) Composer, keyboardist, and pioneer in electronic music. Working with Robert Moog in the early 1960s, she helped develop one of the first keyboard synthesizers and used it on her 1968 hit album *Switched-On Bach*, which won three Grammy Awards.

Carmen French opera in four acts composed by Georges Bizet, with libretto by Ludovic Halévy and Henri Heihac. Originally produced in Paris in 1875, it is one of the best-loved and most-produced operas in the repertoire. The story is set in Seville, Spain, in 1820.

Carmina Burana Scenic cantata composed by Carl Orff and produced in Frankfurt, Germany, in 1937. Based on 25 medieval poems written about thirteenth-century secular life and the perils of gambling, drinking, gluttony, and lust. Written in Latin, Middle High German, and Old French, this popular work is scored for three soloists, an orchestra, a boys' choir, and a full chorus.

carol A traditional song currently used to celebrate Christmas. Many are based on medieval carols that have a popular or dancelike nature. Examples include "Silent Night, Holy Night" and "Away in the Manger."

Carpenters, The A 1970s light-rock duo that consisted of Karen Carpenter, the singer and drummer, and her brother, Richard, who wrote many of the songs, arranged the music, played keyboards, and sang. Winners of three Grammy awards, the Carpenters sold more than 100 million records and were the number-one selling American music group in the 1970s.

Caruso, Enrico (1873–1921) Italian operatic tenor and most famous male opera star of his era. He was a pioneer in the recorded music field, making more than 260 recordings with the Victor Talking Machine Company (later renamed RCA Victor), and was seen in several newsreels and silent movies of the time.

Cash, Johnny (1932–2003) American country music singer-songwriter. Wrote in the folk, gospel, blues, and rock and roll styles, which he sang with a deep, bass-baritone voice. Dubbed "The Man in Black," his black clothes, drinking, and drug abuse gave him an outlaw image. Later in his career, he appeared on his own TV variety show and many other shows and films. Inducted into the Country Music Hall of Fame in 1980 and Rock and Roll Hall of Fame in 1992, he received 17 Grammy Awards during his career. His life and career were portrayed in the 2005 Academy Award–winning film *Walk the Line*. His most popular songs include "Ring of Fire," "I Walk the Line" and "A Boy Named Sue."

castanets   Percussion instrument used by Spanish dancers. Made of two shell-shaped hardwood clappers, hinged together and strung over the player's first finger and thumb, then clapped together in rhythm while dancing.

castrato   Castrated (the testes are removed) male singer. Castration was practiced on young male singers between the sixteenth and eighteenth centuries to preserve the soprano or alto character of the young voice while the chest and lungs of the grown male adult could sing with great power and unique timbre. Farinelli (1705–1782) was considered to be one of the most famous castratti of his time.

Cavalleria Rusticana (It., *Rustic Chivalry*)   Italian opera in one act composed by Pietro Mascagni, with libretto by Giovanni Targioni-Tozzetti and Guido Menasci. Originally produced in Rome in 1890, it is set in a Sicilian village in the late nineteenth century. This is a prime example of verismo (real or true) opera, a style that used a highly dramatic plot and realistic musical style. Because it's a one-act opera lasting approximately one hour, it often shares a double bill with another one-act verismo opera, *Pagliacci*, by Ruggero Leoncavallo.

cavatina   Shorter than an aria (operatic song), this type of vocal piece found in eighteenth- and nineteenth-century operas and oratorios is written in a simplified style using no repetition of words or phrases.

CD (compact disc)   An optical disc that is used to store digital information. From 1982 to 2010, it has been the standard medium for audio recordings and can hold approximately 80 minutes of digital audio.

celesta   Part of the percussion section of an orchestra, this keyboard instrument is similar in appearance to an upright piano. Metal plates are struck by hammers when the keys are played, causing a metallic, pitched tone. Similar to the glockenspiel, the celesta has a more delicate and softer timbre (color of tone) and comes in either the French four-octave or German five-octave version. "Dance of the Sugarplum Fairy" from *The Nutcracker Suite* by Tchaikovsky is the most well-known piece using the celesta.

cello (also violoncello)   A member of the string family that is similar in appearance to the violin but approximately twice as large and tuned an octave and a fourth lower. It is tuned in fifths like its smaller family member, the viola, and is typically made of spruce and other woods.

Cenerentola, La (It., *Cinderella*)   Italian opera composed in two acts by Gioachino Rossini, with libretto by Jacopo Ferretti. First produced in Rome in 1817, it is Rossini's twentieth opera and is set in Italy in the eighteenth century.

cent   The smallest unit of musical interval measurement. A cent equals $\frac{1}{100}$ of a half step (semitone), with an octave (12 semitones) equaling 1,200 cents. A musical tuning system established by Alexander Ellis in the mid-nineteenth century.

Ceremony of Carols, A   Composed in 1942 by Benjamin Britten, a popular classical composition arranged for harp and treble voices with Middle English poem texts by Gerald Bullett.

chamber choir   A small, select, choral SATB (soprano, alto, tenor, and bass) ensemble usually associated with a larger choir.

chamber music   Unlike orchestral music, chamber music uses one player on each part. Traditional chamber ensembles include the trio (three instruments), quartet (four), quintet (five), sextet (six), septet (seven), and octet (eight). Chamber ensembles include string quartets, piano trios, woodwind octets, and many other varieties of instrumentation.

chamber opera   An opera composed for singers and a chamber orchestra of 25 players or fewer. Chamber opera was invented in the 1940s by Benjamin Britten to be performed in small venues. The term is also applied to smaller operatic works of the baroque period.

chamber orchestra   An orchestra of 25 players or fewer.

changes   Jazz slang for chord progressions.

chanson   The French term for a popular art song. The chanson was not an artistic form until the end of the nineteenth century.

chant   Liturgical music of Christian churches that features a single, unaccompanied melody line sung in a free rhythm. The melody consists of two or more pitches called reciting tones.

chanting   The singing of liturgical music (canticles and psalms) on one or two pitches (reciting tones) in the Roman Catholic and Anglican Church.

character piece   Short, nineteenth-century piano compositions meant to express a particular mood or feeling. Examples include Robert Schumann's *Nachtstücke* (*Night Pieces*) and Jean Sibelius's "The Oarsman."

Charles, Ray (1930–2004)   American singer and piano player of soul, pop, and country-western music. Blind since childhood, he was inducted into the Rock and Roll Hall of Fame at its inaugural ceremony in 1986. *Rolling Stone* magazine ranked him 10 on its 2004 list of the 100 Greatest Artists of All Time, and he won 17 Grammy Awards. The 2004 biographical film *Ray*, starring

Jamie Foxx as Charles, won two Academy Awards and two Grammy Awards. Two of his most famous songs are "Georgia on My Mind" and "I Can't Stop Loving You."

Charleston, The   A song and dance popular in the 1920s, introduced in 1923 by composer James Johnson in the Broadway show *Runnin' Wild.*

chart   A musical manuscript written for popular or jazz music.

Checker, Chubby (b. 1941)   American singer-songwriter famous for popularizing the 1960 R&B hit "The Twist."

Cher (b. 1946)   American popular singer-songwriter and actress who has won an Emmy Award, Grammy Award, Academy Award, Golden Globe Award, and People's Choice Award. In her 40 years performing, she has sold more than 100 million records. Born Cherilyn Sarkisian, she started her career when she was 19 with her future husband, Sonny Bono, in the pop rock duo Sonny and Cher. Their singles "I Got You Babe" and "The Beat Goes On," along with their TV variety show from 1971–1975, set Cher up for a solo career after her divorce from Sonny in 1975. Her song "Believe" was the number-one selling single in 1999.

chest voice   Refers to a specific vocal timbre and coloration made in the lower of the two voice registers. It is the register used when speaking and yelling, and when used correctly can add vitality and strength to these two aspects of the voice.

Chicago   American pop-rock and jazz-fusion band formed in Chicago, Illinois, in 1967. Selling more than 120 million albums, they have earned 18 platinum, 8 multi-platinum, and 22 gold albums. Only the Beach Boys have been more successful and performed longer as an American rock-and-roll group. Some of their most famous tunes include "Colour My World," "Does Anybody Really Know What Time It Is?", and "25 or 6 to 4."

chill-out music   Slow, smooth electronic music introduced in the early 1990s. Lounge music, easy listening, ambient house, and New Age are all subgenres of this style. Artists of the genre include Mystical Sun, Boards of Canada, Single Cell Orchestra, and Electric Skychurch.

chimes   A percussion instrument consisting of a series of suspended, tuned, tube-shaped bells.

Chinese block   A hollow, wooden percussion instrument played by a drumstick, producing a dry, hollow sound.

choir   Also called a chorale or chorus. A musical vocal ensemble that sings choral music in a church, theater, or concert hall. The term is also used with instrumental groups such as string, brass, and woodwind choirs.

Chopin, Frédéric (1810–1849)   Polish Romantic period composer and pianist. Primarily wrote solo works for the piano and was very important in developing innovations in the waltz, mazurka, impromptu, and piano sonata.

chops   Jazz slang for a performer's ability to play technically difficult music. Also refers to the lips of the performer.

chorale   *See* choir.

chord   Three or more notes or tones sounding at the same time. Studying chords, their relationships to each other, and their function within the composition is a music theory technique called harmonic analysis.

chord chart   Musical notation indicating the main melody and a series of chord symbols showing the harmonic and rhythmic information of a song. Used primarily in jazz and popular music by the rhythm section as a guideline to improvisation.

chord progression   In music theory, a succession of musical chords with the purpose of establishing a piece's tonality and to provide harmony and musical form to a composition.

chord voicing   The order and spacing in which pitches are placed on a staff or staves of music. This order indicates the instrumental placement or harmonic preference of the composer or arranger.

chordophone   Any musical instrument that creates sound by vibrating a string stretched between two points. Some examples are a harp, violin, guitar, and even a piano.

chorus   *See* choir.

Christian metal   A form of heavy metal music that references Christianity in its lyrics and themes. Originating in the United States in the late 1970s, the band Stryper brought this genre to the mainstream in the mid-1980s.

chromatic   Division of a whole step into two half or semitone intervals, such as C–C♯ and C♯–D. If this principle is applied to all 5 whole tones of a regular (diatonic) scale, it subdivides into the 12 tones of a chromatic scale. A chromatic scale is played on the piano by striking a white key, the next black key, white key, black key, and so on. Often used in jazz and impressionistic music.

church modes   The type of scales used in early church music. All eight scales use notes from the C-Major scale and have a limited range (higher than approximately an octave).

ciphering   A defect in the mechanism of an organ that makes the pipe sound continuously.

circle of fifths   Used in music theory analysis as a tool to remember the 12 different keys. By using this visual aid, a person is able to see more clearly that by ascending clockwise by fifths (C, G, D, A, and so on), the original key is eventually reached again. This aid is also helpful in determining how many sharps or flats are in each key.

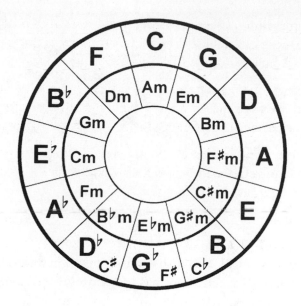

circle progression In music theory, the most common chord progression that travels along the circle of fifths.

clams Jazz slang meaning mistakes made while performing. For example, "Boy, Sam really laid some clams tonight."

Clapton, Eric (b. 1945) English singer-songwriter and guitarist. Ranked 4 in *Rolling Stone* magazine's 100 Greatest Guitarists of All Time, he has been inducted into the Rock and Roll Hall of Fame three times as a member of the groups Cream and the Yardbirds and as a solo performer. He has been awarded 18 Grammy Awards, among many others. "Layla" and "Cocaine" are two of his hit singles.

clarinet Member of the woodwind family. The body's shape is a cylindrical tube of ebonite or wood with a flared bell on one end and a beak-shaped, single-reed mouthpiece on the other. The most popular form of modern clarinet is tuned in the key of B♭ and sounds one whole note lower than what is written. Played in all forms and genres of bands and orchestras, the clarinet's range is E below middle C to the third G above middle C.

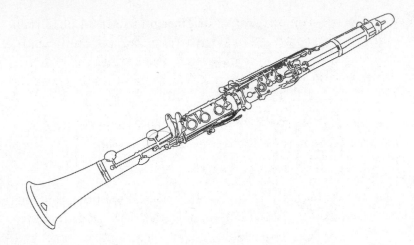

Clark, Petula (b. 1932) English popular music and music-theater singer and composer. Her career has lasted 56 years, from 1954 to 2010, and she has been named the most successful British female recording artist ever by the *Guinness Book of World Records*. Among her hits from the 1960s are "Downtown" and "I Know a Place."

classical period Lasting approximately 70 years, from 1750–1820, this era lies between the baroque and romantic periods. Its musical characteristics are not as complex as the baroque and emphasize beauty of the melody and form, with a bigger variety of rhythms, keys, and dynamics. In the classical period, instrumental music's importance grew along with instrumental forms such as the symphony, concerto, string quartet, and especially the sonata. Orchestras grew bigger, and the harpsichord gave way to the piano. Important composers during the classical period include Franz Joseph Haydn (1732–1809) and Wolfgang Amadeus Mozart (1756–1791), with Carl Philipp Emanuel Bach (1714–1788) and Ludwig van Beethoven (1770–1827) being instrumental in changing the style from classical to romantic.

clavecin (F., harpsichord) *See* harpsichord.

claves   A percussion instrument originating in Afro-Cuban music. Two thick, cylindrical rods, made generally of wood, are struck together to a specific rhythmic figure (called a clave) through an entire piece. Salsa is a type of musical form that uses this instrument.

clavichord   A keyboard instrument, similar to a piano, used between the fifteenth and eighteenth centuries.

clavier (F., keyboard)   *See* keyboard.

clef   A musical sign indicating the pitch of written notes and placed at the beginning of the musical staff. Treble clef (used for the right hand on the piano, higher instruments and soprano, and alto and tenor voices) and bass clef (used for the left hand on the piano, lower instruments, and baritone and bass voices) are the most commonly used.

Clemenza di Tito, La (It., *The Clemency of Titus*)   Italian opera composed in two acts by Wolfgang Amadeus Mozart, with libretto written by Pietro Metastasio. Produced in Prague in 1791 for Emperor Leopold II's coronation as king of Bohemia. The story takes place in Ancient Rome.

climax   The most exciting part of a composition. The composer creates this effect intentionally through tempo changes, key changes, fuller orchestration, chromaticism, and—in the matter of vocal music—following the poet's text to its natural climactic highpoint.

clinker   Jazz slang signifying the performance of a bad note; for example, "That was some clinker you hit, Sam."

coda   A passage or section added to the end of a composition to emphasize or confirm the feeling of finality.

✆

collegium musicum   A musical association, usually formed on a university campus, that uses amateurs in its performance of early music (medieval, renaissance, and baroque).

Collins, Phil (b. 1951)   English drummer, singer-songwriter, keyboardist, and actor. Originally starting in 1970 as the drummer for Genesis, an English progressive-rock group, he took over as lead singer when Peter Gabriel left the group in 1975. He later became an Academy and Grammy Award–winning solo artist. "In the Air Tonight," "Sussudio," "Don't Lose My Number," and the title track for the film *Against All Odds* (which became a number-one and number-two hit in the United States and United Kingdom) were three of his greatest hits.

color   1. Often referred to as "timbre," the tone quality of the musical sound. Color is affected by the materials from which an instrument is made (different qualities of wood or metal produce different color) or how well a voice is trained. 2. The visual aspect of sound associated with frequencies. Composers such as Rimsky-Korsakov and Alexander Scriabin have associated colors with notes of the scale.

color organ   Keyboard instrument that provides the audience with a visual representation of the music being played (color music) by bathing a screen (or audience) in constantly changing colored light. Composers Alexander Scriabin and Olivier Messiaen were both exponents of color music.

coloratura   Rapid runs, trills, and ornaments used primarily in vocal passages of eighteenth- and nineteenth-century opera arias (songs). Handel and Bach were famous for writing coloratura for singers in the baroque period, and Mozart wrote a famous example of coloratura singing with "The Queen of the Night" aria in his opera *The Magic Flute*.

coloratura soprano   An operatic soprano who sings in the highest female vocal register and specializes in music exemplified by lively leaps and runs. Lighter voices in this range are called lyric coloraturas, and heavier voices are called dramatic coloraturas. Gioachino Rossini, Gaetano Donizetti, and Vincenzo Bellini were all famous composers who wrote in this style.

Coltrane, John (1926–1967)   American saxophonist and jazz composer. One of the most influential tenor saxophonists in the history of jazz, he began his career playing bebop and hard bop and later played free jazz (featuring limited organized tempos and chord changes). He was one of the most recorded jazz artists, working with other jazz legends such as Miles Davis (trumpet) and Thelonious Monk (piano).

combo   A small jazz ensemble of 3 to 10 performers. Compare to a "band" in rock.

comic opera   An opera with a lighter or more sentimental subject matter, usually with spoken dialogue that resolves in a happy ending. Reflects a more popular style than serious opera (*opera seria*). Italian *opera buffa* is the same as comic opera but with no spoken dialogue.

common chord   A chord that is commonly shared by two different musical keys and is helpful in modulation.

common practice period   1. Also called the classical music period. This includes the baroque, classical, and romantic music periods from 1600–1900. 2. Classical music from around 1600–1900 that follows the music theory rules of conventional chord sequencing and counterpoint.

common time   A musical notation in the shape of a semicircle. The same as 4/4 or 2/4 time.

Como, Perry (1912–2001)   American singer of Italian descent with a career spanning more than 50 years who sang every popular style of music. His success as a recording artist and television personality (he had a weekly variety show) sold millions of records for the RCA Victor label—so many that Como asked them to stop counting. His most famous songs were "Till the End of Time," "Catch a Falling Star," "Hoop-De-Doo," "Hot Diggity (Dog Ziggity Boom)," and "Round and Round." He won a Grammy Award for Best Vocal Performance in 1958 and a Lifetime Achievement Grammy in 2002.

compass   The range of an instrument, defined by the span between and including the highest and lowest notes.

comping   In jazz, the simpler accompaniment to a solo or improvisation, consisting of chords and harmonies usually played by a keyboard or guitar.

composition   A musical work or the process of creating a musical work.

compound meter   A musical bar or measure divided into two uneven or three or more parts. Examples of compound measures are 6/8, 9/8, or 12/8.

computer music   The application of computing technology concerning music composition, sound design (sequencers), sound synthesis (synthesizers), and acoustics; any music created by computers or computer technology.

concert   A performance by a group of musicians set before the general public. This is a fairly new venue, because until the end of the seventeenth century, performances were usually set in the church or in wealthy persons' homes.

concert band   Also called a wind ensemble or symphonic band, a group consisting of brass, woodwind, and percussion instruments. Composers have written scores specifically for concert band and arranged other music for this type of ensemble.

concert grand   The largest piano, used for solo, small ensemble, and concert performance; longer than the parlor grand and baby grand. In contrast, the upright piano (spinet, console, studio, and upright grand) is made for less-formal use in homes, schools, and other institutions.

concert pitch   The standard used by piano tuners and instrument makers that assigns a certain pitch to written notes. When an instrument is pitched at concert pitch, a C will sound like a C, while a clarinet or trumpet that is pitched at B♭ will play a C and it will sound as a B♭.

concertmaster   The first-chair violinist in an orchestra. He or she tunes the orchestra, plays the solo violin passages, represents the orchestra in management and conductor negotiations, and occasionally substitutes for the conductor.

concerto   A classical musical composition in which a soloist and orchestra perform on equal terms.

concerto form   A three-movement musical form used in the concerto (solo instrument accompanied by orchestra), most commonly starting with the sonata-allegro form in the first movement, ternary form in the second movement, and rondo form in the third movement.

conductor   The leader of the band, choir, or ensemble who uses his or her hand or a baton to coordinate the group and indicate the music's tempo, phrasing, and volume.

conservatory   A school specializing in teaching music and in some cases other performing arts. American conservatories include the Juilliard School of Music, Eastman School of Music, Peabody Conservatory of Music, and Curtis Institute of Music.

console   1. The case that holds the keyboard and other hand-operated parts of an organ. 2. The second tallest upright piano.

consonance   A "stable" effect in a composition produced by consonant (agreeable) intervals consisting of octaves, unisons, and perfect fourths and fifths. The opposite of dissonance.

Consul, The English opera composed in three acts by Gian Carlo Menotti to his own libretto. First produced in 1950 in New York City, the story takes place in the present day in a European country.

contemporary music Music composed in the twentieth and twenty-first centuries.

Contes d'Hoffmann, Les (F., *The Tales of Hoffmann*) French opera composed by Jacques Offenbach in three acts, with libretto by Jules Barbier and M. Carré. Produced in Paris in 1881, the story takes place in Italy in the nineteenth century.

continuo A bass accompaniment part that is performed by organ, harpsichord, cello, or viola da gamba (or a combination of all these) in baroque music. (Also continuous bass, basso continuo.)

contrabass Musical instrument pitched one octave lower than the bass clef. Instruments include the double-bass (largest string instrument), contrabass clarinet, contrabassoon, and contrabass flute.

contrabassoon Also known as a double bassoon, an instrument that sounds an octave lower than the bassoon. The contrabassoon is twice as long and uses a larger double reed than the bassoon. A redesigned contrabassoon called the contraforte, which features an improved tone and fingering capability, has recently been developed by a German company.

contralto The lowest (and rarest) female voice type with a range from the F below middle C to two Fs above middle C.

contrapuntal Any musical composition that uses counterpoint, the simultaneous use of two or more independent melodic voices.

contrast The change of moods in a musical piece. Loud and soft, fast and slow, and major and minor all help develop and enrich the contrast of musical ideas in a composition.

controller Electronic interface used by a performer to transmit notes or rhythmic data of a composition through a MIDI (Musical Instrument Digital Interface) device to an electronic musical instrument. Types of controllers include a musical keyboard, computer, synthesizer, drum pad, and/or sequencer.

cool jazz   A type of jazz that started during World War II when white jazz musicians from California moved to New York and started working with African American bebop musicians. This type of jazz was less abstract and avoided aggressive tempos, concentrating on the intellectual characteristics of the music. The tenor saxophonist Lester Young was a major influence on players of this genre.

Copland, Aaron (1900–1990)   One of America's most famous composers. His style of composition exemplified the spirit of America, making him a nationalistic composer of great importance. His music is influenced by both popular (jazz) and classical music that he used in numerous film scores and orchestral pieces. *Fanfare for the Common Man*, *Rodeo*, and *Appalachian Spring* (which incorporates the Shaker tune "Simple Gifts") are three of his most recognized works.

copyright, musical   Grants the composer of a musical composition exclusive legal rights to his or her work for a period of time, after which it enters the public domain and can be used by anyone free of charge.

Corelli, Arcangelo (1653–1713)   Italian composer and most prominent violinist of the late baroque period. He laid the groundwork for modern violin performance technique and composed only instrumental music.

Corigliano, John (b. 1938)   American composer and winner of a Pulitzer Price for Music and an Academy Award. Composer of the film scores *Altered States*, *Revolution*, and *The Red Violin* and the two-act opera *The Ghosts of Versailles*.

cornet   A member of the brass family that looks much like a trumpet but is shorter, more compact, and emits a mellower tone. Louis Armstrong and Nat Adderley were two famous cornet performers.

countermelody   A group of notes forming a less-prominent melody and serving a subordinate role to the primary melody. The countermelody is heard as a textural component alongside the accompaniment.

counterpoint   An element of music composition that uses two or more melody lines simultaneously, creating "melody against melody" or "note against note."

countersubject   A melodic line played against the primary melody in a contrapuntal piece of music, such as a fugue or invention. With a tempo faster or slower than the primary melody, the countersubject is also called a countermelody.

countertenor   The highest register of the male voice, equivalent to the mezzo-soprano range, and often used in early classical music. This falsetto style of singing is also used by modern popular singers such as Michael Jackson.

counting off   The action by a big band or jazz combo director to set the tempo, vocally counting the beats before the group begins playing.

country music   Popular music form originating from folk, Appalachian, Southern, Celtic, and gospel music. Earlier known as hillbilly music, it gained popularity in the 1970s and is now one of the most popular genres of music in the United States. Willy Nelson, Dolly Parton, and Garth Brooks are a few of the biggest performers in country music.

country pop   A subgenre of country music that became popular in the 1970s; a blend of adult contemporary music and country that was first characterized by crossover artists going from country to Top 40. Glen Campbell, Olivia Newton-John, and Dolly Parton are all country acts who crossed over into this genre.

country rock   Music written with elements of both rock and roll and country music. This genre has been typically performed by rock musicians of the later 1960s and early 1970s, such as Bob Dylan, the Band, the Grateful Dead, and the Eagles, who were influenced by rockabilly and country music.

countrypolitan   Nashville pop-country songs of the 1960s and '70s, known for lush string and backup-singer arrangements. Aimed at the mainstream American audience, it sold well into the late 1970s. Countrypolitan artists include Charlie Rich, Charley Pride, Glen Campbell, and Tammy Wynette.

Couperin, François (1668–1733)   French composer and keyboard player from the baroque period.

cover version   A version of a previously recorded song. Many versions of the original indicate the success of the song. A "cover band" plays popular music written by other musicians.

cowbell   Named after a similar bell attached to cattle collars, this percussion instrument is present in different styles of music (particularly Latin music).

crash cymbal   A percussion instrument placed on a stand and hit with a mallet or stick, or played in pairs that are crashed together for occasional accents in the music.

Creation, The   An oratorio composed by Joseph Handel in 1797. Lyrics are based on a poem from *Paradise Lost* by John Milton, which describes the creation of the world.

crescendo (*cresc.*)   This musical term indicates an increase in the volume of the note or phrase of music. The opposite of decrescendo.

crooning   Singing popular ballads in an intimate manner into a microphone, usually accompanied by a big band or orchestra. Introduced in the early 1930s by singers such as Bing Crosby, Rudy Vallee, and later Frank Sinatra and Dean Martin.

Crosby, Bing (1903–1977)   American singer and actor. The biggest star of radio, movies, and sound recordings between 1934 and 1954, Crosby was the first to win the Global Achievement Award and also received the Academy Award for Best Actor in 1944. He is the fourth best-selling recording artist in history, with more than 500 million records sold.

cross rhythm   Using conflicting rhythmic patterns at the same time, such as a 4/4 meter against a 3/4 meter. Also called polyrhythm.

crossover A singer's change of musical genre, as with an opera singer who "crosses over" into performing and/or recording musical theater or jazz music. Also refers to any switch among pop, country, gospel, jazz, or rock styles.

crossover jazz A type of jazz music developed in the late 1970s that incorporated popular sounds while retaining improvisation as a major element. Grover Washington, Spyro Gyra, and Al Jarreau were a few crossover jazz artists.

Crucible, The American opera composed by Richard Ward, with libretto taken from Arthur Miller's play. First produced in 1961 in New York City, the setting is Salem, Massachusetts, in 1692 during the Salem witch trials.

Crumb, George (b. 1929) An American composer famous for avant-garde (experimental) and modern music, Crumb works with different timbres and instruments in unusual ways. Winner of the Pulitzer Prize for Music in 1968 and a Grammy Award in 2001.

crunk A fusion of hip-hop and electro music. Originating in the United States in the late 1990s, the term "crunk" referred to the manic, out-of-control crowds at concerts. Lil John and Three Mafia 6 are among the groups who play crunk.

cubop A Latin subgenre of bebop jazz music developed in the 1940s, most notably by Dizzy Gillespie, that mixes Cuban and African rhythms with traditional bebop harmonies and rhythms.

cue A short passage of another instrument's music printed in small notes in a performer's part to ensure that the player or singer will make his or her entrance at the correct time.

cut time Also known as "cut common time" or "alla breve," a time signature in which the half note instead of the quarter note defines the beat. Cut time is notated in a score by a C with a vertical slash through it or 2/2.

cycle   1. An acoustical term for a complete sound wave vibration.
2. A section of music that is repeated indefinitely.

cymbal   A percussion instrument made of various metals and
alloys shaped into thin discs. Used in a variety of ensembles such
as jazz bands, orchestras, marching bands, and heavy metal bands,
types of cymbals range from hi-hat, crash, ride, splash, clash,
swish, and sizzle.

C

D   Pitch name for the second pitch of a C-Major scale. On the piano, the second white note above middle C.

d'Arezzo, Guido (Guido of Arezzo) (991–1033)   Italian Medieval music theorist who invented modern music notation.

da capo (D.C.; It., from the beginning)   1. Musical notation instructing the performer to return to and repeat the piece from the beginning or from a designated place within the piece (*da capo al fine*). 2. A popular musical form used in baroque-period opera arias.

D.C. al Fine

da capo aria   An operatic or oratorio aria written primarily during the baroque period using a ternary form in three sections (ABA form). The first (a) section is fully repeated using improvised ornaments and variations to give the piece variety. "The Trumpet Shall Sound," from Handel's oratorio *Messiah*, is a well-known example of a da capo aria.

dal segno (D.S.)   Indicates that the performer must repeat from the dal segno sign.

Daltrey, Roger (b. 1944)   Lead singer for the rock group the Who. He was also a singer-songwriter and later in his career an accomplished actor, starring in television and film.

damper   The device that keeps the string on a piano or harpsichord from sounding by terminating the vibration of the string. Its construction consists of a piece of wood attached to a felt pad.

damper pedal   The left foot pedal under the piano that controls the damper.

damping   A soft surface that absorbs sound or acoustic energy. This surface does not reflect sound waves and keeps optimal resonance from occurring. For example, in singing, the tongue can have a damping effect if it's in a particular position.

dance music   Music used to accompany a dance or dancing.

Darin, Bobby (1936–1973)   American big band and rock-and-roll singer and actor from the late 1950s and '60s. Hugely popular with the teenage population (a "teen idol"), "Splish Splash" and "Mack the Knife" were two of his hits. He was also a record producer and won several Grammy Awards.

Davis, Miles (1926–1991)   American jazz trumpet player, composer, and bandleader. As one of the leading and most influential musicians of the twentieth century, he was at the forefront of many jazz styles of the 1940s through 1980s, such as bebop, cool jazz, hard bop, jazz funk, and jazz fusion. Davis played with all the great jazz performers, such as Charlie Parker (alto saxophone), Coleman Hawkins (tenor saxophone), Max Roach (drums), John Coltrane (tenor saxophone), and Herbie Hancock (keyboards).

D.C. al fine   Musical instruction telling the performer to repeat from the da capo sign to the end.

D.C. al Fine

dead interval   The space between the end of the first melodic phrase and the beginning of the second phrase, often signified by a rest.

death metal   An extreme subgenre of heavy metal, started in the 1980s and building on thrash metal. Although it has loud, distorted guitars, blast-beat drumming, and growling vocals, the term comes from the morbid themes of the lyrics (although some have ascribed it to one of its earliest bands, Death). Bands such as Morbid Angel and Possessed were pioneers of this sound.

Debussy, Claude (1862–1918)   French composer who had the most pivotal influence on music and composers of the early twentieth century. He was a central figure in the transition from late romantic music to modernist and impressionistic music (approximately 1900). His music established a new perception of tonality by using pentatonic and whole-tone scales and frequent bitonal and parallel chords.

decibel   Acoustical measurement dealing with pressure, or loudness, of sound. One decibel is the smallest unit of intensity that can be heard by the human ear. The threshold where pain begins is 130 decibels.

decrescendo (*decresc.*)   Italian term meaning to reduce in volume; become softer.

deep blues   Blues music that developed in the Mississippi Delta region. Played on makeshift instruments in juke joints, bars, barns, and dance halls, it eventually migrated to Chicago and was instrumental in the birth of a number of jazz and rock genres of the twentieth century. Robert Johnson and Muddy Waters were two performers of this music style.

Delta blues   Early blues music that originated in the southern United States in the Mississippi Delta around the beginning of the twentieth century. Instruments consisted of guitar and harmonica, and lyrics spoke of sadness, melancholy, narrative ballads, and work songs. This music was first recorded in the late 1920s and was the basis for later types of music such as country and rock and roll.

démancher   In playing a string instrument, the changing of the left hand from one position to another.

Denver, John (1943–1997)   American singer-songwriter and actor. A famous country, folk, and pop artist, he won two Grammy Awards, one Emmy Award, and many other awards and recognitions. His song "Rocky Mountain High" was declared Colorado's state song in 2007. Five of his songs were number-one chart hits, including "Annie's Song," "Sunshine on My Shoulders," "Thank God I'm a Country Boy," "Calypso," and "I'm Sorry." He died in 1997 in a plane he was piloting.

descant   An obligato (optional) line that soars above the melody line in a hymn.

Desprez, Josquin   *See* Josquin Desprez.

détaché   A type of bowing on a string instrument. Used for loud passages of a slower speed, the performer uses broad, energetic strokes with minor articulation on notes of equal value.

development   The use of variations or restatements of the original musical material throughout a composition. The sonata form exploits this device to its fullest.

Devil's Trill Sonata (Violin Sonata in G Minor)   Written by Giuseppe Tartini (1692–1770), a virtuosic, technically demanding violin piece inspired, according to the composer, by a dream he had in which the devil played this music.

dialogue   A music composition from the seventeenth century that is written for two alternating voice parts, much like a conversation between two singers. Often used in opera and cantatas.

Dialogues de Carmélites, Les (F., *The Dialogues of the Carmelites*) French opera in three acts composed by Francis Poulenc, with libretto by Georges Bernanos. First performed in Milan in 1957, it is set in France in 1789 during the French Revolution.

diatonic   A term used for a natural or major scale. Consists of five whole tones with two half (semi) tones. The C-Major scale, or any scale using only the notes of its own scale, would be considered diatonic.

dice music   Also called "chance" or "aleatory" music. The composer incorporates elements of unpredictability and chance in the composition and/or its performance. John Cage's *Music of Changes* (1951) is an example of this type of composition.

Dido and Aeneas   English baroque opera composed in three acts by Henry Purcell, with libretto by Nahum Tate. Produced in London in 1689, the story takes place in Carthage after the fall of Troy.

diminished   A musical interval that is shortened by chromatically altering it downward by a half step.

diminished scale   In jazz theory, the name for the octatonic scale. A symmetrical eight-note musical scale that alternates intervals by half step, whole step, half step, and whole step.

diminished seventh   A music theory term indicating a four-note chord that contains a minor third, diminished fifth, and diminished seventh note. In the key of C, it's represented by the letter notation C°7.

diminished triad   A music theory term indicating a triad (three-note chord) with a minor third and diminished fifth. In the key of C, this is called a C° chord.

diminuendo (*dimin.* or *dim.*)   Also means decrescendo; Italian term meaning to reduce in volume or get softer.

Dion, Céline (b. 1968)   All-time best-selling female artist who has sold more than 200 million albums worldwide. Winner of five Grammy Awards, two Academy Awards, and over a hundred others.

dirge   A composition used at funerals and memorials, written for either voice or instruments.

disc jockey (DJ)   Person who chooses and plays recorded music for a selected audience. Various types of disc (compact disc) or disk (phonograph record) jockeys include radio DJs, club DJs, and hip-hop DJs.

disco   A genre of dance music that came out of New York City and Philadelphia in the late 1960s and early '70s. Disco has its roots in funk and soul and is characterized by soaring vocals over a driving, "four-on-the-floor" dance beat. Donna Summer, KC and the Sunshine Band, and the Bee Gees were major artists of the genre. Disco hit its peak in the mid-1970s but suffered a big backlash and was all but wiped out by 1980.

dissonance   A music theory term identifying a quality of sound that seems "unstable" or transitional. May be referred to as a "sour" or "bad" note or chord because it demands a stableness (consonance) to resolve it. Also denotes an intentional note or chord that is meant to invoke a sense of grief, conflict, or pain; the opposite of consonance.

distortion   The alteration of any sound or waveform's original shape. It is usually, but not always, unwanted. Distortion differs from noise because noise is the addition of extraneous signals.

diva   A celebrated female singer with superior talent in the world of opera. Popular female music, film, and theater stars are sometimes also called divas. The term "prima donna" is closely related, and divo is the male equivalent.

divided stop   A Spanish organ design element that allows the different registers (right and left hands) to be played separately by dividing the keyboard manuals to upper and lower.

Dixieland jazz   A form also known as New Orleans jazz, developed in that city in the early twentieth century, that combined ragtime, blues, and brass band marches. A Dixieland band consists of a trumpet or cornet, clarinet, and trombone soloists who improvise over a rhythm section of drums, piano, tuba or double bass, and guitar or banjo. "Basin Street Blues" is a famous Dixieland piece.

D.M.A. (Doctor of Musical Arts)   The highest academic graduate degree (terminal degree) for musical performance, composition, or conducting majors.

Dolby Digital (DD)   An audio compression technology developed by Dolby Laboratories.

dolce (It., sweet)   A soft and sweet musical tone quality.

dominant chord   The fifth step in a major or minor musical scale. After the tonic (first degree or root of the chord), it is the most important. Represented in harmonic analysis by the Roman numeral V.

dominant seventh chord   In music theory, a four-note chord built around the dominant or fifth step of a major key: the tonic (the root note of the chord), a major third, the dominant fifth, and a flat seventh note. For example, in the key of C, the dominant seventh chord consists of G, B, D, and F.

Don Giovanni (It., *Don Juan*)   Italian opera or *drama giocoso* (mixture of comic and serious action) composed in two acts by Wolfgang Amadeus Mozart, with libretto by Lorenzo da Ponte. Premiered in Prague in 1787, the opera's action takes place in Seville, Spain, in the seventeenth century.

doo-wop   Vocal rhythm and blues music developed in the 1940s that gained popularity in the 1950s and '60s with groups such as the Platters, the Moonglows, Little Anthony and the Imperials, and the Drifters. Famous tunes from this period included "Golden Teardrops," "Earth Angel," and "The Great Pretender."

doom metal   A subgenre of heavy metal music characterized by slow tempos and dark, low-toned guitars and vocals to produce a sense of doom or despair. Starting in the mid-1980s, doom metal was influenced by Black Sabbath; some of the prominent bands are Pagan Altar, Pentagram, and Trouble.

Dorian mode   A minor scale defined by the following sequence of whole (W) and half (H) steps: W–H–W–W–W–H–W. Two popular songs that use the Dorian mode are "Eleanor Rigby" by the Beatles and "Smoke on the Water" by Deep Purple.

dotted notes   A dot behind a musical note causes one half the value of that note to be added to its duration. A two-beat half note with a dot will then count as three beats (six eighth notes). A double dot adds one half the value plus one quarter the value. So a double-dotted half note would be seven eighth notes (4 + 2 + 1).

double bar line   Two vertical lines used on a music staff to indicate the end of a musical section. When the second line is thicker, it indicates the end of the piece.

double bass   Also called the upright bass, contrabass, and *bass viol*, it is the largest bowed string instrument. It appears in many genres of music, including classical, jazz, bluegrass, blues, rockabilly, and rock and roll. The modern double bass has four strings and is tuned in fourths.

double chorus   A choral ensemble consisting of two complete choirs, which provides an echo effect and a stereo sensory experience. Gustav Mahler's Symphony No. 8, also known as the "Symphony of a Thousand," is one renowned work that includes a double chorus.

double concerto   A composition written for orchestra and two solo instruments, such as Brahms' Double Concerto in A Minor for violin, cello, and orchestra.

double flat   A musical sign used to lower a note by two half steps. It's indicated by two flat signs side by side in front of a note or one flat sign placed before a note that is already flatted in a certain key.

double pedal   An organist's technique of using both feet to either play chords or two single-lined passages simultaneously.

double sharp   A musical sign used to raise a note by two half steps. It's indicated by two sharp signs side by side in front of a note or one sharp sign placed before a note that is already sharpened in a certain key.

double time   A time signature that contains two beats to a measure.

double whole note   A note with a duration twice as long as a whole note. Also called a "breve," it is not usually used in modern musical notation.

double-stop   A performance technique in which two strings are simultaneously played with a bow on a string instrument.

double-tongue   A technique used on wind and brass instruments to play a staccato (detached) passage too rapid for normal articulation. Each instrument uses a different technique, but when mastered, all allow the flow of air to stop by regularly and quickly by alternating the tip and the base of the tongue.

doubling   1. When one performer alternates between two instruments, such as switching from saxophone to flute. Used often in (jazz) big bands. 2. Arranging a composition by assigning the melody to two or more instruments.

Down Beat   American trade journal for jazz musicians established in Chicago in 1934.

downbeat   The first beat of a measure of music.

dramatic music   Incidental (extra) music composed for a play or drama.

Drifters, The   A popular African American R&B/doo-wop vocal group from the 1950s and early '60s. *Rolling Stone* magazine ranked them 81 on the 100 Greatest Artists of all Time list, and they were inducted into the Rock and Roll Hall of Fame in 1988. Two of their most famous songs were "Dance with Me" and "Under the Boardwalk."

drone   A long, sustained tone used, usually in the bass line, to establish a tonality on which a composition is built. Great Highland bagpipes have a characteristic drone.

drum   A percussion instrument consisting of a skin or membrane stretched across a vessel or frame and struck with the hand or a stick.

drum-and-bass   A style of music that evolved from the jungle music genre of the mid-1990s, this electronic genre uses ragga vocals, a heavily integrated synthesized bass and percussion structure, and a simple two-step breakbeat.

duet   1. A composition written for two performers. 2. A musical ensemble made of two performers.

duple meter   A meter that has two beats to the measure. There are two types: duple (2/4) and compound duple (6/8).

duration   The length of a sound, which occurs in three stages: attack, sustain, and decay.

Dvořák, Antonin (1841–1904)   A Czech romantic composer who is famous for his use of folk-music melodies and idioms of Bohemia and Moravia. His best-known compositions include *Slavonic Dances*, Cello Concerto in B Minor, and *New World Symphony*.

Dylan, Bob (b. 1941)   American singer-songwriter. For 50 years, he has been a major influence in popular music. His influence as a poet and political, social, and philosophical figure is incorporated into several styles of his music: rock and roll, gospel, folk, and rockabilly. His honors include 11 Grammy Awards, 6 Grammy Hall of Fame Awards, an Academy Award, and 5 songs in the Rock and Roll Hall of Fame: "Like a Rolling Stone," "Blowin' in the Wind," "The

Times They Are a-Changin," "Subterranean Homesick Blues," and "Tangled Up in Blue."

dynamic accent Also called a "stress" accent, its a musical notation symbol used above a note to indicate an emphasis of sound or articulation of the note.

dynamics Words, symbols, abbreviations, and signs that indicate degrees of volume in a musical composition. See Appendix B, "Visual Index."

E   Pitch name for the third step in the C-Major scale. The third white key above middle C on the piano.

ear training   A form of musical training designed to teach students basic elements such as rhythms, chords, and musical intervals, with the objective of having students first hear musical pitches in their heads and then sing them correctly.

Earth, Wind & Fire   American R&B band that formed in 1969 in Chicago. The winner of four American Music Awards and six Grammy Awards, Earth, Wind & Fire has sold more than 90 million albums around the world. Known for their dynamic horn section and vocals, they use a mixture of funk, soul, pop, rock, and jazz in their music. Their more famous songs include "Shining Star," "Got to Get You Into My Life," and "Serpentine Fire."

echo   A natural phenomenon occurring when a sound is reproduced by acoustically reflecting it off a surface, such as a cave or canyon wall. It may also be produced by an electronic device meant to imitate this effect. An echo effect was often used by composers to emphasize a melody or section of music by immediately repeating it with another instrument or section of the orchestra or choir.

eight to the bar   A phrase meaning eight musical beats played to a measure, often creating a boogie-woogie effect.

eighth note   A musical note equivalent to one eighth of a whole note or one half of a quarter note. The notation consists of a filled-in note attached to a staff with one flag.

eighth rest   A pause equal to the length of an eighth note, half of a quarter rest, or one eighth of a whole rest.

Eine Kleine Nachtmusik (G., *A Little Night Music*)   Also known as Serenade No. 13 for Strings in G Major, K. 525, a popular piece written by Wolfgang Amadeus Mozart in 1787. Instrumentation consists of a chamber ensemble of double bass, cello, viola, and two violins.

electric blues   Blues and blues-rock music played by amplified instruments including drums, bass guitar, guitar, and occasionally the harmonica. Some of the more famous electric blues musicians include B. B. King, Bob Dylan, Stevie Ray Vaughan, and Eric Clapton.

electroacoustic music   Refers to all music made with electronic technology, utilizing sounds that traditional electric instruments cannot make as well as techniques such as prerecorded sound, audio feedback, and circuit bending. Compositions do not focus on meter or melody but manipulation of sound. Originating in the late 1940s in Paris and Cologne, some prominent composers are Pierre Boulez, Edgar Varese, and Brian Eno. A popular instrument created for this genre is the theremin.

electronic instruments   Instruments that use electricity as a power source (instead of breath or manual exertion) to create an audio signal that drives a loudspeaker. All use a controller, such as a keyboard, to activate and control notes on the instrument. The first electronic instrument (the Telharmonium, by Thaddeus Cahill) was made in 1897.

electronic music   Musical production or composition that uses electronic music technology or electronic musical instruments, such as a synthesizer. The opposite of acoustic music, which only uses acoustical (natural-sounding) instruments.

electropneumatic action   Used in pipe organs to control air pressure and to open and close the valves of the organ pipes using an electric current. Electric cables enable the keyboard console to be physically detached from the body of the organ.

Elektra   German opera composed in one act by Richard Strauss, based on Sophocles' tragedy. First produced in 1909 in Dresden, the story takes place in a royal courtyard after the Trojan War.

elevator music   Instrumental arrangements of popular songs designed to play in the background in public places such as malls, department stores, and yes, elevators. The Muzak Corporation is the biggest supplier of this type of music.

eleventh chord   A musical chord used typically in jazz that is an extension of the normal basic chord structure (in the key of C) of C, E, G, and B♭, continuing with D (the ninth) and F (the eleventh).

Elfman, Danny (b. 1953)   American composer best known for his film and television scores. Winner of a Grammy Award and four Academy Awards, Elfman wrote the main title TV theme songs for *The Simpsons* and *Desperate Housewives* as well as all but two Tim Burton film scores, including *The Nightmare Before Christmas.*

Elijah   An oratorio (a composition using an orchestra, vocal soloists, and a choir) composed by Felix Mendelssohn and produced in both English in 1846 and German in 1847. The libretto is taken from the Old Testament.

Elisir d'amore, l' (It., *The Elixir of Love*)   Italian opera composed in two acts by Gaetano Donizetti to the libretto of Felice Romani. First produced in 1832 in Milan, the story takes place in an Italian village in the early nineteenth century.

Ellington, Edward Kennedy "Duke" (1899–1974) African American composer, bandleader, and pianist. Recognized as possibly the greatest and most influential person in jazz history. He led his orchestra (big band) from 1923 to 1974 and helped elevate the respectability of the jazz form to that of classical music. Awarded 13 Grammy Awards (4 of them posthumously), he also was in two films. Songs made famous by his orchestra include "Take the A Train," "It Don't Mean a Thing (If It Ain't Got That Swing)," "Mood Indigo," and "Sophisticated Lady."

embellishment These improvised and written-out ornamentations enhance and decorate the melody of a piece. *See* ornamentation.

embouchure The position of a player's mouth on the mouthpiece of a musical instrument.

emo A type of rock music with melodic themes and expressive, emotional, and often confessionlike lyrics. Started in the mid-1980s as the hardcore punk movement, it converged with pop and indie rock and went mainstream in 2000 with groups such as Jimmy Eat World and Dashboard Confessional.

Emperor Concerto Also known as Piano Concerto in E-flat, op. 73, written in 1809–1811 by Ludwig van Beethoven.

Emperor Quartet String quartet composed by Franz Joseph Haydn in 1797. Also known as String Quartet in C, op. 76, no. 3, this was formerly Austria's national anthem.

encore An additional piece of music played at the end of a concert or recital that is not included in the printed program.

Enführung aus dem Serail, Die *See The Abduction from the Seraglio.*

English horn Double-reed instrument from the woodwind (aerophone) and oboe family. Pitched in the key of F, the English horn has a three-octave range and uses the same fingering as the oboe. Played primarily in symphony orchestras and wind ensembles.

enharmonic   In music theory, this term defines a tone of a chromatic scale that shares the same degree but is written and named differently: A♭ = G♯; D♯ = E♭.

ensemble   A group of instrumentalists or vocalists who perform musical compositions together. Examples include a vocal choir, orchestra, big band, and wind ensemble.

equaled temperament   The main tuning system of Western music, defined by an octave divided into 12 equal steps and frequency ratios.

Erlkönig (G., *Alder King*)   A poem by Johann Wolfgang von Goethe put to music, most notably by Franz Schubert in one of his lied (German art song for piano and voice). First performed in December 1820 in Vienna. Schubert's song is a difficult piece of vocal repertoire accompanied by an equally difficult piano part.

escaped tone   A note that is not part of the musical chord in a piece of music. A nonharmonic or nonchord tone.

ethnomusicology   The study of any music and its cultural aspects from a sociological and anthropological perspective. Involves historical study and long-term observation of different cultures' compositions and performance of local ethnic music. Béla Bartók and Zoltán Kodály were pioneers in the science of ethnomusicology.

étude (Fr., study)   A difficult instrumental composition written to help performers perfect a specific technical skill. Two composers, Carl Czerny and Muzio Clementi, wrote many études for the piano repertoire.

euphonium   A brass instrument commonly confused with the baritone horn because of its similar appearance and identical range. The euphonium is also pitched in B♭ and has three valves, and it has replaced the baritone horn in American schools.

Europop   A type of pop rock that was wildly popular in the 1970s. Groups came from the Netherlands, Germany, Italy, and France, but the most successful were from Sweden. The pinnacle of Europop was the group ABBA.

even scale   A musical scale in which the registers, dynamics, and color of tone are executed in a blended and uniform fashion.

experimental music   A genre that sprung up in the mid-twentieth century and can mean several different types of music. It can refer to music that is composed in a way that its end is incomprehensible, such as the music of John Cage; it can also refer to any music that pushes the boundaries of a certain genre.

exposition   A term used in music theory analysis indicating the part of a movement that introduces the main theme or melody of a musical composition, usually starting in the tonic (root) key and ending in the dominant (fifth step) key.

expression   The manner in which a performer interprets a piece of music and the composer's expressive intent. The interpretation accounts for the emotional effect the music has on the audience.

expression marks   Tempo and dynamic markings (words or signs) indicating the directions performers require to interpret the music the way the composer intended.

expressionism   A musical genre and movement of the early twentieth century associated with the atonal and 12-tone music of the Second Viennese School. Members of this movement include composers Arnold Schoenberg, Alban Berg, and Anton Webern.

extended chord   A triad (chord) with notes added to it beyond the seventh (such as ninth, eleventh, and thirteenth chords).

extended chords   Chords that extend past the seventh chord; most commonly the ninth, eleventh, and thirteenth chords.

extension   Notes that are written on ledger lines either above or below the musical staff outside the standard range.

eye music   Visual features written into a score of music that are not noticed by the listener. Examples of eye music include the use of text painting and puzzle canons such as John Bull's *Sphera Mundi*, a six-part circular canon.

F

F Pitch name for the fourth step of a C-Major scale. Fourth white key above middle C on the piano keyboard.

F-hole The shape of the sound hole on string instruments.

fa 1. Fourth degree in the solfège system (do, re, mi, fa, so, la, ti, and do). 2. Italian, French, and Spanish name for the note F.

fach system Used in Germany to categorize professional singers into specific voice and character types. Women: coloratura soprano, lyric soprano, lyric-spinto soprano, dramatic soprano, lyric mezzo-soprano, and dramatic mezzo-soprano. Men: countertenor, lyric tenor, lyric-spinto tenor, dramatic tenor, heldentenor, lyric baritone, dramatic baritone, bass-baritone, basso contante, and basso profundo.

fagott German word for bassoon, a member of the woodwind family. *See* bassoon.

fake book A collection of song outlines or lead sheets that help the performer learn new songs quickly. These lead sheets contain only the lyrics, melody, and chords. Used most often in jazz where improvisation is a major element.

falsettists Male vocalists who sing in the falsetto (highest) register of the voice.

falsetto   Also "false" voice. Usually referring to a male singer's highest singing register. Also called the "head voice" in women, it often has an extremely "breathy" or "hooty" quality. Singers who are famous for their falsetto singing include Michael Jackson, Al Green, and the Bee Gees.

Falstaff   Italian opera in three acts composed by Giuseppi Verdi, with libretto by Arrigo Boito. Produced in Milan, Italy, in 1893 and based on Shakespeare's *The Merry Wives of Windsor* and *Henry IV.* This was Verdi's last opera. The story takes place in Windsor, England, during the reign of Henry IV (1399–1413).

familiar style   1. Vocal music usually using four voices singing uniformly together with the same text and note values, as sung in a church hymn. 2. Chordal or homophonic.

Fanciulla del West, La (It., *The Girl of the Golden West*)   Italian opera written in three acts by Giacomo Puccini, with libretto by G. Civinini and C. Zangarini. Premiered in 1910 at the Metropolitan Opera House in New York City starring the legendary tenor Enrico Caruso and conducted by Arturo Toscanini. Story takes place in a mining camp in the Sierra Madre Mountains of California in 1849 to 1850.

fancy (fantasy)   A sixteenth- and seventeenth-century term for English instrumental music consisting of several themes written in imitation with sections that overlap. Origins stem from the Italian *fantasia*, popular in the sixteenth century. William Byrd (1543–1623) and Thomas Morley (1557–1602) were two famous composers in this style.

fandango   A Spanish dance appearing first in the early eighteenth century to be danced by a couple with guitar and castanets accompaniment.

fanfare   A short military or ceremonial tune composed for trumpets.

farce   Humorous and comical elements incorporated chiefly in eighteenth-century plays and operas. Similar to current light comedy that incorporates bawdy subject matter.

Farinelli (1705–1782)   Stage name for one of the most famous castratti (castrated male singer) singers of the eighteenth century. Born Carlo Maria Broschi, he was the rock star of his day.

Fauré, Gabriel (1845–1924)   French composer, pianist, organist, and teacher. A prolific composer and master of French art songs, he was the leading French composer of his age. His musical style was very influential on many twentieth-century composers.

Faust   French opera in five acts composed by Charles Gounod and produced in Paris in 1859, with libretto by Jules Barbier and Michel Carré. The story is based on Johann Wolfgang von Goethe's tragic tale of Faust, who sold his soul to the devil, set in Germany in the sixteenth century.

Favola d'Orfeo, La (It., *The Fable of Orpheus*)   Italian opera written in four acts by Claudio Monteverdi (1567–1643), with libretto by Alessandro Striggio. First performed at the annual carnival in Mantua, Italy, in 1607. One of the first operas, it is set in Ancient Greece.

feedback   The phenomenon in which a microphone or string instrument's vibration is amplified and multiplied through a loudspeaker, causing a loud, electronic buzz or shriek. This is often caused if the microphone is too "hot" (volume too high), or the microphone or guitar is placed in front of the loudspeaker.

feeders   Small bellows used to supply air to the large bellows on a pipe organ.

feldmusik (G., field music)   A seventeenth- and eighteenth-century description of brass music to be performed outside.

Fender   Modern manufacturer of acoustic and electric guitars, basses, amplifiers, and accessories founded by Leo Fender.

fermata   Also called a bird's eye, an Italian musical notation telling the performer to hold the note below the symbol for a length of time determined by the performer or conductor.

fiddle   Common name for the violin or string instrument resembling it.

Fidelio   German opera composed in two acts by Ludwig van Beethoven (1770–1827), his only opera, with the French libretto by Jean-Nicolas Bouilly and adapted to German by Joseph Sonnleithner. First performed in Vienna in 1805, the story takes place in a prison in eighteenth-century Spain.

fife   A small flute used in military bands and drum corps with six, seven, or eight finger holes. Later replaced by the piccolo.

fifth   Also called a perfect fifth, an interval made of seven half steps between the two tones of the musical scale. In the key of C, this would be C–G.

Figaro, Le Nozze di (It., *The Marriage of Figaro*)   Italian opera in four acts composed and produced in Vienna, Austria, in 1786 by Wolfgang Amadeus Mozart, with libretto by Lorenzo Da Ponte. Considered an opera buffa (comic opera), the story is set in a castle near eighteenth-century Seville, Spain.

figure   A short musical succession of notes often repeated throughout a composition. Also called a motif or motiv. Beethoven's Ninth Symphony starts with an eight-note figure.

figured bass   A bass part with numbers indicating chords, nonchord tones, and intervals in the attached harmony.

Fille du Régiment, La (F., *The Daughter of the Regiment*)   Italian opera in two acts by Gaetano Donizetti, with libretto by Jules-Henri Vernoy de Saint-Georges and Jean-François Alfred Bayard. Composed in the opera comique (comic opera) style and first performed in Paris in 1840, this was Donizetti's first opera and is set in Bologna, Italy, in the early nineteenth century.

film music   Music written and performed to accompany and describe the action taking place in a screenplay. Famous film music composers include John Williams, Erich Korngold, and Jerry Goldsmith.

final bar   The last measure of music in a composition, indicated by a double bar line.

finale   1. The last movement of an opera, sonata, or related forms, such as a symphony or quartet.

Finale   A music-notation software by MakeMusic, Inc.

fine   Musical term indicating the ending of a composition.

Fine

fingerboard   A long strip of hardwood fixed to the neck of string instruments. The strings stretched over this hardwood may or may not have frets. *See* fretboard.

fingering   An organized system of using fingers to play musical instruments.

Finn, William (b. 1952)   Award-winning American composer and lyricist of musical theater. Works include the musical *The 25th Annual Putnam County Spelling Bee*, which won two Tony Awards in 2005.

Finzi, Gerald (1901–1956)   British composer most famous for his choral and solo vocal music. The cantata *Dies natalis* (1939) and Clarinet Concerto (1949) are two of his most famous works.

Fitzgerald, Ella (1917–1996)   Also called the "First Lady of Song," she was one of jazz music's most famous singers for more than 50 years. She sold more than 40 million records and won 13 Grammy awards. Famous renditions of songs include "One O'Clock Jump" with the Count Basie big band, "The Man I Love" and "Bewitched, Bothered and Bewildered."

Five, The   A group of Russian composers who united to create a national school of Russian music around 1875. They include Nicolay Rimsky-Korsakov, Modest Mussorgsky, Miley Balakirev, Alexander Borodin, and César Cui.

fixed-do   System of teaching music students sight-reading in which each note of the scale is sung to a special solfège syllable (do, re, mi, fa, so, la, ti, and do). In the fixed-do system, musical pitches always use the same solfège syllable no matter what scale they are in; for example, "re" is always the pitch D, and pitch G is always the syllable "so." Two other solfege systems include movable-do and numbers.

flag   In music notation, the flag is attached to a note to indicate rhythm or duration of the note. Connected to a stem, it indicates an eighth note; two flags indicate a sixteenth note or twice as fast, and so on.

flamenco   A song type from southern Spain with traits of folk and art music performed by trained singers with guitar accompaniment.

flat   1. The lowering of a note pitch by one half step. 2. Indicates incorrect intonation lower than the actual pitch.

flat top   A steel-string guitar's flat soundboard.

Fledermaus, Die (G., *The Bat*)   Operetta in three acts composed by Johann Strauss Jr., with libretto by R. Genée and C. Haffner. First produced in Vienna in 1874, the show is set in Austria in 1874.

Flemish School   Active between 1450–1600, the leading school of composers originating in Flanders, northern France, and southern Belgium. Composers who developed this style of polyphonic vocal music include Dufay, Ockeghem, Obrecht, Josquin, Willaert, and Lassus.

Fliegende Holländer, Der (G., *The Flying Dutchman*)   Opera in three acts composed by Richard Wagner to his own libretto. Produced in Dresden, Germany, in 1843. One of his earlier works.

floating pickup   Usually attached to arched-top guitars, a pickup microphone that is suspended over the end of the pick guard or fingerboard to amplify the acoustical properties.

Floyd, Carlisle (b. 1926)   American opera composer who based his works on Southern themes. *Susannah* (1955), his third opera, was his greatest success.

flugelhorn   A brass instrument developed in the early nineteenth century resembling a trumpet, only bigger and with a more mellow and dark tone. Famous jazz artists who have played this instrument include Chuck Mangione, Miles Davis, Freddie Hubbard, Maynard Ferguson, and Woody Shaw.

flute   A woodwind instrument shaped like a cylindrical tube closed at the top end. Usually made from silver, nickel, or gold; older instruments were made from wood. To produce the sound, the flute player or flautist must blow air across the side hole. The flute is one of the world's oldest and most widespread instruments.

flutter-tonguing   A special type of technique in playing wood-wind instruments that uses the tongue in a rolling movement. Used as a special effect or in Vaudeville or New Orleans–style jazz.

FM (frequency modulation)   Used in radio and other telecom-munications to convey information. Digital data is sent via carrier wave by changing its frequency (frequency-shift keying).

focused tone   Well-defined, clear tonal characteristics resulting from the singer or instrumentalist as he or she adjusts to the changing conditions of the vowel, intensity, pitch, and musical concept.

folk music   Music traditionally involving singing (folk songs) that deals with a rural community's poems or songs and different aspects of everyday life, such as love songs, drinking songs, mourn-ing songs, and work songs. Found in almost every corner of the earth, these songs often express nationalistic characteristics.

folk rock   A combination of folk and rock music that came about in England and the United States in the mid-1960s. Cat Stevens, Donovan, Bob Dylan, and Simon and Garfunkel were some of the main players of this genre.

form 1. Styles or genres of music (country western, rock, classical, and so on). 2. The shape of elements within a composition (intervals, phrases or rhythm, and so on).

formant Frequency components of speech and singing. The frequency in these formants creates a resonance that identifies vowels in speech or song to the listener.

forte (*f*) Italian term indicating the volume should be loud.

$$f$$

fortepiano (*fp*) Italian term: 1. Loud followed by soft. 2. The name for the first type of piano, which evolved from the harpsichord by using hammers to strike the strings instead of pluck them.

$$fp$$

fortissimo (*ff*) Italian term directing the performer to play "very loud."

$$ff$$

fortississimo (*fff*) Italian term, louder than fortissimo, that is an indication to perform a musical passage "very, very loudly."

$$fff$$

Forza del Destino, La (It., *The Force of Destiny*) Opera composed in four acts by Giuseppi Verdi, with libretto by Francesco Maria Piave. Premiering in St. Petersburg in 1862, the opera's action takes place in eighteenth-century Spain and Italy.

forzando (*fz*) Italian term indicating a forced or accented note or chord.

Foss, Lukas (1922–2009)   American pianist, composer, and conductor. Born in Berlin on August 15, 1922, Foss made his conducting debut at age 17 and studied with Paul Hindemith.

Foster, Stephen (1826–1864)   The best-known American songwriter of the nineteenth century. He was the "father of American music" with songs such as "Camptown Races," "Oh! Susanna," "My Old Kentucky Home," and "Beautiful Dreamer."

Four Seasons, The   Set of four violin concertos composed in 1723 by Antonio Vivaldi. One of the most popular classical works of all time.

fourth   An interval made of five half steps between two tones of the musical scale. In the key of C, this is C–G.

fox trot   A ballroom dance in duple meter developed in America around 1915.

Franck, César (1822–1890)   Born in Belgium, Franck was a major composer, music teacher, and organist of the romantic period (1820–1900). He lived most of his life in France. He is best remembered for his Symphony in D Minor (1888) and Symphonic Variations for Piano and Orchestra (1885).

Franklin, Aretha (b. 1942)   Grammy Award–winning singer known for her interpretation of soul tunes as well as gospel, jazz, blues, rock, pop, and R&B. She has had 20 number-one and 45 Top-40 hits on the *Billboard* charts.

free improvisation   An outgrowth of improvised jazz that developed in the United States in the 1960s. Free improvisation disregards any formal rules used in traditional improvisation.

free jazz   An avant-garde style of jazz that tries to break down any fixed conventions of bebop or any other modal type of jazz. Introduced in the 1950s, free jazz pioneers include John Coltrane (tenor saxophone), Archie Shepp (tenor saxophone), and Sun Ra (keyboards).

free music   A style of music invented by Percy Grainger (1882–1961) that uses pitches in an untraditional way, replacing a scale with a controlled, uninterrupted glide.

free throat   When the throat is free of tension, allowing phonation (speaking or singing) to occur naturally.

free time   A time signature with no identifiable rhythm. The composer may provide a time signature of 4/4 (common time) to make the notation easier to read, but a composition written in free time does not contain a specific rhythmic pattern.

Freemason music   Music used in Freemason ceremonies and rites. This music uses singing of popular or operatic songs with suitable texts and dance tunes. The most famous Masonic composer was Wolfgang Amadeus Mozart, whose opera *The Magic Flute* uses many elements taken from Masonic rites.

Freishütz, Der (G., *The Freeshooter*)   German opera composed in three acts by Carl Maria von Weber, with libretto by Friedrich Kind. First performed in Berlin in 1821 and set in Bohemia after the Seven Years' War.

French harp   Old name for the mouth harp or harmonica.

French horn   A brass instrument pitched in the key of F with three valves, a funnel-shaped mouthpiece, a round conical bore shaped in a spiral, and a large flared bell. Often simply called the "horn."

French overture   A musical form popular in the baroque period (1685–1750) and developed by the French composer Jean-Baptiste Lully. It is composed in three parts: slow, fast, and slow.

French Suites   Six harpsichord suites composed around 1720 by Johann Sebastian Bach.

frequency   An acoustic term indicating a pitch generated by pressure pulses or cycles per second and created by a sound source such as vocal chords or a string. Measured in Hertz (Hz).

frequency modulation   *See* FM.

Frescobaldi, Girolamo (1583–1643)   Important composer and keyboardist of the late renaissance and earlier baroque periods. His vocal works include many masses, motets, and madrigals, but the major volume of work consisted of keyboard music. He made a major contribution on the modern idea of tempo and was organist at St. Peter's Cathedral in Rome from 1608 until his death.

fret   Narrow strips of metal or wood fixed to the fingerboard of certain string instruments, including the guitar and banjo, to help the player find the finger position needed in the melody or chord.

fretboard   The string-instrument fingerboard to which frets are attached.

friction peg   Round and made of wood; holds the strings onto a solid headstock.

frog   An arch made of wood or plastic that is fastened onto string instruments at the upper end of the neck to help raise the strings over the fingerboard.

front   Jazz slang referring to the music before the beginning of the melody at the top of a song; an intro.

front man   The lead singer in a rock band or jazz group who is often also the leader of the band.

fry voice   A gravelly sound produced at the very low end of the vocal range.

fugue   A contrapuntal composition or technique using a fixed number of voices in imitative counterpoint. The form reached maturity in compositions by Johann Sebastian Bach.

full voice   Singing with a loud and technically masterful technique, using the vocal mechanism to the fullest extent.

functional harmony   A modern harmonic analysis technique based on the premise that within any given key, there are only three functional chords: the tonic (I), the dominant (V), and the subdominant (IV). The rest of the chords are variations of these three chords.

fundamental   The lowest frequency in a complex sound wave, which the listener perceives as pitch.

fundamental bass   The lowest note played or noted on a piece of music. It is often, but not always, the root note of the chord.

fundamental tone   The base note and lowest tone of a chord.

funk   American musical style blending R&B, soul, and jazz in a rhythmic, danceable form. Originating in the mid-1960s, funk emphasizes rhythm and "groove" over melody or harmony, often using extended vamps on a single chord. James Brown, Earth, Wind & Fire, Kool and the Gang, and Average White Band are a few of the artists identified with this genre. Funk influenced the development of disco, hip-hop, new wave, and punk music.

fusion   A jazz style that combines the energy and attitude of rock music with the more harmonically sophisticated and improvisational jazz music. Modern instruments such as the electric guitar and synthesizer replace traditionally acoustic instruments such as upright bass, saxophone, and trumpet. The complexity of the music, using high-intensity rock, also requires performers to have the virtuosity needed to play complex meters, time signatures, and improvisation. Miles Davis and Gary Burton were major influences on this style.

futurism   A term introduced in 1909 to explain a radicalism in the arts. Within music, futurism is the use of instrumental effects imitating machines, factory sounds, electricity, and other sounds that represent the everyday lives of the modern masses.

fuzzy tone   A poorly defined vocal quality usually caused by a lack of laryngeal muscular coordination.

G Name for the fifth pitch of a C-Major scale. On the piano, the fifth white note above middle C.

gallant style A light and elegant style of the classical period (1750–1820) that uses less ornamentation than the baroque period. This style was more appreciated by the middle class and secular audiences because of its more direct and simple style. Johann Sebastian Bach's son, Carl Philipp Emanuel Bach (1714–1788), was one of the main composers of this style.

gangsta rap A type of hip-hop music reflecting urban youth's violent lifestyles. Rap groups such as N.W.A. and Ice T made this genre popular in the late 1980s and early '90s. It's a controversial genre due to its use of lyrics promoting drug use, promiscuity, violence, and materialism.

garage band An amateur band that practices in someone's garage.

garage rock A genre of rock and roll that gained popularity between 1964 and 1967. With fuzzy guitars, growling vocals, and an almost amateurish sound, the term came from the perception that these bands were practicing in their garage. Influenced by the British Invasion, bands such as the Troggs, the Kingsmen, and ? and the Mysterians brought this genre into the mainstream.

GarageBand   A music editing and sequencing software developed by Apple Inc. and shipped in its iLife software suite that helps users create podcasts or music.

Garfunkel, Art (b. 1941)   American singer known for being half of the folk duo Simon and Garfunkel. This Grammy Award–winning duo was one of the most popular groups of the 1960s, with number-one hits such as "The Sound of Silence" and "Bridge over Troubled Water."

gathering note   With this note, the organist signals a church congregation to the pitch of the upcoming hymn.

gavotte   A popular seventeenth-century French dance, in a moderate tempo of 4/4 time, starting with a pickup of two quarter notes with phrases ending in the middle of the measure.

Gaye, Marvin (1939–1984)   American singer-songwriter. Motown's number-one selling artist in the 1960s, he had hit singles such as "How Sweet It Is (To Be Loved by You)," "I Heard It Through the Grapevine," "What's Goin' On," and "Let's Get It On."

general MIDI   A standardized system of synchronizing music synthesizers to MIDI (Musical Instrument Digital Interface) messages produced by a digital keyboard. Enables the synthesizer to play at least 24 notes at a time and defines which of the 128 instrument sounds should be played.

general pause (*G.P.*)   Also called a grand pause, which occurs when an entire orchestra unexpectedly stops with a big rest following a climactic passage only to vigorously restart again. An innovation made popular in the late eighteenth century by the Mannheim School.

//

general probe   Orchestral concert dress rehearsal that is open to the public.

Gershwin, George (1898–1937)   American composer and pianist who composed in both the classical and popular genres. His most famous compositions include *Rhapsody in Blue, An American in Paris,* and what he called his "folk opera," *Porgy and Bess.*

Getz, Stan (1927–1991)   Grammy Award–winning American jazz musician nicknamed "The Sound." One of the most recorded and loved tenor saxophonists from the 1940s to the 1980s. He played with most of the greats in jazz, including Woody Herman, Stan Kenton, Jimmy Dorsey, Benny Goodman, Nat King Cole, Dizzy Gillespie, Oscar Peterson, Max Roach, and many others.

Gibson   American manufacturer of acoustic and electric guitars. Orville Gibson started making mandolins in the late nineteenth century and eventually flat-top guitars in the 1930s. Starting in the early 1950s, Gibson introduced the iconic Les Paul solid-body electric guitar, which has been its best-selling guitar to date.

gig   Slang for a musical job or live performance.

gigue   A baroque period dance originating in the sixteenth century from a British folk dance called the jig. Usually set in 3/8 meter, the accent is traditionally on the third beat of the measure.

Gilbert and Sullivan   The Victorian-era songwriting partnership of William Gilbert (1836–1911), librettist, and Arthur Sullivan (1842–1900), composer. Together, they composed 14 comic operas including *The Gondoliers, The Mikado,* and *H.M.S. Pinafore.*

Gillespie, John "Dizzy" (1917–1993)   American jazz trumpeter and bandleader. With Charlie Parker (alto saxophone), he helped develop modern jazz and more specifically bebop. His rhythms, phrasing, and amazing speed made him one of the greatest trumpeters of his age. He could be easily identified by his pouched cheeks and bent trumpet bell.

Gioconda, La (It., *The Ballad Singer*)   Italian opera by Amilcare Ponchielli, with libretto by Arrigo Boito and based on a play by Victor Hugo. First performed in Milan, Italy, in April 1876, the story takes place in Venice in the seventeenth century.

glam rock A genre that developed in Britain in the early 1970s whose performers wore outrageous hairstyles, clothes, and makeup for theatrical effect while playing hard rock music. Glam-rock performers included David Bowie, T.Rex, KISS, and Queen.

Glass, Philip (b. 1937) American composer of minimalist works, opera, musical theatre, symphonic works, and film scores, three of which were nominated for Academy Awards. A student of Nadia Boulanger, Glass founded the musical group the Philip Glass Ensemble.

glee A type of unaccompanied men's choral music popular in England in the eighteenth and nineteenth centuries that caught on in American universities.

glide A musical effect performed on wind instruments by lipping up or lipping down the pitch to another note, and on string instruments by running the finger up or down the string while bowing the string. In singing, it is used as an effect and also for training the voice.

Glinka, Mikhail (1804–1857) Russian composer who is often regarded as the "father of Russian classical music." He was a great influence on future Russian composers and helped develop a distinct Russian style.

glissando A rapid scale executed on the piano with the thumbnail or middle fingernail being drawn across the white or black keys in a quick movement. This effect is often used on the harp but is harder to perform on woodwind, brass, and especially bowed string instruments.

glitch A type of electronic music developed in the 1990s. A subgenre of electronica, glitch concentrates on the effects that happen when a malfunction in digital technology takes place, such as CD skipping, a computer crash, distortion, or hardware noise.

glockenspiel A member of the percussion section, a glockenspiel is a xylophone with metal bars encompassing a range of two and a half to three octaves. Also called a bell lyre or orchestra bells, it's played by striking it with metal, plastic, or rubber mallets.

glottal attack An abrupt air and sound release of the vocal chords used in speech in words such as "ice" or "good." Also known as a "hard onset." It's the opposite of an easy onset, which uses a breath lift to start the vowel.

go-go A type of propulsive funk music that started in the mid-1970s in Washington, D.C., which uses a syncopated, dotted rhythm with two different-sized congas (tall Cuban drum). With go-go, the nonstop groove takes precedence over individual songs. There is also audience participation, with the performer singing or yelling a phrase and the audience repeating it back.

Goldberg Variations An expressive melody and 30 of its variations for harpsichord written by Johann Sebastian Bach in 1741. This work is an important example of variation form and one of the most popular pieces in the piano repertoire.

Goldsmith, Jerry (1929–2004) Prolific American composer for television and film. His television theme songs included *Gunsmoke*, *The Twilight Zone*, and *Star Trek: The Next Generation*, and his more than 200 famous film scores included *Alien*, *Star Trek: The Motion Picture*, *Poltergeist* 1 and 2, and the *Rambo* movies. He received one Academy Award and six Emmy Awards.

gong A member of the percussion family that comes from the East and Southeast Asia. Constructed from various metal alloys, categories include suspended gongs (a circular metal disc suspended by a chord), bossed gongs (metal disc with a raised center played horizontally), and bowl gongs (bowl-shaped).

Goodman, Benny (1909–1986) American jazz clarinetist and leader of one of the most popular swing bands of the mid-1930s. His band was also one of the first racially inclusive groups, featuring vibraphonist Lionel Hampton and pianist Teddy Wilson. He was nicknamed "The Professor" and "King of Swing."

gospel music   Developed from sacred Christian hymns and African American spirituals, these popular-sounding songs of praise are used in religious worship services and for entertainment as an alternative to mainstream secular music. Written as a personal expression of thanks to God, Jesus, or the Holy Spirit, it is also called Black Gospel. Aretha Franklin, Sam Cooke, and Lou Rawls got their starts in gospel music.

gothic rock   A type of alternative rock that grew from English punk rock in the late 1970s. "Goth" uses a lot of keyboards, dirge-like rhythms, high-pitched bass lines, dark soundscapes, and morbid, depressing lyrics. Bauhaus, the Cure, and Siouxsie and the Banshees are prime examples of gothic music.

Gould, Glenn (1932–1982)   Canadian pianist renowned for his interpretation of Johann Sebastian Bach's keyboard music. One of the twentieth century's most renowned classical pianists. His mannerisms while playing the piano were unorthodox, and he often hummed the tune while he was playing. He quit performing live when he was 31 years old and concentrated on studio recording.

Gounod, Charles (1818–1893)   French composer from the romantic period, best known for his operas *Roméo and Juliette* and *Faust*. His song "Ave Maria" is one of the most performed church vocal pieces.

grace note   An ornamental notation written before the note it embellishes, printed in small type. A grace note with a slash through the stem is played quickly before the downbeat of the regular note, while a plain grace note usually indicates that it should share the beat with the regular note (a plain grace note embellishing a quarter note, for example, would create two eighth notes).

Grainger, Percy (1882–1961)   Australian composer and pianist well known for his piano piece "Country Gardens." He was known for his musical innovations and a style he called "free music."

Grammy Award   Established in 1958 by the National Academy of Recording Arts and Sciences, this award recognizes exceptional achievement in the music industry.

gramophone   1. Original British name for the American "phonograph," which was the earliest mechanism for recording and playing back sound. 2. A British classical music magazine.

Grand Opera   An opera of unusually large proportions typically associated with the Paris Opera House from the 1820s to 1850. Lavish stage effects, spectacular design, and oversized orchestra and cast, along with a ballet, were typically used. Rossini, Gounod, Meyerbeer, Donizetti, Halévy, and Verdi were some of the most notable composers who wrote for this musical genre.

grand staff   Two staffs with different clefs held together using a measure or bar line; used in piano music.

graphic notation   A type of musical notation used in experimental music that uses symbols and illustrations to represent the music. John Cage and George Crumb are among the prominent contemporary composers who have used graphic notation.

Grateful Dead, The   American rock band that fused all types of musical genres together into a psychedelic whole. Formed in 1965 in San Francisco, the band's devoted fans are called "Deadheads." Three of their best-known songs are "Truckin'," "Sugar Magnolia," and "Touch of Grey."

grave   Italian term instructing the performer to perform part or the whole piece in a solemn or serious manner.

Gregorian chant   Liturgical (religious) chant, also known as plainsong, believed to have been developed by Pope Gregory I (reigned 590–604 C.E.) for the Roman Catholic Church. There are approximately 3,000 chant melodies, and most are based on prose text taken from the Book of Psalms in the Bible. Each chant consists of a melody line sung by a cantor (soloist) or unison choir in one of the eight church modes.

Grieg, Edvard (1843–1907)   Norwegian composer and pianist from the romantic period. One of the major nationalist composers, he is perhaps best known for his Concerto in A Minor for Piano and *Peer Gynt Suite.*

grindcore   A genre of rock from the United Kingdom in the 1980s influenced by death metal, industrial music, hardcore punk, and rock. Characterized by distorted guitars, screaming vocals, and blast-beats, some of the bands include Siege, Napalm Death, and Agoraphobic Nosebleed.

groove   1. Jazz slang to describe the state of a musician who is experiencing a good performance; playing "in the groove." 2. A track cut into a phonograph record for the needle or stylus to follow.

ground bass   A four- or eight-measure melodic bass line that is repeatedly played below a changing harmony and melody. A strong characteristic of baroque music, this is also called an *ostinato* bass, *chaconne*, or *passacaglia.*

ground beat   The basic beat of a song, usually the quarter-note beat, whether played or implied.

grunge   A type of alternative rock also called the Seattle Sound. Heavy electric guitars and anguished, lethargic lyrics typify this rock genre developed in Washington State in the mid-1980s. A hybrid of heavy metal, hardcore punk, and indie rock, the groups Nirvana, Pearl Jam, and Soundgarden were the prototypical grunge bands.

Guidonian hand   A picture of the human hand used as a memorization aid to teach students the notes of a scale and to sight sing. Each part of the hand represents a note within a three-octave range. Named after Guido d'Arezzo, the inventor of musical notation and music theorist from the Medieval period.

guitar   Evolving from the lute, a stringed musical instrument used to play many musical styles. Most guitars are constructed from wood and usually have six strings. Types include the classical guitar (with animal gut or nylon strings), acoustic guitar (steel strings), and electric guitar (steel strings with electrical pickups built in). The electric (developed in the 1930s) and acoustic guitars have had a major influence on the sound of all pop, jazz, rock, and country bands and are as effective as a solo instrument as they are an accompanying instrument. Major brand names include Fender, Martin, Gretsch, Ibanez, Gibson, Yamaha, and Ovation.

Guthrie, Woody (1912–1967)   American singer, songwriter, and folk musician. Best known for his song "This Land Is Your Land," he wrote hundreds of ballads, folk songs, and children's songs while traveling with migrant workers on their way to California during the Great Depression and the Dust Bowl (1930s) era. Father of Arlo Guthrie, another famous American folk musician.

G

habenera   A Cuban dance that is an ancestor to the modern-day tango. Popular during the Spanish-American War (April to August 1898), it was made famous in Georges Bizet's opera *Carmen*.

half bar   A measure that does not completely fit on the line of a staff, which is separated into two, with one half at the end of a staff and the other half at the beginning of the next staff.

half diminished scale   A musical scale often used in jazz that contains a minor seven and a flat five (m7♭5).

half mordent   Used during the baroque and classical periods, it is a musical ornament that alternates two notes that are a second interval apart, starting with the written note. Shorter duration than a mordent.

half note   A musical note with a hollow oval body and straight stem with no flags. This note equals 2 beats or 2 quarter notes, 4 eighth notes, 8 sixteenth notes, or 16 thirty-second notes.

half rest   A pause or rest that is equal to two quarter rests, one half note, or one half of a whole rest.

half step   Also called a semitone or minor second, the smallest interval used in Western music. Twelve half steps equal an octave.

half time   *See* cut time.

half voice   A low-volume sound produced by singers as an artistic effect and rehearsal technique (marking) to reduce voice fatigue. A composer uses the Italian term *mezza voce* to signify that the half voice effect is to be used in a passage of music.

Hamlisch, Marvin (b. 1944)   American composer, conductor, and pianist. He is best known for his theater and film scores, including the musicals *A Chorus Line*, *Seesaw*, and *The Goodbye Girl* and soundtracks for *The Sting*, *Ice Castles*, *Ordinary People*, *The Spy Who Loved Me*, and *The Informant*. A recipient of four Emmy Awards; an Oscar, Grammy, and Tony Award; and a Pulitzer Prize, he is one of the most celebrated musicians in American popular music.

hammer-on   A string instrument technique in which the performer sharply brings down his or her finger on the fret board behind the fret, causing the sounding of a note.

Hammond organ   An electric organ invented in 1934 by Laurens Hammond as an alternative to higher-priced pipe organs used in churches. The most well-known type of this organ was the Hammond B-3, used extensively in jazz, rock, and gospel music.

Hampton, Lionel (1908–2002)   American jazz vibraphonist and bandleader. One of the greatest jazz artists of the twentieth century. One of the original jazz vibraphone performers, he worked with most of the great jazz musicians of his day.

Hancock, Herbie (b. 1940)   American jazz pianist and composer. A leader and definer of different jazz styles and the jazz rhythm section. Hancock was pianist in Miles Davis's second great quintet and later embraced the use of synthesizers and experimentation, often successfully crossing over into popular music. Two of his most famous songs are "Watermelon Man" and "Cantaloupe Island."

Handel, George Frideric (1685–1759)   German English baroque composer and organist who, along with Bach, Beethoven, and Mozart, is known as one of the greatest composers of all time. Born in Germany, he trained in Italy and after 1712 spent the rest of his life in England. His compositions consist of 42 operas, 29 oratorios, 122 cantatas, keyboard works, concerti grossi, English songs, and many other types of compositions. He is most known for his oratorio *The Messiah*, with its famous "Hallelujah Chorus."

Hansel and Gretel   German opera composed in three acts by Engelbert Humperdinck, with libretto by his sister, Adelheid Wette. First produced in Weimar in 1893, the story is based on the fairy tale and is set in the Hartz Mountains in Germany.

hard bop   A type of jazz music incorporating syncopated, hard-swinging, up-tempo, and hard-cutting sound with a mixture of bebop, gospel, and blues. A product of East Coast black musicians who contrasted with the cool, West Coast musicians of the 1950s and 1960s. Horace Silver (piano), Art Blakey (drums), Sonny Rollins (tenor sax), and Clifford Brown (trumpet) were leaders in this genre of jazz.

hard rock   A type of rock music starting in the mid 1960s that was influenced by blues, garage, and psychedelic rock. It features heavy distorted guitars, drums, and keyboards. Early hard rock groups included Led Zeppelin, Iron Butterfly, and the Who; later groups included Van Halen, Metallica, and Guns N' Roses.

hardcore punk   A faster, heavier style of punk rock developed in the late 1970s. It also differs from punk with its off-beat drums and vocals. The bands Bad Brains, Black Flag, and Hüsker Dü were famous hardcore punkers.

H

harmonic   Also called an overtone or partial. An acoustical term used to describe certain characteristics of a vibrating body. Harmonics resonate faster than the fundamental (original) vibration at the half, third, fourth, and fifth. A string vibrating at 100 Hz when pressed in the middle will vibrate twice as fast at the octave or 200 Hz, which is the first harmonic.

harmonic analysis   In music theory, the practice of analyzing harmonies and individual chords in a music composition. It is a fundamental aspect of musical training.

harmonic rhythm   When chords change the rhythmic pattern or harmonic tempo in a composition. This underlying harmonic change affects the rhythmic life, style, and texture of the piece.

harmonic series   Vibration patterns inherent in a certain instrument. When blowing a flute with all the keys closed, for example, the player can play seven or eight notes above the fundamental (original) tone. Harmonics resonate faster than the fundamental vibration at the half, third, fourth, and fifth.

harmonic spectrum   The strength of harmonic overtones compared to the strength of the fundamental tone.

harmonica   Also called a mouth organ or blues harp, a popular instrument used in American folk, country, jazz, blues, and pop music. This small metal box with small holes along its side was first invented in Germany in the early nineteenth century. When the harmonica is blown with the mouth, the air pressure goes through the holes and vibrates a pair of reeds that sound at different pitches upon inhalation and exhalation. Famous performers on this instrument include Bob Dylan, Stevie Wonder, and Billy Joel.

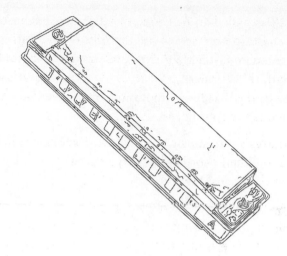

harmonium   A reed organ that uses a foot-operated bellows to push air through a set of reeds. Also called a parlor or pump organ. A portable harmonium is very similar to an accordian.

harmony   The vertical chord structure in a musical composition. Compared to melody, which is played only one note at a time, harmony can consist of many different notes played simultaneously.

Harmony of the Spheres   A medieval concept that the heavenly bodies of the solar system, when moving around Earth at different speeds, produce different sounds, with the moon, Venus, Mercury, the sun, Saturn, Jupiter, and Mars producing the seven notes of a scale.

harp   A string instrument that ranks among the oldest in the world, dating back to 3000 B.C.E. The modern harp was introduced in the early 1800s and is constructed of a triangle frame with six and a half octaves of strings made with wire, nylon, gut, or silk strung from the top to the bottom soundboard. Seven pedals are used to adjust the pitch of the harp's strings, and it is used as a solo instrument and in chamber and symphony orchestras.

harpsichord   Predecessor to the piano, a keyboard instrument with a mechanism that plucks a string when a key is hit, producing a bright sound. It is widely used in baroque and renaissance music, especially as a thoroughbass accompaniment. In addition to the sound, one of the primary differences between a harpsichord and a piano is the instrument's inability to change dynamics, or louder or softer volume.

Harrison, George (1943–2001)   English singer-songwriter and lead guitarist for the rock band the Beatles. *Rolling Stone* placed him at 21 on its list of the 100 Best Guitarists of All Time. After the Beatles broke up in 1970, he had a successful solo career and produced films. His biggest original hits include "Something," "Here Comes the Sun," "Taxman," and "My Sweet Lord."

Hawkins, Coleman (1904–1969)   American tenor saxophone player, one of the first jazz performers on that instrument in the early 1920s. He remained a prominent performer throughout the big band era and into the development of bebop music in the 1940s. His improvisatory take on "Body and Soul" was a major influence on the bebop movement.

Haydn, Franz Joseph (1732–1809)   Austrian composer who, with Mozart, was one of the most prominent and prolific composers of the classical period (1750–1820). Known as the "Father of the Symphony" and the "Father of the String Quartet," he also developed the sonata form and the piano trio.

head   1. Jazz term indicating the composed part of a performance, as opposed to the improvised sections. The head contains the main tune or melody that the soloists improvise upon. 2. The stretched skin or plastic part of a drum that is struck to produce sound.

head arrangement   Jazz slang for an arrangement of a song that is not written out but is remembered by the members of the band.

head voice   A coordinated mixture of the singer's falsetto (highest) and chest voice (lowest) registers. Also known as head register or head tone.

headbanger   Also called a "metalhead," a fan who follows heavy rock and metal bands.

headbanging   Violent shaking of the head in rhythm to rock and heavy metal music.

heavy metal   A type of rock music developed in the late 1960s and 1970s, primarily in the United States and England. Early metal bands such as Led Zeppelin, Black Sabbath, and later Metallica and Mötley Crüe developed this highly amplified, distorted, thick sound that used long guitar solos and vigorous rhythms. Its roots come from psychedelic and blues rock.

heldentenor   One of the rarest voice fachs (types). Its sustained tessitura (most comfortable singing range) is lower than that of a dramatic tenor and is usually thicker, larger, and more dramatic. Parts for this voice are most often in German opera by composers such as Richard Wagner. Lauritz Melchior (1890–1973) was one of the leading heldentenors of his time.

hemiola   A metrical music pattern in which two measures of triple time (3/4 or 3/2) are articulated and performed as if there were three measures of duple time (2/4 or 2/2). Used frequently in baroque music and later by composers such as Johannes Brahms and Robert Schumann.

Hendrix, Jimi (1942–1970)   American rock guitarist, songwriter, and singer. Most famous for his rock rendition of "The Star-Spangled Banner" at the Woodstock music festival in 1969. He was considered the number-one guitarist by many musicians and was 1 in *Rolling Stone* magazine's 100 Greatest Guitarists of All Time list. His preference for guitar effects such as the wah-wah pedal and overdriven amplifiers were expanded in the recording studio, where he was known to experiment with stereophonic and special effects.

Herbert, Victor (1859–1924)   German American composer, conductor, and cellist who composed many Broadway operettas such as *Naughty Marietta*, *Sweethearts*, and *Eileen* as well as orchestral, piano, and concert band compositions, cantatas, and incidental music.

Herman, Woody (1913–1987)   American big-band leader and clarinetist. His band, the Herd, was one of the most popular big bands of the 1930s and '40s.

heroic tenor   *See* heldentenor.

Hertz (Hz)   A frequency unit defined by the International System of Units. In sound analysis, 1 hertz equals 1 cycle per second. Named after Heinrich Hertz, a nineteenth-century German physicist.

heterophony   A performance technique in which the same melody line is played simultaneously by two performers who either improvise or somehow modify the tune.

hi-hat   A cymbal instrument found on a typical drum kit that consists of two cymbals suspended on a steel rod. The performer steps on a pedal that causes the two cymbals to crash together.

hi-NRG   A genre of electronic dance music originating in the United Kingdom and United States in the 1970s. Pronounced "high energy," its major influence is disco and is epitomized by songs such as Donna Summer's "I Feel Love."

hide hitter   Jazz slang meaning "drummer."

high fidelity (or "hi-fi")   A term used to describe the reproduction of sounds and images with lower amounts of distortion, noise, and frequency response. Important to home stereo audio enthusiasts who desire a sound recording that sounds as close to the original performance as possible.

high life   A mixture of twentieth-century American and European music featuring the steady rhythm of West African popular music.

hillbilly music   A stereotypical and derogatory term for folk and traditional music of the Ozark and Appalachian Mountains of the United States. Rockabilly and bluegrass music came from this genre. Also, when mixed with country swing and cowboy music, it resulted in what is now known as country-western music.

Hindemith, Paul (1895–1963)   German American composer, violist, and educator. His distinctive modern style developed from traditional classical forms. In the 1940s, he taught composition at Yale University to notable students such as Lukas Foss and Norman Dello Joio. He wrote 11 operas and many chamber and orchestral pieces, including Symphony in B-flat for Concert Band.

Hines, Earl (1903–1983)   American jazz pianist prominent in shaping the history of jazz. Also known as Earl "Fatha" Hines, he played with early jazz artists such as Louis Armstrong and later played and recorded albums with most of the jazz greats of the twentieth century. His numerous awards included a six-time designation as the world's number-one jazz pianist by *Down Beat* magazine.

hip hop   A style of rap music that began in New York City's Borough of the Bronx in the 1970s. The performer speaks in a specific rhythm to beats that are from a drum machine or sampled from sections of other songs and played through synthesizers or drum machines. The poetry or rhyme is either improvised or prepared before the performance. Prominent hip hop artists include Notorious B.I.G., Jay-Z, and Eminem.

Histoire du soldat, L' (F., *A Soldier's Tale*)   A 1918 composition by Igor Stravinsky, based on a Russian folk story, with libretto by Charles Ramuz. The piece is to be read, danced, and played by an ensemble consisting of a double bass, bassoon, cornet, clarinet, trombone, percussion, and violin septet. This composition premiered on September 28, 1918, in Lausanne, Switzerland.

Hodges, Johnny (1906–1970)   American saxophonist renowned as the lead alto sax player for the Duke Ellington Orchestra for 38 years.

hold   The direction to hold a note or chord while playing a composition. Also known as a fermata, this direction is indicated by a musical notation called a "bird's eye."

Holiday, Billie (1915–1959)   American jazz singer. Her vocal style, influenced by jazz instrumentalists, was one of the first to bend the tempo and phrasing of a song in a new way. Her approach to singing, as demonstrated in a couple of her most famous renditions, "God Bless the Child" and "Lady Sings the Blues," express her intimate and personal style.

holy hip hop   Christian rap music that launched in the 1990s. The Grammy-nominated group Gospel Gangstaz pioneered this type of music.

home chord   *See* tonic chord.

homophony   A composition technique in which the melody is the main component of the song supported by a chordal or more elaborate accompaniment. The opposite of polyphony.

homorhythmic   When all the voices in a composition move in the same rhythm. This produces a succession of chords or intervals also known as a "chordal style."

honky-tonk   1. A type of bar in the southern United States patronized by the working class. Honky-tonks also sprang up in the north after the 1933 repeal of Prohibition. 2. Country music written for patrons of honky-tonks using lyrics that dealt with everyday working-class problems. The instruments used in the bands were later amplified to be more easily heard in these loud and rowdy establishments. Hank Williams's recording of "Your Cheatin' Heart" is typical of the honky-tonk style.

Honegger, Arthur (1892–1955)   Swiss composer who lived most of his life in Paris and was a member of Les Six, a group of six composers whose music was written as a reaction to impressionistic music and Richard Wagner's musical style. His works include symphonies, oratorios, ballets, and chamber works.

hook   A catchy phrase or passage in a piece of popular music, usually found in the chorus of the piece.

hooking   A vocal technique used by a singer attempting an abrupt change from the chest voice register to just above the vocal break to the head voice register. Often used in musical theater for emotional effect.

horn   1. Also known as the French horn, a member of the brass family that consists of 12 feet of wrapped tubing with a flared bell and three rotary or piston valves. This is the modern relative of the natural horn, which has no valves and was used for hunting and military purposes. Tuned in the key of F. 2. Nickname for any wind or brass instrument.

Horne, Lena (b. 1917)   American jazz singer and actress who performed with greats such as Duke Ellington, Billy Eckstein, and Artie Shaw. Winner of four Grammy Awards as well as many other awards. She is perhaps most remembered for her 1943 hit song "Stormy Weather."

Horowitz, Vladimir (1903–1989)   Russian American pianist known for his exciting playing technique. Many consider him one of the greatest pianists of the twentieth century. In his 75 years of performing, he was awarded 20 Grammy Awards for his classical piano recording.

hot jazz   Also known as Dixieland music, a type of jazz developed in New Orleans in the first part of the twentieth century. Combines brass-band marches, blues, and ragtime and uses improvisation by a trumpet, trombone, and clarinet over a rhythm section of banjo (or guitar), piano, tuba (or double bass violin), and drums.

house music   Becoming popular in the discos of the mid-1980s, a type of electronic dance music greatly influenced by elements of disco, soul, and funk. This music uses electronic drums, samples of pop, and a prominent synthesizer for the bass line.

Houston, Whitney (b. 1963)   American singer and actress. One of the highest-paid and most famous female performers of the 1980s and 1990s, she accumulated 6 Grammy Awards and sold 50 million singles and more than 140 million albums. Her hit single "I Will Always Love You," from the film *The Bodyguard*, was one of the best-selling singles in the history of music.

Huguenots, Les (Fr., *The Huguenots*)   A French opera in five acts composed by Giacomo Meyerbeer, with libretto by Émile Deschamps and Eugène Scribe. A prime example of grand opera, it premiered at the Paris Opera House in 1836. The story takes place at the time of the St. Bartholomew's Day Massacre, when thousands of French Protestants (Hugenots) were killed by the Catholics in 1572.

humming   A vocal sound made without articulation when the lips are closed.

hurdy-gurdy   A string instrument from the medieval era that is shaped similarly to a lute or violin. Also called a "wheel fiddle," the strings are made to vibrate when a crank turns the wheel that acts like a bow.

hymn   A religious song that comes from the Greek word *hymnos*, meaning "a song of praise." Published in collections called hymnals or hymnbooks and meant to be sung by the congregation of a church.

iconography of music   The study and interpretation of music-related subject matter in art. Used by musicologists and historians in the study of obsolete instruments, historical performance techniques, and traditions.

idiomatic style   A method of composition in which the style of the music is appropriate for the instrument. This is an important consideration in orchestration for composers who seek to exploit the specific sound and technical qualities of each instrument.

idiophone   A musical instrument that sounds without the use of a membrane, reed, or string. There are concussion, friction, percussion, plucked, scraped, shaken, stamped, and stamping idiophones.

IDM (Intelligent Dance Music)   An electronic music genre developed in the United States in the early 1990s. The style features a slower beat than techno and emphasizes melody instead of a driving techno beat. Artists in this genre include Boards of Canada and Aphex Twin.

Idomeneo   Italian opera composed in three acts by Wolfgang Amadeus Mozart, with libretto by Giambattista Varesco. Originally produced in 1781 in Munich, Germany, the story takes place in Crete shortly after the Trojan War.

imitation   When a melody is repeated by another instrument or voice in quick succession. This theme, or motif, is an integral element of the canon, fugue, or motet, as well as many other earlier forms. An example of imitation is the well-known round (a type of canon) "Row, Row, Row Your Boat."

imitative counterpoint   A style of composition in which a melody or line of music is used in one or more other lines of music later in the piece, either identically or at a different interval. A canon and fugue are two examples of imitative counterpoint. Johann Sebastian Bach was a master of this compositional technique.

imperfect cadence   Also known as a half or open cadence, it refers to any cadence that ends on the V (fifth) chord. Because the cadence does not end on the I (tonic or root) chord, the cadence sounds unfinished and is known as a "weak" cadence.

imperfect interval   An interval that is one half step (semitone)— either up or down—from perfect. An imperfect fifth would be C–G$\sharp$ instead of C–G.

impresario   Term used in the entertainment business for a person who orchestrates and produces music concerts, theater, and opera.

Impresario   A one-act comic opera written by Wolfgang Amadeus Mozart, with libretto by Gottlieb Stephanie. First produced in 1786 in Vienna as an entry to a musical competition held by Holy Roman Emperor Joseph II.

impressionism   A musical style and movement of the late nineteenth and early twentieth centuries. This genre has a close relationship to the artistic movement of Manet, Monet, and Renoir and major poets of the day. Main features of impressionistic music include unresolved dissonances, chords used in parallel motion, the use of the whole-tone scale, fragmented phrases, and the repeated use of tritones. Claude Debussy is the most famous composer of this period.

impromptu   A free-form, casual style of music usually composed for piano in the nineteenth century. Schubert and Chopin were two romantic composers famous for writing these types of character pieces.

improvisation (improv)   The art of creating music spontaneously, in real time. Most commonly used in jazz but also in sections of written classical compositions such as the cadenza, a standard element of many concerti and sonatas.

incantation   A spell that is sung as part of a magic ritual.

incidental music   Music composed for a dramatic play or television show to set the mood or emphasize the action or drama of the piece.

Incoronazione di Poppea, L' (It., *The Coronation of Pompei*)   Italian opera composed in three acts by Claudio Monteverdi, with libretto by Giovanni Busenello. First performed in Venice in 1642, the story takes place in Ancient Rome and Italy.

independent voice   A single voice, section of voices in unison, or instrument that is playing or singing a solo line independent of the main body of the composition. Used for emphasis or to show the importance of a text.

indie folk   A genre combining indie pop, rock, and folk, the style became popular in the 1990s with artists such as Beck, the Dodos, and Kings of Convenience.

indie pop   A genre that developed from indie rock in the 1990s and was influenced largely by 1960s pop and post-punk bands from Scotland. This brand of alternative rock music uses jangly guitars and innocent-themed lyrics.

indie rock   A type of 1980s rock music developed in the United Kingdom and United States, attributed to the production of independent underground music. Indie-rock musicians and labels maintain complete control of their careers and music, producing albums on their own record labels and promoting their albums on the strength of Internet marketing, independent radio stations, word of mouth, and touring.

industrial rock   An aggressive blend of electronic and rock music that initially experimented with electronic instruments and effects, noise, and controversial subjects. The performance groups Cabaret Voltaire and Throbbing Gristle were prominent forerunners of this genre, which gained success with Ministry and Nine Inch Nails.

inflection   The technique of "bending" a note, or deviating it from its original pitch. Inflection is utilized at the end of a plainchant phrase as a type of punctuation and in jazz as a form of ornamentation and expression.

inner voice   A harmonic element used in choral and piano music. In a choir, this would include the altos, tenors, and baritones, with sopranos and basses as the outer voices. In piano, the inner voice would include the inner harmonies.

instrument, musical   Any object used to make music or organized sound. The three categories of instruments are wind, string, and percussion, and the study of instruments is called organology.

instrumental music   Music that is performed on instruments in either a solo or ensemble capacity.

instrumentation   The craft a composer or arranger uses to designate notes to specific instruments in a musical composition. Also called orchestration.

interlude   Music of one or more movements inserted within another composition. Rarely found in printed music of earlier pieces because interludes were often improvised. *See* intermezzo.

intermezzo   1. Music interjected within a musical composition or between acts of a serious drama or opera. 2. A character piece written in the nineteenth century by composers such as Johannes Brahms and Robert Schubert.

interpretation   A performer's personal taste, feeling, and creative response to a musical composition. In an ensemble performance, this responsibility is largely reserved for the conductor or musical director.

interval   The pitch space between two tones of a musical scale. The intervals in a diatonic scale are named: C–C, unison; C–D, second; C–E, third; C–F, fourth; C–G, fifth; C–A, sixth; C–B, seventh; and C–C, octave.

intonation   The aspect of a musical sound related to its "in-tune-ness," or accuracy of pitch. Correct intonation involves a combination of a good instrument and a well-developed technique and listening ear.

introduction (intro)   The opening section of a piece of music or movement that often sets up harmonic, melodic, and/or rhythmic material related to the larger part of the work.

introit   A piece of music performed after the musical prelude at the beginning of a mass or other Christian church service. Originally designed as a choral accompaniment to the entrance of the clergy, it is essentially a signal that the gathering is transitioning from personal meditation to a community of worship.

invention   The name that Johann Sebastian Bach gave to his piano compositions that were studies in double (two-part inventions) or triple (three-part inventions) counterpoint.

inversion   A reversal or alteration technique in music composition. A melodic conversion occurs when the direction of a musical line is reversed, such as an ascending melody line followed by a descending one. In the second type, harmonic inversion, the root of a chord is changed from the lowest pitch to the third or fifth of the chord (third when the root is called first inversion; fifth when the root is called second inversion).

invertible counterpoint   A type of harmonic inversion in which the lowest note in a chord is switched with the highest note. When two notes of the chord are moved in this way, it is called double counterpoint. *See* inversion.

ionian mode   A musical scale defined by the following sequence of whole (W) and half (H) steps: W–W–H–W–W–W–H. This mode is most commonly known today as the major scale.

isometric A type of polyphonic composition in which all the voices of the chord move at the same time in the same rhythm, forming a succession of chords.

Israel in Egypt An English oratorio by George Frideric Handel that premiered in London in 1939. Handel's text is taken from passages in the Old Testament books of Exodus and Psalms.

Italiana in Alger, L' (It., *The Italian Girl in Algiers*) An opera in two acts that premiered in Venice in 1813. Composed by Gioachino Rossini when he was only 21 years old, with libretto by Angelo Anelli. The plot is a lighthearted, comic romp about love and marriage.

J

Jackson, Michael (1958–2009)   American singer/entertainer born in Gary, Indiana. At the age of six, he started singing lead vocals in the Jackson 5 (consisting of four of his brothers), and after splitting off as a solo act became one of the top three commercially successful musical artists of all time (along with the Beatles and Elvis Presley). Known as the "King of Pop," Jackson had 17 number-one singles, 13 Grammy Awards, record sales of up to $750 million, and was named the "Most Successful Entertainer of All Time" by the *Guinness Book of World Records*. His 1982 *Thriller* album is the best-selling album of all time, and his *Off the Wall*, *Bad*, *Dangerous*, and *HIStory* albums are all among the all-time top-selling albums. Known for his complicated dance style, he developed moves such as the robot and the moonwalk and was the first to make use of the new media of music videos as an art form, with videos of his songs "Billie Jean," "Thriller," and "Beat It."

Jackson, Milt (1923–1999)   American vibraphonist known for his important contribution to the jazz style of bebop. He is renowned as one of the best players of vibraphone in musical history and has played with most of the leading jazz musicians of the twentieth century. Besides being a member of the Modern Jazz Quartet, he has played with jazz greats such as Dizzy Gillespie (trumpet), Thelonious Monk (piano), Charlie

Parker (alto sax), B. B. King (guitar), and Ray Charles (vocals/piano). His tune "Bags' Groove" is a jazz standard.

Jackson 5, The   American family pop-soul group that performed together from 1964 to 1989. The five brothers in the group, from oldest to youngest, were Jackie, Tito, Jermaine (later replaced by brother Randy), Marlon, and Michael. Later known as the Jacksons, their music repertoire consisted of pop, soul, R&B (rhythm and blues), and disco. As black teen idols, they were just as popular with white audiences as with black and sold more than 100 million records. Their number-one hits include "ABC," "I'll Be There," "The Love You Save," and "I Want You Back."

Jagger, Mick (b. 1943)   British singer, songwriter, and lead vocalist for the British rock band the Rolling Stones.

jam session   An informal gathering of musicians to experiment and perform for themselves. The rhythm section plays the underlying chords and rhythms (often a blues progression) while members of the jam take turns improvising solos.

Jarrett, Keith (b. 1945)   American jazz/classical pianist and songwriter. His style is a mixture of jazz, classical, blues, and gospel, and he has performed with many of the great jazz musicians of the late twentieth century.

jazz   The only original American art form, jazz is a musical genre that originated in New Orleans at the turn of the twentieth century. The earliest jazz was played by small marching bands or by solo piano or banjo. Since then, jazz has developed into more than two dozen styles, all of which are still performed today. The basic elements of all jazz styles are improvisation, syncopation, varied and expressive tone colors, "blue notes" that slur into each other, percussion, and rhythm. Jazz styles, from earliest to latest, include the blues, swing, bebop, R&B, cool, soul, fusion, and smooth jazz.

jazz standard   A popular, commonly performed jazz piece.

jazz-rock   *See* fusion.

Jephtha   1. The last oratorio written by George Frideric Handel in 1752, with English words by Thomas Morell. 2. Oratorio written by Giacomo Carissimi in 1650 with Latin text taken from the Bible.

jew's harp   Also called a "jaw harp," a small, lyre-shaped instrument made of a metal frame and thin, flexible "tongue." The frame is placed against the teeth as the player plucks the tongue, which vibrates and produces the sound, which the player changes by changing the shape of his or her mouth and throat. An ancient instrument, the jew's harp is a traditional folk music instrument.

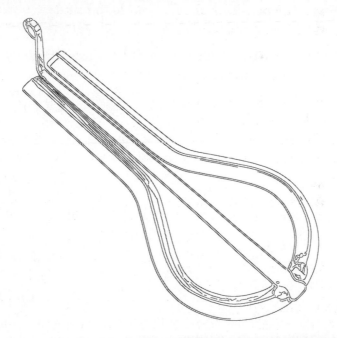

jig   A lively dance in triple (waltz) time that originated in the sixteenth century.

jingle   1. The small metal disc attached to the frame of a tambourine. 2. A short, catchy song designed to advertise a product.

jitterbug   A dance in 4/4 time from the swing era of the 1930s and '40s. 2. A popular term for a swing dancer.

jive   An African American dance style in 4/4 time from the early 1940s that was an exaggerated version of the jitterbug.

John, Elton (b. 1947) English pianist, singer-songwriter, and composer of pop and rock music. In four decades, he has won 5 Grammy Awards, recorded more than 50 Top 40 hits (9 of which hit number one), and sold more than 200 million records. He was knighted Sir Elton John in 1998.

Jolson, Al (1886–1950) American singer and actor whose career spanned 40 years and more than 80 hit records. He was considered "the world's greatest entertainer" in his time and was the highest-paid entertainer in 1920. Jolson is best known for his leading role in the 1927 film *The Jazz Singer*, the first movie to feature sound for musical numbers.

Jones, Quincy (b. 1933) American record producer, film composer, conductor, and music arranger. One of the most famous producers in the entertainment business, he has won 27 Grammy Awards. His biggest producing credit goes to Michael Jackson's album *Thriller*, the number-one selling album of all time.

Joplin, Janis (1943–1970) The legendary American rock and blues singer and songwriter of the 1960s, renowned for her raspy and emotionally charged voice. Her best-known songs include "Piece of My Heart" (with Big Brother and the Holding Company) and "Me and Bobby McGee" (written by Kris Kristofferson).

Joplin, Scott (1867–1917) African American pianist and composer of ragtime music. Dubbed "The King of Ragtime," he wrote 44 rags, 2 ragtime operas, and a ragtime ballet. His "Maple Leaf Rag," published in 1899, became the most popular rag for a century, and his rag "The Entertainer" was made famous in the 1970s film *The Sting*. He was awarded the Pulitzer Prize, posthumously, in 1976. *See also* ragtime.

Jordan, Louis (1908–1975) American alto saxophone player, songwriter, and bandleader hailed as "the father of rhythm and blues." His first million-selling hit, "Is You Is or Is You Ain't My Baby," recorded with his swing band the Tympany Five, featured his distinctive upbeat take on the blues. Jordan was ranked fifth on Billboard's list of the best African American recording R&B artists of the twentieth century.

Josquin Desprez (c. 1455–1521)   Also called Josquin des Prez and simply Josquin, the influential Franco-Flemish composer was considered the greatest composer of the Renaissance. He invented word painting, a technique in which the music reflects the meaning of the text, and other musical techniques that continue to define Western music. Among his hundreds of motets, masses, and secular vocal music, his most renowned works include the masses *Missa Pange Lingua* and *Missa La sol fa re mi*.

Judas Maccabaeus   Oratorio composed by George Frideric Handel and produced in London in 1747 about the Old Testament hero.

jug band   A band of instruments made from common household items, including a jug. The jug player would fill the jug partially with liquid and blow into the opening, often producing a two-octave range. Other items of the band may be a washboard, a comb with tissue paper, a washtub bass, and spoons.

Juilliard School   One of the most prestigious performing arts conservatories in the world. Located in New York City at the Lincoln Center for the Performing Arts, it was established in 1905 and later given its name after Augusta D. Juilliard, a wealthy textile merchant.

juke joint   Also called a barrelhouse, a drinking establishment in the southeastern United States often run by African Americans, used for drinking, playing music, dancing, and gambling.

jukebox   An automated music-playing machine that usually takes coins to operate. When buttons with numbers are pressed, it plays a particular song by either automatically picking up a record and placing it on a turntable or by choosing either a CD or another source of digital sound file. Most jukeboxes are decorated with colored lights and eye-catching designs.

jump   Jazz slang meaning "to swing."

jump band   A small jazz band in the 1940s and early '50s that used a stronger beat than the larger big bands. The jump band also featured a blues vocal style, shuffle rhythm, strong backbeat, more syncopated riffs, and a smaller horn section than a big band.

jump blues   A fast-tempo blues music popular in the 1940s that used a small group with horns and evolved from big band, swing, and boogie-woogie music. This music was much cheaper to hire than a big band and was meant for jitterbug-type dancing. Louis Jordan was one of the leading jump-blues artists of the day. A good example of this music is the Andrews Sisters' song "Boogie Woogie Bugle Boy" (1941).

jungle   An electronic style of music that combines elements of techno, breakbeat hardcore, raregroove, and other styles, which was most popular in the mid-1990s. Jungle music uses synthesized effects, fast tempos, samples, and percussive loops. Artists in this genre include Ed Rush, Total Science, Goldie, and Reprazent.

Jupiter Symphony   The nickname for Wolfgang Amadeus Mozart's last symphony, one of his most popular, the Symphony no. 41 in C Major, K. 551, which was written in 1788.

K., K.V. (Köchel-Verzeichnis)   A list of all the works of Wolfgang Amadeus Mozart, in chronological order, developed by L. von Köchel. Each of Mozart's compositions is referred to by one of the numbers on this list.

Kamen, Michael (1948–2003)   American composer of film scores, including *X-Men*, *Highlander*, and the *Lethal Weapon* and *Die Hard* series.

Kenton, Stan (1911–1979)   American big-band leader and pianist. He was instrumental in developing a new style of big band jazz on the West Coast called "progressive jazz," which featured an expanded orchestra and exploited new orchestration techniques such as nontraditional harmonic changes, frequent chromatic shifts, and changes of tempo. This made his band sound more concertlike than traditional dance bands.

Kern, Jerome (1885–1945)   American composer of more than 700 songs exclusively for musical theater and film. Kern wrote classic songs such as "All the Things You Are," "Ol' Man River," "Smoke Gets in Your Eyes," and "A Fine Romance."

kettledrum   Also known as a timpani. A member of the percussion family of musical instruments. Large bowl-shaped drum with a skin head stretched across the top. Made of copper or fiberglass, it is struck with a timpani mallet or drumstick to produce a pitch. Evolved from the military drum and is now used in classical orchestras.

key   1. Part of the action used on a keyboard instrument. 2. The tonal center of a musical composition.

key signature   The flat and sharp symbols used at the beginning of a musical staff that indicate the key of the composition.

keyboard   Used on the piano, organ, harpsichord, and other instruments to produce musical pitches. These black and white keys are usually made of wood with ivory or plastic on the playing surface. On the modern piano, there are 88 keys and 7 octaves (the organ has 61 keys).

keynote   Also called the tonic or first note of a musical scale.

King, B. B. (b. 1925)   Stage name for Riley B. King, American jazz electric guitarist and singer-songwriter. King has won 15 Grammy Awards and was ranked 3 in *Rolling Stone* magazine's list of the 100 Greatest Guitarists of All Time. His solo style of bending strings and vibrato were a great influence on almost all electric guitarists who came after him.

King, Carole (b. 1942)   American singer-songwriter of many hit rock and pop singles since 1960. Four of those hits include "Take Good Care of My Baby," "The Loco-Motion," "Will You Love Me Tomorrow," and "Go Away Little Girl." She has been awarded four Grammy Awards for her songwriting.

Konitz, Lee (b. 1927)   American jazz alto saxophonist and composer who is one of the leading cool jazz artists. He has played with many of America's jazz greats since he started his career in 1945 and has recorded 132 albums as a bandleader and 9 albums as a sideman.

Kool & the Gang   American funk, soul, R&B, and disco band that has sold more than 70 million albums since 1964. "Celebration" and "Jungle Boogie" are two of their biggest hits.

Korngold, Erich Wolfgang (1897–1957)   Austrian American film composer who won an Academy Award for his score for *The Adventures of Robin Hood* in 1938. After a successful early career composing opera in Austria, the most famous being *Die Tote Stadt* when he was 23, Korngold was asked to come to Hollywood to compose for film. Because of the deteriorating conditions for Jews in Germany, he stayed in the United States, where he became a citizen in 1943.

Krupa, Gene (1909–1973)   One of the most influential American big-band drummers of the twentieth century. He helped design and shape the modern drum kit, invented the rim shot, and set the standard for playing different cymbal techniques.

K

L

la Sixth degree in the solfège system that assigns a word to a pitch: do, re, mi, fa, so, la, ti, do.

Lakme A French opera in three acts composed by Léo Delibes, with libretto by Philippe Gille and Edmond Gondinet. Produced in Paris in 1883, Lakme takes place in India in the late nineteenth century.

lament A composition written to commemorate the death of a famous person.

lamento Musical compositions written in a sad or somber manner. In seventeenth-century opera, a lamento was a scene expressing immense despair.

largo A musical tempo of a very slow speed equaling 40 to 60 beats per measure. The same tempo as *lento*.

Lark Quartet Award-winning New York City–based string quartet.

Lark Quartet Nickname for a string quartet (String Quartet in D Major, op. 64, no. 5) by Franz Joseph Haydn. This piece was named so because of the first violin's high-soaring passage at the beginning of the first movement.

laryngoscope Device invented by the famous singing teacher Manuel Garcia II in 1854 for viewing the larynx and vocal chords.

larynx   The bone and cartilage housing that surrounds the vocal chords in the throat. One of its main functions is to produce the vocal tone. By closing the vocal chords, the larynx also helps to keep foreign matter out of the windpipe.

Latin music   Music originating from Latin American and Caribbean countries. The common unifying feature is Latin-based languages, and stylistic types include the salsa, mambo, tango, chacarera, tropicalismo, cueca, mariachis, bossa nova, cha-cha, and bolero.

lead sheet   A type of music notation that outlines the melody, harmony, and lyrics of a song by using chord symbols instead of spelling out in detail all the voices in the accompaniment.

leader   1. The conductor or concertmaster of a musical ensemble. 2. Empty sections between tracks on a recording.

leading tone   A music theory term indicating a pitch one half step above or below the tonic pitch that resolves or leads to the tonic pitch. This is usually the seventh degree of the scale: in a C-Major scale, this would be the white B key one half step below middle C.

leap   A jump between two notes that are at least a third interval apart.

Led Zeppelin   English hard-rock band that played from 1968 to 1980. The most popular rock band of the 1970s, the group consisted of Robert Plant on vocals, Jimmy Page on guitar, John Bonham on drums, and John Paul Jones on keyboards and bass guitar. The band ranked first on VH1's *100 Greatest Artists of Hard Rock*.

ledger lines   Small lines drawn above or below the staff for notes that are too high or too low to be placed on the regular staff.

legato   A musical term that directs the performer to play or sing a series of notes smoothly and without any perceptible interruption. Legato is also indicated in the music by a curved line above the notes that are to be played in this manner. The opposite of *staccato*.

legit   Abbreviation for "legitimate," referring to a trained, classically experienced voice being used in a different genre; for example, "He sang the Rodgers and Hammerstein piece in a legit style."

Lehmann, Lilli (1848–1929)   German operatic soprano and voice teacher who helped popularize the music of Richard Wagner in the United States.

leitmotif   A compositional technique most commonly used in Richard Wagner's later operas in which a musical theme is used repeatedly throughout the work. Each leitmotif consists of a short melody, rhythm, or chord progression and represents a certain place, person, or idea.

Lennon, John (1940–1980)   English rock singer, songwriter, guitarist, and founding member of the Beatles. With Paul McCartney, another Beatles member, he was one of the most successful rock songwriters of the twentieth century.

letter notation   The system of naming the notes of the scale with letters. Their trailing symbols, such as flats, sharps, and chord symbols, are also a form of letter notation.

Lewis, Jerry Lee (b. 1935)   American country and rock and roll singer, pianist, and songwriter. Ranked 24 on *Rolling Stone* magazine's list of the 100 Greatest Artists of All Time.

librettist   The person who writes the words to a musical work such as an opera, musical, oratorio, or cantata.

libretto   The dialogue and words that go with extended musical works such as opera, musical, oratorio, and cantata.

lied (G., song)   German art song composed for solo voice and piano. Franz Schubert was the most proficient and well-known composer of this kind of music.

line The legato tonal flow of a melodic musical phrase.

liner notes Writings such as performer biographies, lyrics, and credits that are inserted into a CD case, vinyl record, or cassette packaging.

lineup The members of a band or bands performing at a concert.

lip An embouchure technique for playing a musical instrument in which the player is able to change the pitch by loosening or tightening the embouchure (lip position).

lip trill A musical ornament where two adjoining notes alternate quickly back and forth, causing a shaking effect.

Liszt, Franz (1811–1886)   Hungarian pianist and composer who was often called the greatest pianist of his time. His large output of compositions consisted of piano works and vocal compositions, and he was the inventor of the symphonic poem (a descriptive orchestral piece consisting of one movement).

Little Richard (b. 1932)   American singer, songwriter, and pianist who was instrumental in the early development of rock and roll in the 1950s. Along with Elvis Presley, he was one of the most influential early rock and roll performers who guided the transition of R&B to rock. Three of his most famous songs are "Good Golly, Miss Molly," "Tutti Frutti," and "Long Tall Sally."

liturgical chant Sacred music comprised of an ancient melody (chant). Usually, but not always, performed as a vocal solo or in unison without accompaniment.

lo-fi A term meaning a recording that has flaws, such as distortion, hums, cracks, and pops, or background noise due to the low frequency or limitation of the recording.

Loesser, Frank (1910–1969)   American songwriter of many Broadway musicals, including *How to Succeed in Business Without Really Trying* and *Guys and Dolls*. Winner of one Academy Award and four Tony Awards, he wrote famous songs such as "Heart and Soul," "Baby, It's Cold Outside," and "A Bushel and a Peck."

Lohengrin   German opera in three acts composed by Richard Wagner from his own libretto. First produced in Weimar, Germany, in 1850, the story takes place in Antwerp in the early tenth century. *Lohengrin* marks Wagner's transition from his early operas, which contain separate arias, to his later operas, where he uses a continuous melody and begins the use of the leitmotif (a melody denoting a character, idea, or thing).

Lombardo, Guy (1902–1977)   Canadian American bandleader who, with his orchestra, the Royal Canadians, appeared on North American radio and TV broadcasts each New Year's Eve from 1954 to 1976. Their record sales reached into the hundreds of millions.

long meter (L.M.)   A regular metric hymn pattern that consists of four-line stanzas, with each line containing four iambs (an unstressed syllable followed by a stressed syllable), for a total of eight syllables per line.

long-playing record (LP)   An analogue format for recorded music introduced in 1948. Made of vinyl in either 10- or 12-inch diameters, the records played at $33\frac{1}{3}$ rpm (rotations per minute), each side averaging around 15 to 22 minutes. The LP has been replaced by magnetic tape and then digital recording.

loop   A short section of a song (usually one to four measures) that is repeated continually through a piece of music using tape, samples (digital recording of a live sound), or looping software.

loudness   A strong intensity or volume of sound.

lounge music   A genre that became popular in the 1950s and 1960s and had a resurgence in the 1990s, lounge music encompasses many types, including easy listening, exotica, space-age pop, and mood music. It has a definite retro feel. The term refers to music that is played in lounges, bars, and hotel lobbies.

Lucia di Lammermoor (It., *Lucy of Lammermoor*)   Italian opera written in three acts by Gaetano Donizetti, with libretto by Salvadore Cammarano. With the story taken from *The Bride of Lammermoor*, a novel by Sir Walter Scott set in seventeenth-century Scotland, it was first produced in Naples in 1935.

Lulu   German opera composed in three acts by Alban Berg, who also wrote the lyrics. First produced in Zurich in 1937, it is set in early twentieth-century Germany. This work utilizes a 12-tone technique. *See* serial music.

lute   The predecessor of the guitar, the lute appears in images dating back 2,000 years to Ancient Babylon. It is a string instrument with a half pear-shaped body and flat neck with up to 11 frets.

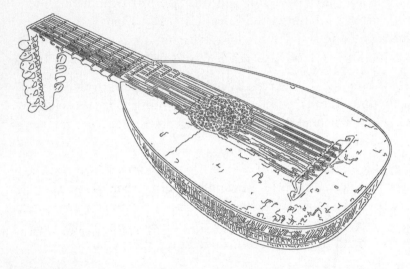

Lydian mode   A scale defined by the following series of whole (W) and half (H) steps: W–W–W–H–W–W–H.

lyre   An ancient string instrument similar to a small harp that is strummed instead of plucked.

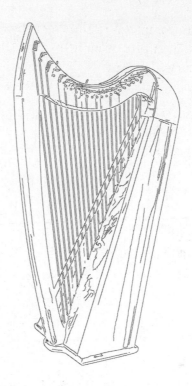

lyrics The words or text sung in a musical composition. The person who writes the text to a song is a lyricist.

L

Macbeth Italian opera composed in four acts by Giuseppi Verdi, with libretto by Francesco Maria Piave, taken from Shakespeare's play of the same name. First produced in Paris in 1847 in Florence, Italy, the story is set in Scotland in the eleventh century.

MacDowell, Edward (1860–1908) American composer and pianist of the Romantic period known for his piano works and especially "Woodland Sketches," piano suites, and the short piano piece "To a Wild Rose."

Madama Butterfly Italian opera composed in three acts by Giuseppi Verdi, with libretto by Giuseppe Giacosa and Luigi Illica. First produced in Milan, Italy, in 1904, the setting is Nagasaki, Japan, around 1900.

Madonna (b. 1958) American rock singer and actress. According to the Recording Industry Association of America, she is the number one selling female rock artist of the twentieth century. *The Guinness Book of World Records* says she is the most successful female recording artist in history, with more than 200 million albums sold worldwide. Some of her most famous songs include "Like a Virgin," "Vogue," and "Material Girl."

madrigal   A secular type of composition for two to eight singers, with or without instruments. First written in Italy in the 1520s through the renaissance and early part of the baroque period, madrigals evolved from the *frottola*. These short songs set to lyric love poems were a major influence on the development of opera.

maestoso   Italian term meaning that the music should be played majestically or "with dignity."

maestro   Italian classical music term used most commonly for opera conductors but also for any master musician, including performers, music directors, impresarios, and composers.

Magic Flute, The (G., *Die Zauberflöte*)   German comic opera with dialogue (*singspiel*) in two acts composed by Wolfgang Amadeus Mozart in 1791, with libretto written by Emanuel Schikaneder. First produced in Vienna in 1791, it is currently the tenth most popular opera in the operatic repertoire in North America.

Magnificat   1. A polyphonic (two melody lines) piece of music about the Virgin Mary written with text taken from the Bible. 2. Major choral work composed by Johann Sebastian Bach and first performed in its current version in 1733. Called the Magnificat in D Major, BMW 243.

Mahler, Gustav (1860–1911)   Austrian composer and conductor who was famous as a leading orchestral and opera conductor and one of the most important late Romantic period composers. Best known for his 10 symphonies and vocal works.

major   Used to describe a type of musical interval, key, scale, or chord. The third step is the determining factor in whether a key is major or minor, with the major being one half step further apart (four half steps).

major scale   A series of seven pitches, starting and ending with the same note (8), played in the following order:

1	2	3	4	5	6	7	8
whole	whole	half	whole	whole	whole	half	

The major scale is also called the Ionian scale. The most commonly used major scale, and simplest to play or compose in, is the C-Major scale, which only uses the white keys of the piano.

mambo   Literally means "conversation with the gods." Cuban music and dance formerly called a *danzón*, descending from European social dances and African folk music. Mambo uses a variety of Latin percussion, upright bass, piano, trumpets, trombones, and saxophones. Some popular mambo musicians include Pérez Prado, Arsenio Rodriquez, and Enrique Jorrin.

mandolin   A musical instrument with four pairs of strings that are picked or strummed. Used most often in folk, country, and bluegrass music, it is a member of the lute family and a descendant of the *mandore* from the mid-eighteenth century.

Mannheim School   Refers not only to the eighteenth-century orchestra in Mannheim, Germany, but to the orchestral techniques used by members of that school. One of its most famous members was Johann Stamitz, who became the orchestra's director in 1750. Two of the famous techniques that came from this school include the *Mannheim Rocket* (a fast, ascending orchestral passage) and the *Mannheim Crescendo* (a sudden growth in volume).

Manon Lescaut   Italian opera composed in four acts by Giacomo Puccini and first produced in Turin, Italy, in 1893. The setting is the second half of the eighteenth century, and the opera is based on a story by Abbé Prévost.

manual   The keyboard, played with hands, on a piano, harpsichord, synthesizer, clavichord, or organ

maraca   Percussion instrument native to Venezuela and several Caribbean countries. A type of rattle made from a dried gourd or coconut shell with beans or seeds inside and attached to a wooden handle; usually played in pairs.

marcato   Italian term indicating that the performer should attack a note or chord with a sforzando (*sfz*) or explosive start, letting the note sustain for two thirds the normal length and ending with a gap or rest before the next note. Sometimes referred to by jazz musicians as a "jazz staccato."

marcato (strong)   Same as marcato, only with more intent.

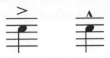

march   A musical genre composed especially for marching and for the military. March is set in 4/4 time and has strong and regular rhythm.

marching band   An ensemble of percussion, brass, and woodwind musicians used to play musical marches for parades, military, and sporting events.

mariachi   Mexican musical genre that uses string instruments, trumpets, and singers. Performers wear silver-studded *charro* (Mexican cowboy) outfits with large-brimmed hats and play the *guitarrón* (a large acoustic bass guitar), *vihuela* (high-pitched guitar), acoustic guitar, violins, and trumpets. Currently, they play most often at weddings, formal affairs, Mother's Day, and to serenade tourists.

marimba   A percussion instrument made up of bars of wood arranged and tuned like a piano keyboard that are struck with mallets to produce musical tones. A marimba is used in a variety of different ensembles, including jazz ensembles, woodwind ensembles, marimba ensembles, and orchestras.

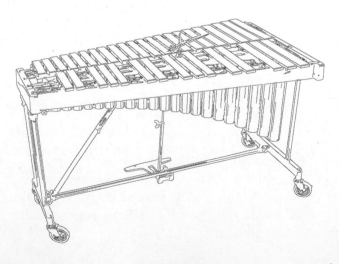

mark   A vocal technique in a rehearsal or practice that involves taking the notes down an octave or singing the music softly to preserve the voice from strain or overuse.

Marley, Bob (1945–1981)   Jamaican singer-songwriter and lead singer for the reggae band the Wailers. The most well-known performer of reggae music, his most famous songs are "Jamming," "I Shot the Sheriff," and "One Love."

Marriage of Figaro, The (It., *Le Nozze de Figaro*)   Italian comic opera composed in four acts by Wolfgang Amadeus Mozart, with libretto by Lorenzo Da Ponte. Produced in Vienna in 1786, it's one of Mozart's most popular and famous operas.

Marsalis, Wynton (b. 1961)   Prominent modern American jazz and classical trumpet player and composer. Awarded nine Grammy Awards and one Pulitzer Prize for Music.

Martin, Dean (1917–1995)   One of the most famous and beloved American singers, recording artists, and movie and television actors of the 1950s and '60s. Three of his most famous songs are "Everybody Loves Somebody Sometime," "Volare," and "Mambo Italiano."

mask   The area in the sinuses around the eyes and nose where a singer finds nasal resonance in his or her tone. This complements the primary resonance produced in the throat and mouth.

Masked Ball, A (It., *Un ballo in maschera*)   Italian opera composed in three acts by Giuseppe Verdi, with libretto by Antonio Somma. First produced in Rome in 1859 and set around the assassination of King Gustav III of Sweden.

masking   An acoustic effect that occurs when one sound is covered or made imperceptible by the frequency or intensity of another sound.

masque   A sixteenth-century stage production performed for nobility using different elements such as instrumental music, dancing, and vocal music.

mass A sacred choral composition performed by singers only or accompanied by instruments used during certain parts of the Eucharistic liturgy in the Roman Catholic Church.

Mathis, Johnny (b. 1935) American pop singer whose career started in the 1950s. He concentrated on jazz, popular, and adult contemporary standards and was awarded Grammy Awards for three of his songs, "It's Not for Me to Say," "Misty," and "Chances Are."

Matthew Passion, St. (G., *Matthäuspassion*) A composition by Johann Sebastian Bach (1727) that sets chapters 26 and 27 of the Gospel of Matthew to music.

mazurka A Polish dance set in 3/4 ("waltz") time. Famous composers known to use this musical form include Frédéric Chopin in his piano works and Modest Mussorgsky in a dance in his opera *Boris Godunov.*

McCartney, Paul (b. 1942) English singer-songwriter, bass guitarist, record producer, and entrepreneur. A former member of the rock groups the Beatles and Wings, he is the most successful songwriter in popular music history according to *The Guinness Book of World Records*, selling 60 gold albums and 100 million singles. His song "Yesterday" is the world's most covered song. He has been a successful composer of classical music, film scores, and electronic music. He owns over 3,000 copyrights of songs written by composers such as Buddy Holly, and as of 2009 his estate was worth $1.2 billion. Some of his most famous songs include "Hey Jude," "Let It Be," and "Band on the Run."

measure A measurement of time in music defined by a set number of beats between two vertical lines on a staff of music. Also called a "bar" of music.

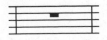

mechanical instruments   Refers to any musical instrument that operates mechanically and not electrically. It can either use a performer or can be operated by a "barrel and pin," "clockwork," or "perforated paper roll" mechanism. One such instrument would be a player piano.

mediant   The third note of a major (diatonic) scale and the middle note of a tonic triad. In the key of C, it is the third note, or E.

Medium, The   A short, two-act opera in English composed by Gian Carlo Menotti and produced in New York City in 1946.

medley   A composition using a number of existing songs placed back to back, sometimes overlapping each other. Most medleys are songs with words rather than instrumental pieces.

megaphone   Funnel or cone-shaped device used to amplify the voice. Electronic megaphones amplify the voice even more and use a microphone, amplifier, and loudspeaker to do so. Megaphones are used to address crowds and large numbers of people in open spaces.

M

meistersinger (G., master singer)   German singers and poets from the fourteenth to sixteenth centuries who were members of guilds organized in the main cities. These guilds established competitive standards for the performance and composition of poetry and music.

Meistersinger von Nürnberg, Die (G., *The Mastersingers of Nurem-berg*)   German opera composed in three acts by Richard Wagner, using his own text. First produced in Munich, Germany, in 1868. The setting is Nuremberg in the middle of the sixteenth century and it takes approximately four and a half hours to perform.

melisma   A musical term indicating the singing of one syllable of text on a succession of different notes.

born

mellophone   Member of the brass family of musical instruments used in place of the French horn in drum and bugle corps and marching bands. This instrument uses three valves with the same fingering as the trumpet and is tuned in the key of F and sometimes G.

mellow tone   A calm, warm sound played by a musical instrument.

mélodie (F., melody)   French song equivalent to an English art song or German lied.

melodrama   A theatrical device that uses dramatic and expressive musical themes to obtain an emotional response from the audience. A melodrama involves music composed almost exclusively for salon entertainment and later for silent movies, where different motifs (themes) represent the hero, heroine, villain, imminent threat, heroic rescues, and other situations. It's usually arranged for piano or a small orchestra.

melody   A succession of notes strung together to form a musical line the ear perceives as most interesting or important. The melody is usually the most singable and memorable part of a piece of music and recurs throughout the piece. The accompaniment, or harmony, reinforces the melody with chords and/or countermelodies.

Mendelssohn, Felix (1809–1847)   German romantic period composer, conductor, pianist, and organist. A true musical genius from early childhood, he was one of the most prolific and talented composers in music history and composed for all combinations of instruments and voices. One of his most-loved compositions is the "Wedding March" from *A Midsummer Night's Dream* that is heard at so many weddings.

Menotti, Gian Carlo (1911–2007)   Italian American composer who composed many operas including the Christmas classic *Amahl and the Night Visitors*. He was also a librettist and wrote the text for most of his own works. He was the winner of two Pulitzer Prizes in music for the operas *The Saint of Bleecker Street* (1955) and *The Consul* (1950).

Mercer, Johnny (1909–1976)   One of the most popular songwriters (lyricists) between 1935 and 1955. He wrote the words to more than 1,000 songs, which included songs for Broadway shows and movies. He was nominated for 19 Academy Awards, 4 of which he won. He was also the co-founder of Capital Records. Two of his most famous songs were "Moon River" and "Days of Wine and Roses," both written with songwriter Henry Mancini.

merengue   Music and dance from the Dominican Republic created in the 1920s by Ñico Lora (1880–1971). *Merengue típico* uses traditional instrumentation including a tambora (two-sided drum), an accordian, and a güira (percussion instrument) and is played in a fast 2/4 meter. *Merengue de orquesta* is the most popular today and uses a large horn section, saxophone, backup singers, electric bass, and traditional instrumentation. Popular artists include Ilegales, Raulin Rodriquez, and Manny Manuel.

messa di voce   Italian vocal term for two vocal effects. It is a musical ornament where the singer's voice grows louder and gets softer on a single note. It is also a vocal exercise where the singer joins the two vocal registers (falsetto and chest voice) at the register's area of transition.

Messiaen, Olivier (1908–1992)   French composer and organist known for his rhythmically complex music that uses harmonies and melodies based on scales and musical modes of his own invention called the "modes of limited transposition."

M

Messiah, The An oratorio composed by George Frideric Handel, with libretto by Charles Jennens. Performed for the first time in Dublin in 1742, it is Handel's most famous composition and one of Western music's most popular choral works. *The Messiah* includes the famous "Hallelujah" chorus.

meter A notation of grouping beats into a regulated pattern to indicate strong and weak beats; also known as a time signature. As a musical notation, the meter is placed at the beginning of the staff to indicate the meter of the song, such as 3/4, 4/4, or 6/8. A waltz has a 3/4 meter, indicating there are three beats to a measure.

metronome A device used while practicing to keep a consistent tempo or "keep time" by listening to it click or blink at a regular pulse. It can be manually wound or electrically powered. Composers use metronome markings in their compositions to indicate to the performer at what tempo the piece should be played.

Metropolitan Opera Housed in the Metropolitan Opera House at Lincoln Center for the Performing Arts in New York City, the Metropolitan Opera is America's largest classical music organization. Founded in 1880, it is one of the leading opera companies in the world and presents nearly 27 operas and 220 opera performances annually.

mezza voce (It., medium voice) Musical term for singing with a subdued tone.

mezzo forte (It., medium loud) In musical notation, this volume description is abbreviated *mf.* It's the volume level between medium soft (*mp*) and loud (*f*).

mf

mezzo piano (It., medium soft)   In musical notation, this volume description is indicated by the abbreviation *mp*. It's the volume level between soft (*p*) and medium loud (*mf*).

mp

mezzo soprano   Soprano voice whose tonal characteristics are darker than a soprano but lighter than a contralto. Although the range is basically the same as that of a soprano, it has a lower tessitura (the place the voice sounds the best and is most comfortable). It's a soloist term for the choral equivalent "alto."

microphone   Also called a "mic," it's an electronic device that converts speech, singing, or acoustical sound into an electrical signal, which is routed through an amplifier and sound speakers to reach bigger spaces. A microphone is also used to convert sound for radio, television, and motion picture production and is present in telephones and hearing aids. Different types include the condenser, dynamic, and ribbon microphones.

microtone   Any musical interval smaller than a semitone (a half step). Not as often used in Western music as in Asian music.

middle C   Also called C4, it indicates the fourth C on a standard 88-key piano keyboard and the key found in the direct center of the keyboard. On the grand staff, it sits between the two staffs and is the dividing point between the pianist's left and right hands. Pitch frequency is 261.626 Hz (hertz).

MIDI   Abbreviation for Musical Instrument Digital Interface. This industry standard, started in 1982, allows electronic musical instruments such as synthesizers, samplers, drum machines, and computers to communicate with each other, exchanging digital data that control instrumental parameters such as volume, tempos, and vibrato.

Midsummer Night's Dream, A   An English opera composed in three acts by Benjamin Britten, with libretto adapted from Shakespeare's play by himself and Peter Pears. First produced in 1960 at the Aldeburgh Festival in Suffolk, England.

Mignon   French opera (later revised to Italian) composed in three acts by Ambroise Thomas, with libretto by Michel Carré and Jules Barbier, based on a Göethe novel. First produced in Paris in 1866, the story takes place in Germany and Italy at the end of the eighteenth century.

Milhaud, Darius (1892–1974)   French composer whose works were influenced by jazz. He was an advocate of polytonality, in which the composition is in more than one key at a time. He was a member of Les Six, a famous group of six French composers.

military music   Music used for military purposes to signal or accompany an army into battle. Early armies used animal horns, but later military groups included trumpets (or bugles), drums (usually with the cavalry), and fife (flutes) and drums for the infantry. A military band consisting of mostly percussion and wind instruments is used for military functions and plays marches and ceremonial music.

Miller, Glenn (1904–1944)   American bandleader of the swing era; also a composer and arranger and one of the best-selling recording artists from 1939 to 1942. He was lost over the English Channel on an entertainment mission during World War II. Some of his most famous songs include "Tuxedo Junction," "Chattanooga Choo-Choo," and "Pennsylvania 6-5000."

Mingus, Charles (1922–1979)   American jazz composer, bandleader, and bassist. A pioneer on bass technique, he made 68 albums as a bandleader and many more as a sideman. He was posthumously awarded a Grammy Lifetime Achievement Award in 1997.

miniature score   Complete musical scores that are printed or photographically reduced and used primarily for study (not for playing).

minimalist music   A type of experimental music originating in the San Francisco underground scene and New York City lofts and alternative spaces of the early 1960s. Some of its traits include a steady beat, a stable harmony, and repetition of short musical phrases or motifs. Steve Reich, Philip Glass, and Terry Riley are the most recognized minimalist American composers. Reich's *Piano Phase* (1967) and Glass's opera *Einstein on the Beach* (1975) are fine examples of minimalist music.

Minneapolis sound   A mixture of rock, pop, funk, R&B, and new wave pioneered by the musician Prince in the 1980s.

minnesinger   German poet-musicians in the twelfth and thirteenth centuries who devoted their songs to courtly love (the rules of sexual behavior between men and women). Minnesingers and their English and French counterparts, called troubadours and trouvères, performed their songs in public, open courts.

minor   Used to describe a type of musical interval, key scale, or chord. The third step is the determining factor in whether a key is major or minor, with the minor being one half step closer apart (three half steps).

minstrel   A European poet who performed songs about historical places, imaginary or real events, and distant travels. They often performed in the streets and became wandering minstrels. They were later replaced by the troubadours in the royal courts.

minuet   A French dance for two people set in 3/4 (waltz) time that was introduced in the court of Louis XIV around 1650. Also, the name for a musical piece composed in the same rhythm and time signature.

mirror composition   An inverted or retrograde (backward) duplicate of the original musical composition.

misterioso   Italian performance direction meaning "mysteriously."

mixed voices   A mixture of soprano, alto, tenor, baritone, and bass voice types singing in a choral ensemble.

mixing board   Also called a "mixing console" or "soundboard," it's an electronic device used in recording studios, broadcasting, public-address systems, and sound reinforcement to route separate channels of sound and change timbre and volume levels of analog and digital signals. All the separate channels (from guitars, vocals, keyboards, and so on) are mixed to come from two speakers simultaneously. Sound effects such as reverb, panning, and EQ (equalization) are used in the mixing of sound.

M

Mixolydian mode   A scale that starts on the dominant (fifth note) of a C-Major scale. It is a major scale with a half step lowered seventh note.

modal jazz   A type of jazz composition that evolved from late-1950s bebop and uses few chord changes and modes for improvisation. It has a meditative and mysterious feel and can be found in Miles Davis's tune "So What." Other musicians of this style include Herbie Hancock (keyboards), Wayne Shorter (tenor sax), Bill Evans (piano), Chick Corea (piano), and John Coltrane (tenor sax).

modalality   Term to describe the church modes other than major and minor used in the Greek scales before modern tonality was developed. The scales were Mixolydian, Lydian, Phrygian, Dorian, Hypolydian, Hypophrygian, and the common scales Locrian and Hypodorian.

mode   The notes and scales that are the basis for a piece of music. For instance, in a major mode, the scales would all be major.

moderato   Italian musical term indicating a moderate speed of performance between *andante* and *allegro*.

modern music   Term used to indicate contemporary music of many types, including classical, rock, popular, twentieth century, and modernism.

modes of limited transposition   A system of scales and modes invented by the twentieth-century French composer Olivier Messiaen (1908–1992) and explained in his book *The Technique of My Musical Language.*

modulation   The action of changing keys within a song. This musical effect is used to build excitement and add interest.

molto   Italian musical term meaning "very much."

Monk, Thelonious (1917–1982)   American jazz pianist and composer. One of the jazz greats who had an unusual improvisational style, he is considered one of the founders of bebop. Two of his most famous tunes include "'Round Midnight" and "Straight, No Chaser."

monochord An ancient instrument using one string stretched across a sound box and a movable bridge to change the length of the string to create different notes.

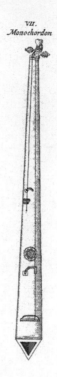

VII.
Monochordon

monocordo A violin technique of playing a short piece or passage of music on a single string.

monody A type of accompanied solo vocal music developed around 1600 using a type of recitative (sung narrative speech) design. It developed from the solo madrigal and evolved into forms such as the operatic aria and Italian art song.

monophonic notation A generic term for the musical notation of several early solo music systems, including Chinese, Byzantine, Greek, Chinese, Gregorian, troubadours, Meistersinger, and more.

monophony Single melodic line of music without the use of harmony. It's performed one note at a time by one or more voices in unison or at the octave.

M

monotone   1. The unvaried repetition of a single musical tone. 2. A person with bad pitch who is unable to tell the difference between different musical intervals (also referred to as "tone deaf").

Monteverdi, Claudio (1567–1643)   One of the greatest composers of the early baroque period (1600–1750), he was instrumental in developing the basso continuo technique and composing one of the first operas, *L'Orfeo* (1607).

Moog   The first commercially manufactured analog synthesizer (electronic sound-generating instrument), invented by Dr. Robert Moog in the mid-1960s.

"Moonlight" Sonata   Piano Sonata No. 14 in C-Sharp Minor, Op. 27, No. 2, by Ludwig van Beethoven. Composed in 1801 for his 17-year-old piano student, Countess Giulietta Guicciardi, whom Beethoven loved.

mordent   Used during the baroque and classical periods, it is a musical ornament that alternates two notes that are a second interval apart, starting with the written note.

Morley, Thomas (1557–1602)   Most famous English composer and organist from Elizabethan England in the renaissance period. He was a composer of secular music and an important member of the English Madrigal School.

Moses and Aaron   German opera composed in three acts by Arnold Schoenberg, with libretto taken from the Book of Exodus. The music from the opera was first performed in 1951 in Darnstadt, Germany, and the first staging was held in Zurich, Germany, in 1957.

motet   Early polyphonic (more than one voice) choral music compositions from around the thirteenth century to 1750.

motif   A recurring musical theme or phrase used to describe or identify characters, places, or ideas represented in a piece of music. Richard Wagner used the motif or motives extensively in his operas.

Motown Records   Originating in Detroit, Michigan, in 1959, it was the first record label owned by an African American to feature African American performers. The "Motown Sound" featured soul music with pop influences and R&B, soul, and hip-hop.

mouth organ   Musical instruments played by blowing air through them. The harmonica is the instrument most commonly known as a mouth organ.

mouthpicce   The part of a musical instrument, brass or wood-wind, that comes in contact with the performer's mouth. There are two types: those that use single or double reeds (such as clarinets and oboes), and mouthpieces that are blown straight into (such as a flute or trombone).

movable do   System (also called Tonic sol-fa) for teaching music students sight reading in which each note of the scale is sung to a special solfège syllable (do, re, me, fa, so, la, ti, do). In the movable do system, "do" is always the tonic or first note of that scale, the second step is "re," and so on. The two other solfège systems are "fixed-do" and "numbers."

movement   A division of a larger piece of music, such as the first movement of a symphony.

M

Mozart, Wolfgang Amadeus (1756–1791)   German composer from the classical period (1750–1820). Undoubtedly, one of the greatest, most influential, and beloved musicians of all time. He wrote more than 600 compositions of all types, including symphonies, chamber works, operas, piano works, and choral works. He was a child piano prodigy and started composing at age five. Some of his most famous compositions include the operas *The Magic Flute*, *The Marriage of Figaro*, and *Don Giovanni*. The 1984 film *Amadeus* is a dramatization of his life.

Mozarteum   A university of music and dramatic arts honoring Wolfgang Amadeus Mozart and based in Salzburg, Austria. Also called the Universität Mozarteum Salzburg.

MTV   A cable television network started in 1981 originally to play music videos using on-air hosts called VJs. Used as a promotional tool to sell music albums, it was also instrumental in breaking the color barrier with videos such as Michael Jackson's hit "Billie Jean." The first video broadcast on MTV was "Video Killed the Radio Star" by the Buggles.

Mulligan, Gerry (1927–1996)   American jazz baritone saxophone player. Besides being one of the leading "bari" players in jazz history, he was a composer, arranger, bandleader, pianist, and clarinetist. Winner of one Grammy Award and three Grammy nominations.

multi-measure rest   Also known as a "multiple" measure rest, it indicates the number of rests that the performer is to wait before playing again.

multiphonics   A twentieth-century extended instrumental technique that takes an instrument that generally plays only one note at a time (monophonic) and produces several notes at once, such as singing while playing a flute.

multimetric   1. A modern musical technique where the time signature in a composition changes in almost every measure. 2. A composition technique used in the eighteenth century for writing different time signatures for different instruments. It was used by Mozart in the first-act menuetto of his opera *Don Giovanni*.

multitrack recording   The separate sound recording of a number of different instruments or sound sources. These tracks are then mixed together to create a complete song.

music   An art form using the elements of sound. These elements include pitch, rhythm, dynamics, texture, and timbre. Musical compositions are created when these elements are systematically arranged using melody, harmony, meter articulation, and tempo.

music appreciation   Teaching individuals how to listen to and appreciate different types of music by explaining the composer's intentions, the history of the music era it came from, and why the people of that era liked the music.

music box   An automatic musical instrument that plays a song by using pins on a disc or revolving cylinder to pluck a steel comb's tuned teeth. Music boxes were first made in the nineteenth century in Switzerland by watchmakers who used clockwork to run them.

music critic   People who review music performances; recorded music; or printed music for either the newspaper, journals, or books.

music drama   Musical theater with a serious tone, first referred to by composer Richard Wagner (1813–1883) in his 1850–1851 book *Opera and Drama*. This concept was intended to bring back Greek drama and all its symbolic forms by using music to express the dramatic action. The texture of this music would be inserted with thematic ideas called leitmotifs at emotional points in the drama. Wagner's cycle of four operas called *Der Ring des Nibelungen* (*The Ring of the Nibelung*) is a fine example of the use of music drama.

music therapy   When a trained music therapist uses music to treat any number of conditions, including psychiatric disorders, substance abuse, physical handicaps, mental illness, and aging.

music video   Short video or film primarily used to market a song, artist, or album. In the early 1980s, this art form became popular when MTV and later VH-1 based their programming around it. Content of the video usually included a scripted and choreographed live or edited version of the band members performing the song.

M

musical director   The person in charge of the musical direction of an orchestra, opera company, choir, band, or musical theater. Other duties include hiring and firing of talent, picking the repertoire, assisting with fundraising, and being the "public face" of the musical organization.

musical form   The harmonic and melodic structure or style of a song; sometimes refers to a specific musical genre.

musical instrument   An object that is shaped or constructed to make sounds with tone. A musical instrument is made and used for human expression through the manipulation of sound.

musical theater   A popular theater production using music, drama, song, spoken dialogue, and dance. Some famous musicals are *Carousel*, *Phantom of the Opera*, *South Pacific*, and *West Side Story*.

musical tone   Pitch, intensity, and duration produced from the vibrating mechanism of an instrument or voice. Good musical tone is produced when the performer produces a vigorous, expressive sound strong enough to keep the pitch sounding at the optimal vibration.

musique concrete   A composition technique that emerged from new music technology in the 1940s, centering on but not excluding the use of nonmusical sound sources that are recorded, spliced, filtered, looped, and mixed. These recorded sounds are obtained by a number of different sources, such as noises, nature sounds, and percussion instruments. Invented by the French composer and theorist Pierre Schaeffer (1910–1995).

Mussorgsky, Modest (1839–1881)   Russian composer of the romantic period known for establishing a nationalistic music style using Russian folklore and history. His opera *Boris Godunov* and piano suite *Pictures at an Exhibition* contained nationalist themes.

mutation   The change that occurs in an adolescent boy's voice, between ages 13 and 16, from alto or soprano to tenor or bass.

mute   Device fitted in the bell of a musical instrument used to change the sound and timbre and reduce the volume.

mystic chord   Also called the "Prometheus" chord, it was used by the Russian composer Alexander Scriabin (1872–1915) in his later pieces as a melodic and harmonic structure. Scriabin was deeply interested in mysticism and used this six-note chord to express this interest.

M

Nabucco Italian opera in four acts composed by Giuseppi Verdi, with libretto by Temistocle Soler. First produced in Milan, Italy, in 1842, the story follows the Jews of the Bible as they are exiled from their homes by King Nabucco of Babylonia.

nasal tone A thin, twangy vocal sound a singer makes as a result of using a constricted throat.

national anthem Composition written as the main song representing a country. Played (and sung) before most major sporting events and during national holidays. The United States' national anthem is "The Star-Spangled Banner."

National Endowment for the Arts An agency of the U.S. government "dedicated to supporting excellence in the arts, both new and established; bringing the arts to all Americans; and providing leadership in arts education." The NEA's slogan is, "A great country deserves great art." It was established in 1965 by the U.S. government and is based in Washington, D.C.

nationalism In music, nationalism uses melodies, rhythms, and different musical ideas and motifs identifying certain regions and ethnicity of its country. Certain folk song themes are often incorporated into the classical programmatic compositions of the host country's leading composers. Nationalistic composers include Russian composer Mikhail

Glinka (1804–1857), Czech composer Antonin Dvořák (1841–1904), Norwegian composer Edvard Grieg (1843–1907), English composer Ralph Vaughan Williams (1872–1958), and American composer Aaron Copland (1900–1990).

natural A symbol that cancels out a sharp or flat in a bar of music. On the keyboard, each of the white keys (the scale of C Major) is natural. The sign for natural is ♮.

natural horn An ancestor of the modern horn (French horn) with the same basic shape but without the valves. This brass instrument's notes are played by modulating the lip position and tension.

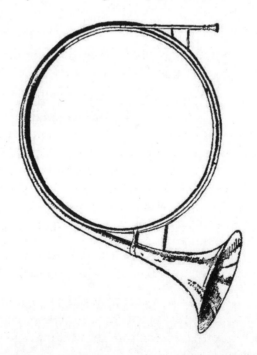

natural tone The fundamental tone (pedal tone) and higher harmonics that are sounded when overblowing a musical wind instrument of a certain length.

Neapolitan school   A school of composition from the eighteenth century originating in Naples, Italy, by a group of famous composers (known mostly for their operas) such as Domenico Cimarosa, Alessandro Scarlatti, and Giovanni Battista Pergolesi.

Neapolitan sixth   Known as a "Neapolitan chord," it is a major chord that usually occurs in first inversion (the root of a chord is changed from the lowest pitch to the third) and is built on the lowered second degree of the scale. Its name is associated with the composers from the Neapolitan school, who frequently used it in their music.

neck   The part of a string instrument that projects away from the body of the instrument and where the fingers push down to stop the strings to make different pitches. The neck also holds the frets, fret board, and peghead (tuning pegs).

neighboring tone   A tone that is one step above or below the next chord. Because it is not part of the next chord, it can create dissonance, which is "resolved" when the next chord is played.

Nelson, Willie (b. 1933)   American country songwriter, singer, and actor known for being a major performer of "outlaw country" music in the 1970s. He is the winner of 10 Grammy Awards and 7 American Music Awards. Willie Nelson has made 100 albums, 3 film soundtracks, and 97 singles, 29 of which have reached number one. Also an actor in 31 movies and an author of 4 books, he has written many famous songs, including "Night Life," "Crazy," and "Mamas, Don't Let Your Babies Grow Up to Be Cowboys."

Nelson Mass   Mass in D minor by Joseph Haydn (1732–1809), written in 1798 and sometimes called "The Imperial."

neoclassicism   A twentieth-century movement that uses contemporary composition techniques taken from seventeenth- and eighteenth-century music. A reaction to the emotionalism of the late romantic period (1820–1900).

neomodal   A modern compositional music technique that uses altered ancient modes as a source of inspiration.

netlabel   A record label that uses the Internet to distribute its music through digital audio formats such as MP3.

neumes   Music notation used between the eighth and fourteenth centuries. Refers to the notation used to create Gregorian chants in the Roman Catholic Church.

neutral clef   Also called a "percussion" clef, it indicates which unpitched percussion instruments are assigned to the lines and spaces of the staff. Neutral clefs usually use one line instead of five lines.

New Age music   Music composed to inspire or relax the listener. Meant to create a peaceful atmosphere and often used to create positive feelings for people involved in massage, yoga, meditation, relaxation, and New Age spirituality. Rhythm and melodies are often repetitive, with modal harmonies and a drone bass line to create a hypnotic effect. This music is often mixed with nature sounds.

new beat   1. The term Americans gave to new electronic and techno music in the early 1980s. Later named techno or house. 2. Local music style from around 1987 in Belgium, an alternative to Eurobeat from the United Kingdom.

new jack swing   A musical style that mixes the sound of R&B's emotional solo and harmonizing vocal lines with hip-hop's production methods, rhythms, and samples. Most popular from the late 1980s to the mid-1990s. Three new jack swing artists are Bobby Brown, Janet Jackson, and TLC.

new music   A term introduced in 1925 designating the different radical and novel trends in twentieth-century music, such as "atonality" and "serial techniques" used by composers such as Alban Berg and Arnold Schoenberg.

New Orleans jazz A music genre and performance art born in New Orleans, Louisiana, using elements of improvisation, syncopation, blues scales, and harmony.

new prog Alternative rock bands that use progressive rock elements. Several recent bands that use this title include Mystery Jets, Radiohead, Mew, the Mars Volta, and Oceanside.

new wave In the 1970s, this music was the same as punk rock (anti-establishment, political, and fast and hard-edged) but later incorporated experimental music, reggae, ska, disco, and electronic aspects.

New Weird America Subgenre of music originating from folk and psychedelic rock groups of the 1960s and 1970s.

New World Symphony Composed by Antonín Dvořák in 1893. Popular name for the *Symphony No. 9 in E Minor "From the New World"* (Op. 95, B. 178).

Newman, Alfred (1900–1970) American composer of more than 200 film scores between 1930 and 1970. Nominated 45 times for an Academy Award and winner of the Oscar 9 times. Three of his most famous film scores include *How Green Was My Valley* (1941), *The Robe* (1953), and *How the West Was Won* (1962).

Newman, Randy (b. 1943) American composer whose satirical pop songs ("Short People" and "Sail Away"), 15 albums, and many film scores (26) have won him 4 Grammy Awards, 15 Academy Award nominations, and 1 Oscar. Several of his most famous film scores include *The Natural, Sea Biscuit,* and Disney/Pixar's *Toy Story 1 & 2* and *Cars*.

ninth chord Musical chord using the tonic (root) note of the scale and the second note of the scale above the octave. Usually used as an extended chord with the root, third, fifth, and seventh included.

N

Ninth Symphony   Choral symphony written by Ludwig van Beethoven in 1824. The last of Beethoven's symphonies and one of Western music's best known and loved classical masterpieces. Full name is the *Symphony No. 9 in D minor, Op. 125 "Choral."*

no wave   Popular music of the mid-1970s that was short-lived but influential on noise and industrial music and on the art performance world in New York City. Two no wave bands were Teenage Jesus & the Jerks and DNA.

nocturne   A romantic piece composed for piano with an expressive melody over an arpeggiated (broken chord) accompaniment. Frédéric Chopin was the most famous composer of nocturnes.

node   A point on an instrument where the string vibrates the least (for example, the bridge and fingerboard of a violin) or air particles don't move (for example, where the highest-density air particles don't move in an organ pipe).

Noel (F., Christmas)   Famous Christmas song taken from the Latin word *natalis* or birthday. Also known as "The First Noel," a traditional English carol first published in 1832.

noise music   Music that features all different types of electronic or acoustical noise, including dissonance, nontraditional musical instruments, distortion, audio feedback, atonal music, vocal elements, and cacophony (unpleasant sound utterances). The avant-garde music of Karlheinz Stockhausen as well as the distortion and loud volume in popular hard rock music are both examples of noise-based music.

noise pop   Term for an alternative rock that fuses punk rock, atonal music, and "noise music" elements. It's more accessible than "noise rock" because of its use of basic pop/rock formulae and length. The Velvet Underground were a major influence on this sub-genre, and the Jesus and Mary Chain are known for being the first noise-pop band.

noise rock   Music of the 1980s that uses the same instrumentation of regular rock but incorporates dissonance and atonality in an unconventional songwriting style. Also called "noise punk."

non troppo An Italian notation instructing the performer of a composition to play "moderately" or "not too much."

nonharmonic tones In music theory, any tone not within the harmonic structure of the moment. Nonharmonic tones include passing tones, neighboring tones, appaggiaturas, and other embellishments.

nonmetric Music without a strong meter or beat.

Norma Italian opera composed in four acts by Vincenzo Bellini, with libretto by Felice Romani. Produced in Milan in 1831.

notation Musical symbols or a method for writing down music. Used for all vocal and instrumental music.

note A musical symbol representing the pitch and length of a sound.

Notre Dame, School of Composers of polyphony (composition with two or more melodic lines occurring simultaneously) at the Notre Dame de Paris cathedral between 1160 and 1250. Léonin and Pérotin were two composers famous for developing polyphony from an earlier form of Medieval composition called *organum*.

novelty tunes Popular songs whose subject matter reflects a current trend, event, person, or time period. Novelty tunes have a short shelf life because, except for certain holiday songs, listeners lose interest when the subject in the song is no longer popular. A few examples include songs such as "1999" by Prince, "Pac-Man Fever" by Buckner & Garcia in 1982, and "Convoy" by C. W. McCall in 1975.

Nozze di Figaro, Le See *The Marriage of Figaro*.

nu jazz Style of jazz that mixes in other styles such as soul, electronica, and funk. Nu jazz emphasizes fresh rhythms and melodies instead of the players' technical abilities and mixes synthesizers and horns with the regular rhythm section setup of bass guitar, electric guitar, and drums.

nuance   The color or tone of a composition or phrase of music; the feeling or meaning of expression in the music.

number opera   The way opera was written until the early nineteenth century, using separate pieces such as arias, duets, ballets, ensembles, and recitative or spoken dialogue. Richard Wagner was instrumental in changing the style to a more continuous music.

number symbolism   The relationship numbers have with the compositions of some of the great masters. Johann Sebastian Bach used number symbolism in his works, such as using a key signature with three flats to represent the trinity (father, son, and holy ghost). An example of number symbolism can be found in Prelude and Fugue "St. Anne" in E flat Major, BWV 552.

nuove musiche (G., new music)   A term introduced in 1925 designating the different radical and novel trends in twentieth-century music, such as "atonality" and "serial techniques," used by composers such as Alban Berg and Arnold Schoenberg.

nut   Also called a "frog." An arch made of wood or plastic that is fastened onto string instruments at the upper end of the neck to help raise the strings over the fingerboard.

Nutcracker Suite, The   Eight numbers taken from Pyotr Ilyich Tchaikovsky's ballet *The Nutcracker*, composed in 1891–1892. These eight selections were intended for concert production, named *The Nutcracker Suite, Op. 71a*, and performed in St. Petersburg in March 1892, eight months before the entire ballet's December premiere.

o

obbligato Italian term that means the musical line written is "fixed" and must be played exactly the way it is written, without any omissions or changes.

oboe A double-reed musical instrument that is a member of the woodwind family. It is known for its clear, penetrating voice and is pitched in the key of C. Used in symphony orchestras (often to tune the rest of the orchestra) and developed in the mid-seventeenth century from its predecessor, the shawm. Members of the oboe family include the English horn, bassoon, and contrabassoon.

ocarina   Ancient flutelike instrument that goes back 12,000 years. It's an oval-shaped instrument with up to 12 holes blown through a mouth tube coming out of its body.

octave   The eighth step of a major scale. It is acoustically double the frequency of the original tone (middle A = 440; one octave higher A = 880).

octave clef   This is used to indicate that the music be performed an octave higher or lower. There are two octave clefs. One has an 8 written above the treble clef sign and is to be performed an octave higher, and one has an 8 written below the treble clef sign (also called a vocal tenor clef) and is performed an octave lower.

octet   Chamber instrumental ensemble of eight performers.

ode   A lyrical verse written about an important person, event, or particular subject and set to music.

Oedipus Rex (L., *King Oedipus*)   Opera-oratorio composed in two acts by Igor Stravinsky with lyrics from Sophocles' tragedy. Produced in Paris in 1927 and set in ancient Thebes.

off-pitch   A faulty or imprecise intonation of a musical pitch as a result of faulty hearing acuteness, uncoordinated vocal muscles, or lack of tuning ability.

offbeat   The weak beat or beats in a measure of music.

Offenbach, Jacques (1819–1880)   Romantic period French composer and cellist who invented the operetta form. His influence in popular music of the nineteenth century made him very famous in Europe and English-speaking countries. Later in his career, he wrote *The Tales of Hoffman*, his one fully operatic hit.

Old Maid and the Thief, The American opera composed in one act by Gian Carlo Menotti from his own libretto. Produced in 1939 at the NBC radio studios in New York City. The setting is the present in a small American town.

Oliver, Joseph "King" (1885–1938) A jazz cornet player, composer, bandleader, and leader in the development of jazz, Oliver was known for his innovative use of mutes and his playing style. He was a teacher and mentor of the famous trumpet player Louis Armstrong.

ombra scene A scene in early opera that takes place in Hades or has ghosts in it. A couple of operas with an ombra scene are *Orfeo* by Claudio Monteverdi and *Mitridate, re di Ponto*, an early opera of Wolfgang Amadeus Mozart.

one-step American dance between 1910–1920 set in a fast duple meter.

onset The beginning of a sound or musical note.

open fifth Musical theory term for a two-note chord using the tonic (first step) and dominant (fifth step) of a scale (for example, C–G).

open notes When a wind or brass instrument is played with no fingers on the keys or valves. Also, a string instrument played on an open string.

open strings When the strings on a string instrument are unstopped (not pushed down).

opera An art form that combines all elements of theater, including drama, music (vocal and instrumental), stage design, dance, and costuming. Opera expresses the feelings and thoughts of the characters through song instead of speech, using recitative (sung speech), arias (solos), duets, ensembles, and choruses. The first real opera produced was in 1597 (*Dafne* by Jacopo Peri), although many of the elements of opera had been incorporated in works before this date.

opera buffa   An opera with a lighter or more sentimental subject matter, usually with spoken dialogue that resolves in a happy ending. Opera buffa reflects a more popular style than serious opera (opera seria).

opera house   Performance venue where opera is performed. The first opera house opened in Venice in 1637. Some of the more famous opera houses include the Metropolitan Opera in New York City; the Royal Opera House in London; La Scala (Teatro alla Scala) in Milan, Italy; and the National Opera of Paris (Opéra National De Paris) in Paris.

opera seria   Opera composed in three acts from the eighteenth century based on a serious plot. An example of opera seria would be *Idomeneo* by Wolfgang Amadeus Mozart (1756–1791).

operetta   1. A light, popular theatrical piece with song, dance, and spoken dialogue from the nineteenth and twentieth centuries. A shorter, less serious opera. American composers Victor Herbert and Sigmund Romberg wrote in this medium. During the 1920s, the more sentimental operettas started to be called "musical plays" and eventually just "musical."

opus (*op.*)   A term used to indicate the chronological publication date within the entire collection of a composer's works.

oratorio   A sacred composition performed in a concert hall or church using an orchestra and chorus. Like opera, it uses vocal soloists, recitatives, arias, duets, ensembles, and a chorus. Unlike opera, it uses only a religious text and is performed without acting, costumes, and scenery. George Frideric Handel (1685–1759) composed the most famous oratorio, *Messiah*.

Orbison, Roy (1936–1988)   American singer-songwriter of rock ballads such as "Only the Lonely," "Pretty Woman," and "Crying," and an inspiration for musicians such as Elvis Presley, Bob Dylan, and Bono. Twenty-two of his songs placed in the Top 40 in the early 1960s. Known for his incredible vocal range, he was sometimes called the "Caruso of Rock."

orchestra   A large instrumental ensemble of about 100 performers (modern orchestra) consisting of string, brass, woodwind, and percussion instruments. These symphony orchestras are used for symphonic works, while smaller pit orchestras are used for the accompaniment of concerts, operas, and oratorios. Small ensembles are called chamber orchestras (usually one performer on each part). Jazz big bands were often called orchestras by band leaders such as Duke Ellington and Stan Kenton.

orchestration   Arrangement and organization of instruments in a musical composition by an orchestrator or arranger (often the composer).

Orfeo (It., *La Favola d'Orfeo*)   Italian opera composed in five acts by Claudio Monteverdi, with libretto written by Alessandro Striggio. One of the first recognized works to be considered an opera (*Dafne*, by Jacopo Peri in 1597, was the very first). Produced in 1607 and published in 1608, it was performed at the ducal palace in Mantua, Italy, for the annual carnival of Mantua. The story takes place in Ancient Greece, with Orpheus attempting to bring his dead lover Eurydice back from Hades.

Orff, Carl (1895–1982)   German composer best known for his oratorio *Carmina Burana* (1937). Orff is also famous for development of the Orff Method (also called Orff–Schulwerk or Music for Children), a children's method of music education.

organ   A keyboard instrument that uses a series of pipes traditionally supplied with wind by feeders (small bellows) to make music. Besides the current electronic and sampled (digital reproduction) organs, there are two types: the tracker organ and the electropneumatic organ. The earliest organ in recorded history appears in 120 C.E. The organ has been the main instrument played in churches of all faiths for 900 years.

organ reform   An organ-building revival movement originating in Germany in the early twentieth century that grew with the interest in historical performances of great organ pieces by composers such as Johann Sebastian Bach.

organ stops   The part of the organ that lets wind into and "stops" wind from entering the organ's pipes. The "stop knob" or "draw-knob" controls this action.

organology   The scientific and analytical study of musical instruments, especially from other cultures and time periods.

organum   A plainchant (Gregorian chant) vocal line with an added voice to make the first harmony (polyphony). *Early* or *parallel organum* (first documented circa 895) started in unison, moved to the same melody a fourth or perfect fifth apart, and ended on the unison. This later developed into *free organum* (1020–1050) and reached its peak with *florid organum* and *melismatic organum* (twelfth century) at the Notre Dame school in Paris, with Léonin and Pérotin being the most famous composers of this style of composition.

ornamentation   Musical flourishes that decorate a melody. A common practice in the baroque period (1600–1750), it was often used on the repeated section of a de capo aria (song form A-B-A) and used extensively by harpsichord and clavichordists to prolong or sustain notes. Types of ornaments include trills, mordents, appaggiaturas, glissandos, and turns. Ornaments are either written out by the composer or improvised. Ornamentation is used frequently in modern songs by singers such as Mariah Carey and Whitney Houston.

ossia   Italian musical term indicating an alternative (usually easier) version to a musical passage.

ossilation   Movement between two points or tones, causing the effect of a vibrato.

ostinato   A succession of repeated rhythmic patterns, melodies, phrases, or motifs in classical music, much like riffs are used in popular music. Ostinato is also used in jazz (for example, the left-handed pattern in the boogie-woogie style).

Otello   Italian opera composed in four acts by Giuseppe Verdi, with libretto by Arrigo Boito from the play "Othello" written by William Shakespeare. First produced in Milan in 1887, it was Verdi's penultimate opera.

ottava (It., octave)   This is used to indicate whether a section of music is to be played one octave higher or lower than it is written. For example, *ottava basso* means that the music is to be played an octave lower than written.

$$8^{va} \qquad 8^{vb}$$

outlaw country   An important musical trend in country music in the late 1960s and 1970s. A reaction to the softened Nashville sound, performers such as Johnny Cash, Waylon Jennings, and Willie Nelson performed music whose "outlaw" lyrics were about working men, drugs, drinking, and fighting, with a general rawness and energy the Nashville sound was lacking. "Take This Job and Shove It" by Johnny Paycheck, "Are You Ready for the Country" by Waylon Jennings, and "Whiskey River" by Willie Nelson are all examples of outlaw country music.

outsider music   Songs written by musicians outside the commercial music industry who have not received formal music training or disagree with formal rules of composition. These artists have more control over their music because they are unwilling to listen to opinion and cooperate with changes suggested by a producer or record label. Famous for her terrible singing ability, American soprano Florence Foster Jenkins (1868–1944) was a performer of this type. In the late 1960s, the Shaggs were a group playing outsider music.

overblowing   Technique of playing a wind instrument by blowing with more force than needed to create an overtone or harmonic of the fundamental (original) note. A note can also be overblown by altering the direction of the airstream to sound higher notes, such as blowing into a glass bottle or a flute or tightening the embouchure for brass instruments.

O

overdubbing   A recording technique that adds extra tracks of music onto a previously recorded performance. Used in professional or home recording studios to add different instruments to the initial recording; the drum track could be laid down first, then the guitar, then vocals, then any other instrument.

overtone   Also called an harmonic or partial. An acoustical term used to describe a certain characteristic of a vibrating body. Overtones resonate faster than the fundamental (original) vibration at the half, third, fourth, and fifth. A string vibrating at 100 Hz when pressed in the middle will vibrate twice as fast at the octave or 200 Hz, which is the first harmonic.

overture   The musical introduction for an opera, oratorio, musicals, and certain movie films. After 1750, the accepted practice for the modern overture was to introduce the basic melodies and musical themes used throughout the show and set up the mood for the first act. Other types of overtures are the *French overture* as a suite and the *concert overture*, written as an independent orchestral work.

Paganini, Niccolò (1782–1840)   Italian composer and most famous virtuoso violinist of his time who developed much of today's modern violin playing technique. He was a great inspiration to prominent artists following him. His composition Caprice in A Minor, Op. 1, No. 24, is one of his best-known pieces.

Page, Jimmy (b. 1944)   Songwriter, producer, and lead guitarist for the English hard-rock band Led Zeppelin. In 2003, *Rolling Stone* magazine ranked him ninth on its 100 Greatest Guitarists of All Time list.

Page, Patti (b. 1927)   American pop singer and best-selling 1950s female artist. Songs such as "Tennessee Waltz," "With My Eyes Wide Open I'm Dreaming," and "(How Much Is That) Doggie in the Window?" helped her sell more than 100 million records.

Pagliacci (It., *Players or Clowns*)   Italian verismo opera (opera composed around the "realistic" emotions of everyday life) composed in two acts and a prologue by Ruggero Leoncavallo to his own libretto. First produced in Milan in 1892, it's set in Calabria, Italy, in 1865. Because of its short length (one hour), it is often combined with another short verismo opera, *Cavalleria Rusticana*, by Pietro Mascagni, in a double bill called *Cav/Pag*.

paraphrase   A reworking or arrangement of a well-known melody. Franz Liszt often composed piano pieces by paraphrasing famous Wagnerian opera motifs.

Parker, Charlie (1920–1955)   Jazz alto saxophonist and composer who was one of the top five most important and influential jazz musicians who played a major role in the development of bebop through virtuosic technique and improvisation.

parlando (It., to speak)   1. A vocal term directing the singer to approximate speech while singing, much like in a "patter song" with rapid articulation. 2. When playing an instrument, parlando indicates that the performer must play in a declamative, expressive manner suggesting speech or song.

parlor songs   Vocal music that was originally meant to be sung in a person's parlor by amateur singers. Parlor songs were very popular in-home entertainment before the advent of phonograph records and radio.

parody   Refers to the imitation of an original piece of music with the exchange of a funny text for the original text or some aspect of the music exchanged with a comical element.

Parsifal   German opera composed in three acts by Richard Wagner to his own libretto. First produced in 1882 at the Bayreuth Festival Opera House in Germany, it tells the story of an Arthurian knight on a quest for the Holy Grail.

part   The music played or meant to be performed by an individual instrument or voice type.

partial   Also called an "overtone" or "harmonic," partial is an acoustical term used to describe a certain characteristic of a vibrating body. Partials resonate faster than the fundamental (original) vibration at the half, third, fourth, and fifth. A string vibrating at 100 Hz, when pressed in the middle, will vibrate twice as fast at the octave or 200 Hz, which is the first harmonic.

passage   A small section of a musical composition.

passaggio (It., passageway)   The tonal passageway where a singer's voice passes from chest voice to head voice. This is also called the "break."

pasticcio (It., pastiche)   1. An eighteenth-century stage entertainment that uses a new libretto to fit the melody of an existing work of music. 2. An eighteenth-century operatic medley of popular songs from different composers.

pastorale   1. Music composed to imitate the music of the Biblical shepherds present at Jesus' birth. Usually played in 6/8 or 12/8 meter with a flowing melody and long drones. 2. Dramatic performance in the sixteenth century that incorporated a pleasant plot; an important predecessor of opera.

Pathétique, Sonata   Piano Sonata No. 8 in C Minor, Op. 13 by Ludwig van Beethoven. Written in 1798 when he was 28 years old, it is one of Beethoven's most beloved works.

patter song   Used for comical effect in operas, this parlando (rapid, speechlike) style tries to get in as many words as possible in the shortest amount of time.

Paul, Les (1915–2009)   Born Lester William Polsfuss. American jazz and country-western guitarist, inventor, and songwriter who invented the solid-body electric guitar and was instrumental in recording innovations such as multi-track recording, overdubbing, and tape-delay effects.

pause   Also known as a "fermata" or "hold," the bird's-eye sign is placed above or below the note or rest that is to be held or prolonged.

Pavarotti, Luciano (1935–2007)   Italian operatic tenor who became the most recorded and most popular tenor of the twentieth century. Called the "King of the High Cs," he has two *Guinness Book of World Records* titles, one for the most curtain calls (165) and one for the best-selling classical album (*In Concert* with the Three Tenors).

P

Pearl Fishers, The French opera composed in three acts by Georges Bizet, with libretto by Michel Carré and Eugène Cormon. First produced in Paris in 1863, the opera's setting is Ceylon (now the Democratic Socialist Republic of Sri Lanka).

pedal An attachment to a keyboard that uses an action operated by the feet; the three pedals of the piano or the foot pedals (that play tones) of the organ.

pedal harp Name for the modern chromatic or concert harp; used as a solo instrument or in small and large orchestral ensembles. There are seven pedals that change the strings' pitches and were first used around 1697.

pedal harpsichord A harpsichord that uses a pedal board of from 8 to 15 pedals, much like an organ. No pedal harpsichords have survived.

pedal piano A piano that uses a pedal board much like an organ. It was not very successful and is no longer used.

pedal point   Long note in the bass line that sustains while the harmonies change in the other parts. Also called a "drone" or "bourdon," it is one of the first devices of polyphony (using two or more different melodies at the same time) and is used extensively in organ works of Bach and Buxtehude.

pedal tone   Another name for the fundamental (harmonic series lowest frequency) tone of a cylindrical-bore brass instrument.

Pelléas et Mélisande   French opera composed in five acts by Claude Debussy, from a libretto adapted from Maurice Maeterlinck's play with the same name. Produced for the first time in Paris in 1902.

pentachord   Five-step portion of a major scale (for example, C to G).

pentatonic scale   A five-step scale used by many ancient cultures, it can be played on the keyboard on all the black keys.

percussion instrument   One of the four musical instrument families. It is usually associated with any instrument that is hit, scraped, shaken, or rubbed. Two categories of percussion instruments are the *idiophones*, which make a musical tone through the vibration of their entire body (for example, bell or marimba), and the *membranophones*, which produce sound when the head or membrane is hit (for example, timpani or snare drum). The name is taken from the Latin *percussio*, meaning "to beat or strike."

percussionization   A sharp attack on a musical instrument, thus creating a percussive sound. An example would be the pizzicato (plucking) effect on a string instrument, often used by the double bass violin as it creates the rhythmic and harmonic foundation in an orchestra. The trend in the 1960s and 1970s to make the bass and electric guitars more percussive involved the new technique of slapping or popping the strings and choking a guitar sound, as heard in the music for the movie *Shaft* and in other funk music of the time.

perfect authentic cadence (PAC)   The strongest type of cadence (two chords that bring finality to a phrase or composition). The chords V to I in major keys (V to i in minor keys) are in the root position.

perfect interval   The distance between two notes of the scale that is neither major nor minor. This would include the perfect fifth and the perfect unison.

performance practice   1. The way a performer practices his or her instrument(s). 2. The study of how early music (fifth to sixteenth century) was performed and the problems associated with playing it accurately in modern performances.

period   In a melody, a natural division or group of around eight measures with two or more complementary or contrasting phrases ending in a cadence.

Peter, Paul and Mary   One of the most popular and successful folk acts of the 1960s. A few of their hits include "Puff the Magic Dragon," "If I Had a Hammer," and "Leaving on a Jet Plane."

Peter and the Wolf   A popular Russian orchestral piece and children's story written and composed in 1936 by Sergei Prokofiev; uses a narrator and orchestra.

Peter Grimes   English opera composed in three acts by Benjamin Britten. First produced in London in 1945, the opera's setting is the east coast of England around 1830.

pharynx   The area of the throat right behind the mouth and above the esophagus and larynx; important for vocalization and tone resonance in singers.

Philadelphia sound   Also called "Philadelphia soul" or "Sweet Philly," it's the predecessor of disco. This 1960s genre of soul music used a mixture of R&B, funk, smooth jazz, and pop vocals in lush orchestral arrangements.

phonation   When a sound is vocalized. This includes singing, speaking, grunts, sighs, burps, or whimpers.

phoneme   Small unit of sound that makes up a phonetic system. The two types of phonemes include consonants and vowels.

phonetic   A system that studies the sounds of speech and its auditory, physiological, and neurophysiological (effect on the nervous system) properties.

phonics   The science of producing the sounds of speech and a system of teaching children to read and pronounce words.

phonograph   Also called the "record player," "gramophone," and later the "turntable." Invented by Thomas Edison in 1877, it was the most common way to play recorded sound from 1877 to the late 1980s. Earlier phonograph recordings were made and played on cylinders, but by 1910 the most common analog recordings were disk-shaped. "Record player" became the universal name by the second half of the twentieth century.

phrase   Any small unit of music with a complete musical reason. Much like a motif, it is part of a larger melody.

phrasing   The separation of a melody into smaller clear and meaningful units or phrases. Often, the term "articulation" is applied with the same meaning.

pianissimo (*pp*)   Italian term indicating "very soft."

$$pp$$

pianississimo (*ppp*)   Italian term indicating "very, very soft."

$$ppp$$

piano (*p*)   Italian term indicating "soft."

$$p$$

piano, pianoforte   The main keyboard used in the United States and Europe since the end of the eighteenth century. This instrument's strings are struck by hammers, which are activated by playing keys with the fingers. Different from its predecessors the harpsichord and clavichord, the pianoforte (abbreviated "piano") can vary its dynamics from soft (*piano*) to loud (*forte*), and its range covers more than seven octaves (88 keys). Created by Bartolomeo Cristofori (1655–1731) in Florence, Italy, a little before 1700. The modern acoustic piano comes in different sizes (from smallest to largest): the uprights stand vertical to the floor and include the

P

spinet (36 inches high), the console (42 inches high), the studio (46 inches high), and the upright grand (anything higher than the studio). Grand pianos sit horizontally to the floor and come in different lengths, extending from the baby grand at about 5 feet, 1 inch to the concert grand at approximately 9 feet long. Other types of pianos include the toy piano (same mechanism with a much smaller range), player piano (plays from a piano roll perforated with holes), prepared piano (piano altered with objects placed in its mechanism and used in contemporary art music), and the digital piano (either electronic or sampled).

piano roll   Perforated rolls of paper used in player pianos to reproduce an actual performance of a pianist. This was the first music storage medium that could be mass-produced. The perforated hole's length and position determined the note and its duration with a "tracker bar" reading the paper and sending the information to the piano mechanism.

picardy third   A major chord used at the end of a musical section that is written in a minor key. This is achieved by raising the third of the chord by a half step as a way of resolving the line.

piccolo (It., small)   A member of the woodwind family, a piccolo is a half-sized flute. Tuned in the key of C, it is pitched an octave higher than a flute with the same fingering.

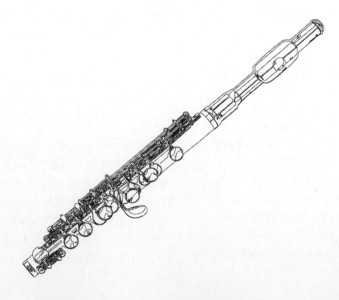

ping   An unnatural, artificial vocal tone characteristic that is sometimes mistakenly used by the singer to give more focus or edge to the tone.

pipe   Generic name for wind instruments, including flutes, earlier instruments in the shape of a tube, and the pipes used on the organ.

piston valve   Used on brass instruments to change the instrument's tubing length. When pressed, the valve diverts air through other tubing and changes the pitch of the tone.

pitch   Position of a sound in the musical scale. A musical tone dictated by a sound wave's frequency.

pitch aggregate   A cluster of musical pitches. Found in alleatory (chance) music.

pitch control   An attempt to stay in tune or regulate intonation, either consciously or subconsciously.

pitch names   Names given to the note positions on a musical scale. These are C, D, E, F, G, A, B, and all the sharps and flats in between, such as C♯ and B♭.

pizzicato (*pizz*)   Italian term or instruction to "pluck" the instrument's string.

placement   The direction of vocal tone or energy into a certain part of the body, usually the "facial mask" in the forward part of the head.

plagal cadence   Also called the "Amen" cadence because of its use at the end of religious hymns. It's a subdominant IV chord to a tonic I chord progression usually sung to the word "Amen."

plainchant   Liturgical (religious) chant, also known as "plainsong" or Gregorian chant, believed to have been developed by Pope Gregory I (reigned 590–604) for the Roman Catholic Church. There are approximately 3,000 chant melodies, and most are based on prose text taken from the Bible's Book of Psalms. Each chant consists of a melody line sung by a cantor (soloist) or unison choir in one of the eight church modes.

P

player piano   A self-playing piano that uses a "tracker bar" to play piano rolls with perforated holes whose length and position determine the note and its duration. The "pianola" was a generic name for the player piano.

plosive   In singing, a sudden release of sound from a stopped air position using one or a combination of the tongue and lips. This creates a voiced or unvoiced consonant sound. Voiced plosives include *b*, *d*, and *g*, and unvoiced plosives are *p*, *t*, and *k*.

plucking   *See* pizzicato.

poco   Italian term meaning "a little."

poco a poco   Italian term meaning "little by little." (For example, poco a poco allegro means "to get increasingly faster.")

point   1. A violin bow's upper end. 2. A placed or focused tone.

polka   A central European dance written in duple meter (2/4) originating in Bohemia in 1830. Often used in classical repertoire but usually associated with popular music and the "Polish-style polka" played in German beer houses.

polonaise   Slow Polish dance in 3/4 time. Frédéric Chopin (1810–1849) is known for his piano polonaises.

poly   Prefix meaning "many."

polychoral   Also called "antiphonal." A sixteenth-century choral performance style that uses two or more choirs in unison or answering each other in a "call and response" or echo effect.

polymetric   Also known as "polyrhythmic," it refers to the use of different musical meters or rhythms performed simultaneously.

polyphony   A composition using two or more different melodies at the same time.

Pomp and Circumstance   Five concert marches written by Edward Elgar from 1901–1930. March No. 1 in D is the best known of the set, frequently played as students process and recess at school graduations.

Pons, Lily (1898–1976)   A French American operatic coloratura soprano who started her career in 1928, she was a principal artist at the Metropolitan Opera house in New York City for 30 years and continued to sing recitals until 1973. Her film appearances include *I Dream Too Much* (1935), *The Girl from Paris* (1936), and *Hittin' a New High* (1937).

pop music   A musical genre developed in the 1950s to reflect current music trends and to appeal to a general audience. A gentler alternative to rock and roll, it was usually a love song that used elements from many different styles and emphasized production and recording (two and a half to three and a half minutes long) instead of live performances. Several subgenres of pop music include disco, Europop, Latin pop, synthpop, and psychedelic pop, among many others.

pop punk   A combination of pop music, which uses strong melodies, crisp vocals, and outstanding guitar riffs with punk's fast tempos and loud guitars. The Buzzcocks, the Jam, and the Undertones were bands that started pop punk in the early 1980s.

popular music   Music that contrasts with art and traditional music in that it appeals to a broad range of audiences. Types of popular music include show tunes, film music, dance music, music hall songs, folk music, and country.

Porgy and Bess   American folk opera composed in three acts by George Gershwin, with libretto by Ira Gershwin. First produced in 1935 in New York City, it is a story of African American life in Charleston, South Carolina, around the early 1920s. Its most famous song is "Summertime."

portamento (It., carrying)   A slide, similar to a glissando, between two pitches, with a pause on the note just above or below the final pitch. (If there is no pause, then it is a glissando.) Often written into violin or trombone music to emulate this effect.

P

portative organ   Used from the twelfth to the sixteenth centuries as a portable organ strapped to the performer's left side. The bellows are employed by the left hand, and the keyboard is played with the right hand.

portato (It., to carry)   An articulated legato (smooth) or slurred staccato (detached) line. Identified in music as staccato notes together with a slurred line.

Porter, Cole (1891–1964)   American composer and lyricist of musical theater shows such as *Kiss Me, Kate* and *Anything Goes.* Some of his most famous songs include "I've Got You Under My Skin," "I Get a Kick Out of You," and "Night and Day."

position   1. In music theory, this refers to the closed and open positions or spacing of chords. 2. In playing a string instrument, it refers to where on the fingerboard the left hand "shifts" to, to make higher or lower notes.

positive organ   A portable organ larger than a portative organ, using one manual (keyboard). Used from the tenth to the seventeenth centuries to play the basso continue (bass accompaniment) in religious and sacred ensemble pieces.

post-grunge   A subgenre of the alternative-rock style that emerged from the grunge and hard-rock scene of the 1980s and lasted most of the 1990s. Bands such as Candlebox, Silverchair, and Bush were popular post-grunge groups. Post-grunge is still active with groups such as Creed and Nickelback.

post-punk   Starting in the late 1970s, post-punk followed the first punk-rock wave of 1974–1978 by taking the essential characteristic of punk (fast with few chords and progressions) and mixing it with a darker, more challenging rhythmic and musical structure and more interesting lyrics. Bands of this genre include Public Image Limited, Gang of Four, and Sonic Youth.

postlude   Organ piece played at the end of a church service as the congregation is exiting the sanctuary.

postmodernism   A style of music that incorporates important cultural messages with traditional, experimental, and unusual sounds and elements into a composition or "sound art" that makes a conscious statement. Jane Ira Bloom is a fine example of a post-modern jazz musician.

potpourri   A medley (songs placed back to back) of different popular songs, operatic arias, or patriotic tunes connected with chord modulations or introductions.

power chord   A rock music guitar effect where the root and the fifth are played, either in quick succession or hit and held, usually by a highly amplified and distorted guitar.

power pop   A musical style that comes from American and British 1960s rock and pop music. Traits incorporated in power pop include a strong drum beat, short but prominent guitar solos, strong melodies, and tight vocals. The main inspiration for most bands of this genre was the Beatles. The Who, the Kinks, and the Monkees were early bands of this type. The Raspberries' 1972 song "Go All the Way" uses most of the elements that identify power pop.

power trio   A rock band configuration of three members (guitar, bass, and drums) that became popular in the late 1960s. Because of amplification, pedal effects, and performance ability, they are able to fill out the sound of the band with no loss of effectiveness. Famous power trios include the Jimi Hendrix Experience, Rush, the Jam, and the Police.

P

practice   The method by which a musician repeats an aspect of music preparation in order to improve upon or master it. This repetition develops muscle memory and mental mastery (confidence and interpretation) of the music. Different aspects of practice include technical facility (fingering, breath control, and rhythmic and dynamic precision), tone production, memorization, mental practice (positive thinking and visualization), text interpretation, language preparation (proper use of vowels and consonants), endurance, ensemble preparation, and stage presence.

prelude   1. A small musical composition used to introduce a larger piece of music or liturgical ceremony (church service). 2. A short nineteenth-century piano composition meant to express a particular mood or feeling (such as a character piece). Frédéric Chopin (1818–1849), Claude Debussy (1862–1918), and Alexander Scriabin (1872–1915) are composers known for writing preludes.

preparation   In music theory, a harmonic device that uses a consonant (agreeable) tone in a proceeding chord first as an anticipation of a dissonant (transitional or unstable) tone, thus softening its impact.

prepared piano   A grand piano encountered in some contemporary art music that has objects placed inside it or has had its mechanism changed in some other way to alter its sound. The scores for music for prepared piano specify the modifications (for example, instructing the pianist to insert pieces of rubber, paper, or metal screws or washers between the strings). These either mute the strings or alter their timbre.

Presley, Elvis (1935–1977)   American rock and roll singer and actor called "The King of Rock 'n' Roll." His blending of blues and bluegrass styles made him one of the first rockabilly performers, but he sang many other styles of music, including gospel, blues, pop, country, and ballads. He began his professional career in 1954 and, by his death in 1977, had made 77 albums and 31 films. He is the number two–selling recording artist of all time (after the Beatles), with 1 billion, 300 million records sold. His influence on performers following him is so great it can't be measured.

pressure drum   Also called a "talking drum," a percussion instrument used in twentieth-century West African popular music. It has a double membrane with an hourglass body and can imitate the glides and tones of spoken language. Pitch can be manipulated by using the left hand to pull the leather thongs, thus tightening the membrane, while the right hand strikes it with a curved stick.

presto Italian term indicating "very fast." Faster than *allegro*, it is the fastest of the tempos.

Previn, Andre (b. 1929) German American conductor, composer, and pianist. Winner of 4 Academy Awards and 10 Grammy Awards. He has been the music director for the Houston, Pittsburgh, and London Symphony Orchestras as well as the Royal and Los Angeles Philharmonic Orchestras. He composed the opera *A Streetcar Named Desire*.

prima donna (It., first lady) Title first applied to the female singer in an opera company who got the lead roles. Prima donnas were often stereotyped as egotistical, irritable, and vain, which is why the term is now used to describe any woman with these characteristics.

prima vista (It., first sight) Playing the musical composition without having seen it before; sight-reading.

primitive music Also called "prehistoric music," it is any preliterate (before written records were kept) music coming before 1500 B.C.E. Refers to any traditional or indigenous folk music before this time.

Prince (b. 1958) American singer-songwriter, guitarist, producer, and actor known for his prolific songwriting (more than 1,000 tunes), his virtuosic guitar playing, and his vocal and performance skills. On many of his albums, he plays a majority of the instruments (up to 27 on his 1978 album *For You*), and his main influences were the groups Sly and the Family Stone, James Brown, Miles Davis, Jimi Hendrix, and Earth, Wind and Fire. The pioneer of the Minneapolis sound (a mixture of R&B, funk, rock, pop, and new wave), he has received a Golden Globe Award, an Academy Award, and seven Grammy Awards. *Rolling Stone* magazine ranked him number 28 in its 100 Greatest Artists of All Time list. For seven years of his career, he changed his name to an unpronounceable symbol (later called "Love Symbol #2") and was called the "The artist formerly known as Prince." This was in response to a dispute with Warner Bros. Records. Some of his most famous songs include "1999," "Little Red Corvette," "When Doves Cry," and "Let's Go Crazy." His 1984 movie *Purple Rain* was a box-office hit.

P

printing, music   The first printed music was done in Germany in 1473–1476 by Ulrich Hahn using woodcuts (block printing). This was the most common method until the advent of freehand music engraving and double printing, where the staff lines and notes were printed separately. Moveable type was gradually refined in the 1700s. The art of lithography was a breakthrough for music printing in 1796 and later was refined through photolithography through the late nineteenth century and continued until the use of notation software (1980s) commonly used today. Two of the most used score-writing or notation software include Finale by MakeMusic Inc. and Sibelius by Avid Technology, Inc.

Prix de Rome (The Roman Prize)   A scholarship established initially in 1663 for sculptors and painters, opened to music composers in 1803. It allowed the winner to study for a year in Rome and paid a five-year pension. The competition was judged by the Paris Conservatoire.

Pro Tools   Software by Digidesign and Avid Technology used for music production editing and recording, television and film post-production, and film scoring. Used on both the Microsoft Windows and Mac OS operating systems.

profession, music   People educated and jobs dedicated to the performance and education of music. *Teaching* music is one of these professions. It requires either a Bachelor of Arts (B.A.), Bachelor of Music (B.M.), Master of Arts (M.A.), Master of Music (M.M.), Doctorate of Musical Arts (D.M.A.), or Doctorate in Music (Ph.D.) degree. These professionals teach privately and in public and private schools, colleges, and universities. *Performing* is another music profession. More glamorous but with fewer job opportunities, a soloist can be found on the operatic, musical, or concert stage or in an instrumental or vocal ensemble. Many professional musicians work in both. Composers, arrangers, and accompanists should also be included. Churches, publishing houses, nightclubs, and concert halls all employ professional musicians.

program music   Music composed as art music (music originating from the classical music tradition) to cater to the listener's imagination by using images, scenes, moods, and nonmusical ideas. In the romantic period (1820–1900), Hector Berlioz's *Symphonie fantastique* and many of Franz Liszt's piano pieces were examples of program music.

progression, chord The action of musical chords moving and changing through a series of harmonic progressions toward a set goal of tonicity (root chord); for example, a cadence with the chord progression IV, V, I.

progressive country A subgenre of country-western music from Texas in the early 1970s also referred to as "redneck rock." Willie Nelson, Waylon Jennings, and Jimmy Buffett are a few performers of this style. It had a big influence on the development of alternative country music in the 1980s and '90s.

progressive folk American progressive folk emerged from the folk-music revival of the 1930s with acoustic artists such as Woody Guthrie and Pete Seeger. Later in the 1960s, it included artists such as Joan Baez and Bob Dylan. The music mixed current political themes and common people's troubles with acoustic folk music. Meanwhile, in the British 1960s underground scene, progressive folk meant a move toward a more psychedelic type of folk, pop, and rock music—examples of which were David Bowie and Marc Bolan, early in their careers.

progressive rock A type of rock music evolving in the late 1960s and peaking in popularity in the mid-1970s; an attempt to make rock more artistically credible by drawing inspiration from different influences and song structures with jazz, classical, and world music elements. Emerson, Lake and Palmer, Pink Floyd, and Yes were bands of this type.

project To propel or send out vocalized sounds with enough tonal energy to be heard from a reasonable distance. Although the speed of sound is always a constant 1,100 feet per second, the ability of the singer to use adequate breath pressure, efficient vocal-fold vibration, and well-formed acoustical placement can result in producing the "singer's formant," or the desirable "ring" needed for the human voice to be heard over an entire orchestra.

P

Prokofiev, Sergei (1891–1953)   Russian composer, conductor, and pianist known as one of the greatest composers of the twentieth century. His composition *Peter and the Wolf* and ballets *Romeo and Juliet* and *Cinderella* are three of his most famous works.

prolongement   Describes the effect or "sustain" of the piano's *sostenuto* pedal.

prompter   In an opera house, the person responsible for giving the singer onstage the opening words of his or her upcoming phrase before singing it. This individual sits in a box sticking up at the front of the stage, facing the performer so the audience can't see him or her, and mouths or quietly says the words to the performer. They are also responsible for preparing the singer for his or her role and attending all rehearsals.

pronunciation   The articulation of spoken and sung language.

psalm   Taken from the Bible, the psalms were originally songs that most likely had an instrumental accompaniment. The combined 150 psalms are undoubtedly the most important sources for music text and are used extensively in Gregorian chant and sacred music through history.

psychedelic rock   Rock music during the mid-1960s meant to enhance and replicate the psychedelic drug experience. This type of rock used Indian music such as the drone and ragas in a mix with progressive rock, hard rock, blues, and art rock. Other instruments used were the theramin, Moog Synthesizer, and tape loop effects. It was very influential on later rock genres. The Yardbirds and the Doors were early bands that played psychedelic rock.

psychobilly   A musical style that uses elements of punk rock, rockabilly, and R&B. It was popular in the 1980s in Europe and later in the United States. Most of the lyrics tend to revolve around subjects relating to horror, science fiction, sexuality, and other taboo subjects, but often in a playful manner. Psychobilly uses an upright bass instead of an electric bass. Bands of this type include the Cramps, the Meteors, Mad Sin, and the Quakes.

psychology of music   The study of the effects of music on the human mind. For example, classical music has been proven to have a positive influence on test scores, pain reduction, anxiety reduction, linguistic enhancement, and the reduction of autism and epilepsy symptoms.

puberphonic voice   A major hormonal malfunction of the voice when a boy's voice fails to change at puberty and continues to be of soprano or alto quality.

publishing, music   Music publishing started in Venice, Italy, in 1481 by Ottaviano dei Petrucci. It is the printing and selling of musical compositions by a music publisher. The songwriter or composer signs a publishing contract and hands over his or her song's copyright to the publisher, who prints, markets, and sells it commercially to music outlets and stores. The publisher then collects royalties and gives the money to the composer, minus a commission.

Puccini, Giacomo (1858–1924)   Italian opera composer. Of his 10 operas, *Madama Butterfly*, *Tosca*, and *La Bohème* are some of the most beloved in the repetoire. His romantic and *verismo* (excessive realism) style of composition emphasized melody and was strongly influenced by Richard Wagner. This is reflected in his use of motifs and the connectivity and flow of his work, although certain arias and songs also stand alone.

punctualism   Also named "pointillism" or "punctual music," a type of musical composition in Europe between 1949–1955 attributed mostly to Anton Webern. It is different pieces of music composed separately and put together in a nonlinear manner. An example of this style is represented in Olivier Messiaen's piece *Mode de valeurs et d'intensités* written in 1949.

punk rock   A rock-music style developed in the early to mid-1970s that was anti-establishment, fast, and hard-edged. Many punk bands self-produced their own records and sold them through informal channels. Several punk bands include the Ramones, the Sex Pistols, the Damned, and the Clash.

P

Purcell, Henry (1659–1695)   The most famous and influential English composer of the baroque period.

purfling   A decorative wooden strip inlaid in the bottom and top plates of well-made string instruments to help stop cracking if the instrument is dropped or bumped.

Pythagorean scale   Named after Pythagoras (570–495 B.C.E.), it is one of the oldest musical systems.

quadruple meter   Basic pattern of four beats to a measure; also known as common time.

quadruple stop   The technique of playing four notes at once on a string instrument.

quadruplet   Four notes played in the amount of time that three notes are played.

quality   The timbre or color of a tone. The quality is a direct byproduct of a well-made musical instrument or well-trained voice and the performance ability of the performer.

quartal harmony   A harmony based on fourths instead of the traditional thirds. Quartal harmony is widely used in twentieth-century music.

quarter note   A musical note that equals one beat or one fourth the duration of a whole note (four beats). The musical symbol has a filled oval head and a stem with no flag.

quarter rest   A musical symbol that indicates a one-beat pause.

quarter tone   Distance in a musical scale that equals one half of a semitone (half a step). Also called a microtone, it uses a 24-tone equal temperament, where there are 24 quarter tones in an octave. Although quarter-step scales have been used in modern music by composers such as Pierre Boulez (b. 1925), Charles Ives (1874–1954), and Béla Bartók (1881–1945), it is not often used in Western music.

quartet   Music composed for four instrumental or vocal performers. Also, the four players performing the music.

Queen   English rock band formed in 1970 whose originality, vocals, and showmanship—due primarily to lead singer Freddie Mercury—made them one of the most popular bands of all time, with more than 300 million albums sold.

Queen of Spades, The (Pique Dame)   Russian opera composed in three acts by Pyotr Tchaikovsky, with libretto by his brother Modest Tchaikovsky. First produced in St. Petersburg in 1890, it is based on a short story by Alexander Pushkin.

quick-step   A ballroom dance in a quick 2/4 or 4/4 time.

quintet   Music composed for five instrumental or vocal performers. Also, the five players performing the music.

quintuple meter   Five beats per measure with a time signature of 5/4.

quintuplet   A group of five notes played in a space of time equal to three or four notes.

quiver   An excessively erratic, tremulous movement of the vocal tone that may come as a result of age, nervousness, or incorrect vocal technique.

quotation music   Works common since the mid-1960s that use quotations from earlier compositions, such as *Concerto Grosso* (1985) by Ellen Zwilich.

Q

radical bass   The same as "fundamental bass"; a progression of root or base notes of a chord.

radio   The transmission, through the air and vacuum of space, of electromagnetic radiation or modulated electromagnetic waves as audio signals. Nikola Tesla was the first to patent radio technology in the 1880s. Since radio's regular public service in the United States beginning in 1920, radio has been a major media source of "live" and recorded performances of music.

raga (Sanskrit, mood or color)   A melody of five or more musical notes used in classical Indian music.

ragtime   A genre that emerged from the marches and jigs of late nineteenth century and the red-light districts of New Orleans and St. Louis. Ragtime was named after its characteristic "ragged" or syncopated rhythm and was popular between 1897–1917, after which jazz became favored. Scott Joplin, dubbed the "King of Ragtime," wrote the first song to sell more than one million pieces of sheet music: "The Maple Leaf Rag" in 1899.

Rake's Progress, The   English opera composed in three acts by Igor Stavinsky, with libretto by Wystan Hugh Auden and Chester Callman. Produced in Venice in 1951, its setting is eighteenth-century England.

rallantando (*rall.*)   A musical direction to gradually slow down a passage in a composition.

rall.

Rameau, Jean-Philippe (1683–1764)   Most important French composer and theorist of the baroque period (1600–1750). He is famous for his opera compositions and his *Treatise on Harmony* (1722).

range   The sounding range is the distance between the highest and lowest pitch a musician can play on his or her instrument or sing (vocal range). The written range is sometimes different than what is actually sounded; for example, the piccolo flute is written an octave lower than what is actually heard.

rank   The pipes on an organ that produce a certain timbre or "color" of sound. By selecting certain ranks, the organist can control the combination of sounds heard.

rap   The performing of rhythmically rhyming lyrics, more spoken than sung, by an MC or musician (called a rapper) against a groove or drumbeat. Rap is a strong element of hip-hop music.

Rape of Lucretia, The   English opera composed in two acts by Benjamin Britton, with libretto by Ronald Duncan and taken from a play by André Obey. First produced in Glyndebourne, England, in 1946, the setting takes place in 510 B.C.E. Rome.

rarefaction wave   The lowest pressure area of a sound wave.

Rastafarian music   Jamaican music of the Rastafarian religion. This includes Nyabinghi music, a drumming and chanting music used at worship ceremonies, and *burru* drumming, both of which kept their African musical traditions nearly pure. Count Ossie and Prince Buster were two of the most important figures in Rastafarian music from the 1950s to the 1970s.

rattle   A member of the percussion family; a generic term for an idiophone that is shaken. It may be made from any hard material, but it is traditionally a dried gourd filled with dry seeds or pebbles. They are one of the oldest and widely used instruments. *See also* maraca.

Ravel, Maurice (1875–1937)   French impressionistic composer known for his use of instrumental textures, orchestral effects, and strong melody lines. He wrote song cycles, ballet music, opera, chamber, and piano works. His most famous orchestral work is *Boléro* (1928).

rebec   A string instrument popular in the Middle Ages (450–1450) that was shaped like a narrow violin and had three strings.

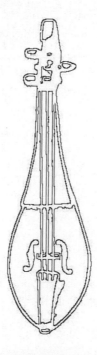

rebop   An early name for the jazz form bebop. This term is mostly used in the United Kingdom.

recapitulation   The place at the end of the development section of the sonata form where the exposition (part of a movement that introduces the main theme) is repeated in an altered form.

recital   A public performance by one or two players.

recitative (*recit.*; It., to recite)   A musical element used in opera, oratorio, and cantatas to set up and carry on the action happening between arias (solos). This vocal style is composed to imitate the natural inflections of speech and is accompanied either by a harp-sichord or piano alone (*recitativo secco*) or with orchestra (*recitativo accompagnato*).

recorded music   Any digital or analog record of organized vocal or instrumental sound waves. Analog recordings use vinyl records (played on a phonograph or jukebox) and magnetic tape (cassette, reel-to-reel, 8-track, or video). This format was taken over by digital recordings in the late 1980s. These playback formats are the compact disc (CD), digital tape (DAT), minidisc, flash memory, MIDI, hard-drive recording, DVD-A, HD DVD, and Blu-Ray disc.

recorder   A member of the woodwind family of musical instruments. An end-blown flute or whistle with a mouthpiece and finger holes bored in the side. Mainly used from the Middle Ages to around 1750, interest in the recorder was revived in the early twentieth century. The main sizes are the soprano, alto, tenor, and bass recorders. They are made from wood and sometimes plastic.

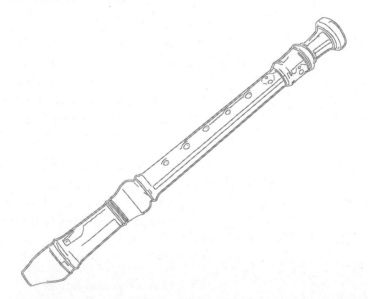

recording industry   The RIAA (Recording Industry Association of America); a group of record labels and recording industry distributors since 1952 who distribute about 85 percent of all legitimate

U.S. sound recordings. Recorded sound has been around since Thomas Edison invented the phonograph in 1878. However, current trends show that major artists are leaving recording agencies and producing, marketing, and selling their own music. The future of the recording industry is tentative.

reed   A thin, elongated piece of reed cane or steel used to make the sound on many woodwind instruments, including the saxophone, clarinet, oboe, and bassoon (both double-reed instruments), bagpipes, harmonica, organ, and accordion.

refrain   Also called the "chorus" of a song, it contrasts dramatically with the verse; it recurs two or three times with its own melody and often adds instruments, volume, and energy. It's a common structure in popular music, hymns, and ballads.

regal   A portable organ popular in the renaissance period (1450–1600) that used two bellows and brass reeds. The regal was played on a table with one person working the keyboard and another person pushing the bellows.

reggae   Musical style developed in Jamaica in the late 1960s and based on the rhythm's accent being placed on the offbeat or the skank (second and fourth beat of the measure) and a complicated bass line. Other types of music influencing reggae in Jamaica were ska and rocksteady. The most famous reggae bands include Bob Marley and the Wailers, Toots and the Maytals, and Peter Tosh.

reggae fusion   A mixture of reggae music with styles such as hip-hop, techno, jazz, R&B, house, rock, and pop. Some reggae fusion bands are Ms. Triniti, Brick & Lace, and Ava Leigh. Fusion hits include "Calabria" by Enur and Natasja and "Say Hey (I Love You)" by Michael Franti & Spearhead.

regional rock   Rock music that describes a specific part of the country, such as the surf music of the Beach Boys and Jan and Dean singing about the surf, cars, babes, and the endless summer.

register   1. Term used to describe an entire set of pipes controlled by one "stop." 2. The different parts of a vocalist's range, such as head voice and chest voice.

R

registration   The skill and ability of the organist to mix organ registers together. Although modern composers indicate registration in their compositions, early composers did not.

rehearsal letter   Used in a music score to help performers have a convenient spot in which to start or rehearse a certain section. It can also be called rehearsal figures; rehearsal marks; or, when used with numbers, rehearsal numbers.

Reich, Steve (b. 1936)   American minimalist composer who has significantly influenced the direction of American music in the twentieth century. His innovations, such as using tape loops, repetitive figures, and slow harmonic canons and rhythms, have earned him the Grammy Award for "Different Trains" and the Pulitzer Prize for Music in 2009 for his composition "Double Sextet."

relative key   The relative minor of a certain major key has the same key signature but a different root note or tonic. For example, C Major has the same key signature as A minor (no flats or sharps).

Renaissance, The   The time period between 1450 and 1600. This "rebirth" of human creativity was a time of exploration and curiosity. Individualism was encouraged, and the intellectual movement of humanism was most focused on human accomplishments. Every educated person was expected to have some musical training, and although the church was still the major contributor to music, much of the activity took place in the royal courts, where the royalty competed for the best composers. This was a time when instrumental music was gaining prominence, and characteristics such as "text painting" and polyphony (composition using two or more different melodies at the same time) were used.

repeat sign A musical notation on the staff indicating where and when a section should be repeated.

repertoire A list of songs or complete shows that an ensemble, instrumentalist, or singer has prepared and rehearsed to perform.

repetition A practice technique used to reinforce muscle memory and technical ability.

reprise Often used in musical theater, the reprise is a repeat of an earlier piece or motif in the show, usually with different words reflecting a development in the story. A reprise is also used as a repetition or recapitulation of the exposition in the sonata form, following the development section.

requiem A mass written to commemorate someone's death. Famous requiem masses include those composed by Mozart and Verdi.

resolution When a chord or note changes or resolves from an unstable sound (dissonance) to a stable or final one (consonance).

resonance When a vibration is amplified, reinforced, and held out after another vibration of the same frequency is added to it. When a voice sings in "acoustically live" places such as shower stalls or dome-shaped buildings, it causes the acoustical reaction called resonance.

resonating system The cavities of the mouth and throat that produce an amplified singing tone after the vocal folds set sound vibrations into motion.

resonator A system, material, or device that exhibits a resonant behavior by oscillating at certain frequencies, such as the empty body of a guitar or violin or the cavity and open throat of the voice. Different resonators include electromagnetic, cavity, mechanical, and—the resonator every musical instrument has— acoustic.

R

response   1. The unison response of Gregorian chant by the congregation to the Catholic church's cantor singing a psalm or other part of a religious service. The antiphonal or "call and response" style of the Antiphon. 2. A form of cultural response brought over from Africa to the New World. Used in many aspects of culture (sporting events and public gatherings) and music, especially gospel, blues, and jazz.

responsorial singing   A sung response by the choir or congregation in unison to a psalm (a book from the Old Testament) sung by the cantor in a Catholic mass or vespers religious service.

rest   An interval of silence or absence, or pause of a certain voice for a set amount of time. Indicated by a rest sign equal to the length of the note value it is temporarily replacing.

restatement   A repetition of the exposition (part of a movement that introduces the main theme) in a sonata form.

resultant bass   An acoustic effect used to emulate a 32-foot stop on an organ by playing a 16-foot stop in combination with a stop pitched a fifth above. Also called a "harmonic" or "acoustic" bass.

retardation   The prolonging or slowing down of chords leading up to a consonant (harmonically agreeable) chord in a piece of music. It differs with a suspension in that it resolves upward instead of downward.

retrograde   A melody that is read backward, from the last note to the first. Although it has been used sparingly throughout music history, it found importance in the serial music of the early twentieth century.

return   When the music repeats a verse or section of a composition; indicated by a repeat sign. *See* repeat sign.

reverberate   A succession of overlapping echoes or violent vibrations.

revue   1. A popular theater production that combines dance, music, and dramatic acts. A little more sophisticated than the vaudeville acts of the day, revues were more expensive and were popular between the years 1916–1932. 2. A critique or first-person account of a music or theater performance by a media reporter.

rhapsody   Music compositions featuring fantasies with heroic, epic, or nationalistic themes, such as George Gershwin's *Rhapsody in Blue* and Johannes Brahms' *Rhapsodies for Piano*.

Rheingold, Das (G., *The Rhine Gold*)   German opera composed by Richard Wagner to his own libretto as the first of four operas in *Der Ring des Nibelungen*, his "Ring Cycle." It was first produced in Munich, Germany, in 1869 and was originally written as an introduction to the other three operas in the "Ring." The other three besides *Das Rheingold* are *Die Walküre*, *Siegfried*, and *Götterdämmerung*.

rhythm   1. A recurring movement; the feel of a musical phrase progressing through a given meter. The two different categories of rhythm are isometric and multimetric. Composers indicate rhythm through the constant change of note values on a staff and an underlying pulse written into the percussion and rhythm section parts. Good rhythm insinuates an ability to be spontaneous to the logical flow of the music.

rhythm and blues   Also called "R&B," a wide-ranging, popular, jazz-based music genre developed by African Americans in the late 1940s. The term was first applied more to blues records and later contributed to the development of rock and roll. The term currently refers to popular music influenced by soul and funk.

rhythm section   Usually refers to the drummer, bass player, electric guitarist, and piano player of a band or musical ensemble who lay down the rhythmic pulse and chord structure of the band.

R

rhythmic modes   Used in the duration patterns of the written notes. Developed between 1170 and 1250 by the Notre Dame School composers (especially Pérotin) using the metric feet or pulses of classical poetry. There are six rhythmic modes, each consisting of a pattern of short and long values.

ribs   Trade name for the thin wood that forms the sides of the violin.

Rich, Buddy (1917–1987)   American jazz drummer and bandleader famous for his speed of playing, power, and amazing technique.

riddim   The instrumental version or background of a Caribbean or Jamaican song made up of a drum pattern and clear bass line. It is also used to describe the entire rhythm section or the feel or beat of a piece.

riff   A repeated melodic figure, chord progression, or pattern played by the rhythm section or soloist. Most often played in jazz, rock, and Latin music, they are catchy little rhythmic figures that are an essential part of the song.

Rigoletto   Italian opera composed in three acts by Giuseppe Verdi, with libretto by Francesco Piave from a Victor Hugo play. Produced in Venice in 1851, it is now one of opera lovers' favorite compositions and a performance vehicle for great tenors such as Enrico Caruso (1873–1921) and Luciano Pavarotti (1935–2007).

Riley, Terry (b. 1935)   American minimalist composer. Along with John Adams and Phillip Glass, he is recognized as a major innovator of this type of composition using two or more different melodies at the same time. His "all-night concerts" were famous in the 1960s. Two of his compositions include "In C" (1964) and "The Cusp of Magic" (2004).

Rimsky-Korsakov, Nikolai (1844–1908)   Russian composer known for his orchestration skills and nationalistic compositions that utilized Russian folk music themes. Two of his most famous compositions showing his orchestration skills include the symphonic suite *Scheherazade* and his *Capriccio espagnol*.

ring   In the voice, a vibrant tone quality produced when strong upper harmonics are present. It's associated with resonance produced in the larynx (voice box).

Ring des Nibelungen, Der (G., *The Ring of the Nibelung*)   Cycle of four operas composed by Richard Wagner from 1848–1874. Wagner was also the librettist for his works, which dealt with Norse sagas (Viking history and stories). The four operas of the "ring" are, in order, *Das Rheingold, Die Walküre, Siegfried,* and *Götterdämmerung.*

ripping   Process of transferring digital audio or video files to a hard drive from a removable media source or media stream.

ritardando (*ritard.* or *rit.*; It., to retard)   Musical instruction indicating the performer to play more slowly.

rit.

ritenuto (*riten.*)   Italian musical term meaning "to immediately slow down" or "hold back."

ritornello (It., to return)   A baroque music word for an orchestra passage that keeps repeating in the first or last movement of an aria or solo concerto. Also, a theme or refrain that opens the tutti section (called ritornello form).

Roach, Max (1924–2007)   American jazz drummer and composer who was a pioneer in the development of bebop jazz (with Charlie Parker, Dizzie Gillespie, and Miles Davis). He was one of the most important jazz drummers of the twentieth century, playing on more than 136 albums.

rock   A popular music genre that revolves around a rhythm section of drums, electric bass, and rhythm guitar, as well as lead guitar and vocals. Usually set in 4/4 or 2/4 time, it also has a guitar backbeat (chord on the second and fourth beat of the measure). Rock influences were folk music, jazz, classical, country, and R&B. Piano, synthesizer (in the 1970s), harmonica, and saxophone are sometimes used as soloing instruments.

R

rock musical A musical theater production that uses rock music. Examples of rock musicals include *Hair*, *Rent*, and *Grease*.

rock opera Different from a regular rock album in that it tells a cohesive story over different sections and songs of the album. The first short rock opera was written by Pete Townshend on part of the Who's second album *A Quick One* in 1966. Later, the group also came out with *Tommy*, a full-scale rock opera, in 1969.

rockabilly The earliest style of rock and roll that started in the early 1950s. "Rock" is taken from rock and roll and "billy" is from hillbilly, referring to what people called country music in the 1940s and 1950s. Boogie-woogie, R&B, and western swing were also strong influences, and most of the original bands were from the South. Basic instrumentation used the double bass, guitar, piano, and drums. Three of the most famous rockabilly artists were Elvis Presley, Johnny Cash, and Buddy Holly. Gene Vincent's "Be-Bop-a-Lula" and Carl Perkins' "Blue Suede Shoes" were two rockabilly hits.

rococo Style of performance from the baroque period (1600–1750) that uses embellishments, flourishes, and ornate notation to express a certain feeling or affection (mood).

Rodgers, Richard (1902–1979) American composer known for being part of songwriting partnerships with Oscar Hammerstein and Lorenz Hart. He wrote 43 musicals and more than 900 songs. He was one of two people to be awarded a Grammy Award, Oscar, Emmy Award, Tony Award, and Pulitzer Prize in music (the other was Marvin Hamlisch).

Rodgers and Hammerstein American songwriting partners who created popular Broadway musicals throughout the 1940s and 1950s. Richard Rodgers (1902–1979) wrote the music, and Oscar Hammerstein II (1895–1960) wrote the lyrics. Their shows included *Carousel*, *Oklahoma*, *South Pacific*, *The Sound of Music*, and *The King and I*. Their musicals and screen adaptations won the duo 15 Oscars, 34 Tony Awards, 2 Grammy Awards, and the Pulitzer Prize for Music.

rolled chord   When a pianist plays a fast *arpeggio* or chord from bottom to top, such as the strumming of a guitar. It's often used when the chord being played is too wide for the pianist to hit all the notes at once.

Rolling Stones, The   English rock group formed in 1962 and still playing to sellout crowds. Lead vocalist Mick Jagger and guitar player Keith Richards write most of their songs, and they have sold more than 200 million albums and released more than 90 singles.

Rollins, Sonny (b. 1930)   American jazz tenor saxophonist; one of the most influential jazz artists of the post-bebop era. Rollins worked with all the greats of jazz, such as Thelonius Monk (piano) and John Coltrane (tenor sax).

Roman chant   Also known as "Old Roman," Roman chant was plainchant sung in the Roman rite of the Catholic church until being replaced by Gregorian chant between the eleventh and thirteenth centuries.

romantic period   Period of music from 1820 to 1900. The "romanticism" of the period stressed imagination, emotion, and individualism and freedom of expression. Among the most important of the romantic composers were Hector Berlioz, Felix Mendelssohn, Franz Schubert, Robert Schumann, Frédéric Chopin, Johannes Brahms, Giuseppe Verdi, Richard Wagner, and Giacomo Puccini.

Romeo and Juliet   French opera composed in five acts by Charles Gounod with Michel Carré and Jules Barbier. Produced in Paris in 1867, it is taken from William Shakespeare's tragedy of two young lovers from two rival families.

rondeau   *See* rondo.

rondo   A musical form often found in the last movement of a string quartet, sonata, or classical symphony. A rondo features a main (A) theme that alternates and repeats itself among other themes (for example, A-B-A-C-A-B-A).

R

Ronstadt, Linda (b. 1946)   American singer of popular music and songwriter with a 40-year career and 30 solo albums. During her career, she has been called the "Queen of Rock," "First Lady of Rock," and "the highest paid woman in rock." She has earned 11 Grammy Awards, 17 Grammy nominations, 1 Emmy Award, and a Tony Award and Golden Globe nomination. Some of her most famous songs are "You're No Good," "Blue Bayou," and "Don't Know Much."

root   The tonic or fundamental note of the chord; the first note of a scale.

Rosenkavalier, Der (G., *The Knight of the Rose*)   German opera composed in three acts by Richard Strauss, with libretto by H. von Hofmannshal. Produced in Dresden, Germany, in 1911, the story takes place in Vienna in the mid-eighteenth century.

rosin   A sticky substance made from pine sap, used on a violin bow's hairs to help the hairs grab the strings as it passes over them and make the strings vibrate.

Ross, Diana (b. 1944)   American singer and actress. Most famous for being the lead singer for the 1960s women's singing trio the Supremes. Her solo career started in 1970, and by 1976 *Billboard* magazine gave her the title of "Female Entertainer of the Century." She has sold more than 100 million records, received 12 Grammy Award nominations, 1 Academy Award nomination, and has won 1 Tony. She has made 61 albums and had 19 number-one singles, including "Upside Down," "Endless Love," and "Chain Reaction."

roulade (F., rolling)   An ornamented or embellished melody sung on one syllable.

round   Two singers singing the same melody and words at different times so that they harmonically and melodically fit together. "Row, Row, Row Your Boat" can be sung as a round. Also called a "circle canon."

round tone   A musical quality that gives the impression of roundness and warmth.

row   Same as "tone row." In serial music, it is a 12-tone system using all 12 tones of the chromatic scale where the composer cannot repeat a note until all 11 of the other notes have appeared. Arnold Schoenberg devised serial music using this system as a composition technique around 1910.

rubato (It., robbed)   A musical term indicating a flexible give and take of a tempo's accelerandos and ritardandos. Two types exist. The first finds a soloist performing the rubato over a strict accompaniment and ending up in the same place as if he or she had stayed in strict time (often used in jazz). The second kind is a full orchestral rubato with give and take throughout the whole ensemble.

rumba   A style of music and dance originating in Cuba (from Spanish and African elements) in the late nineteenth century. Rumba has a fast tempo and starts with the *canto* (extended vocal solo that is sometimes improvised and a call and response section), then the *montuno* (featuring the dancers and instrumental solos). It is accompanied by percussion instruments such as the conga and claves and comes in three types: Yambú (slowest and oldest), Guaguancó (the most popular), and Columbia.

run   A scalelike musical instrumental passage that ascends (usually chromatically).

R

sackbut   A trombone from the renaissance and baroque periods. The term *sackbut* is usually used to differentiate between historic and modern trombones.

sacred music   Also known as religious music; music performed or composed for religious use or that has been influenced by religion in some way.

Salome   German opera composed in one act by Richard Strauss with his own libretto. Based on the French play *Salomé* by Oscar Wilde, it depicts the death of John the Baptist from the perspective of King Herod and his stepdaughter. *Salome* premiered in 1905.

salsa   Music created by Spanish-speaking people from the Caribbean. Salsa is also a dance with European and African roots.

saltbox   A wooden box with a flat, angled lid used to store salt. It was often used extemporaneously as rhythmic accompaniment by flapping the lid and striking the side with a rolling pin.

samba   A Brazilian dance with African and European roots. *Samba* is derived from the Portuguese verb *sombar*, which means "to dance to rhythm." The samba is the national dance of Brazil.

sampling   The act of taking a portion (or sample) of a recording and reusing it. Another form of sampling is using a digital recording device to copy an individual person's sound (instrumental or vocal) for reuse in recording music.

Samson et Dalila (F., *Samson and Delilah*)   French opera composed in three acts and four tableaux by French composer Camille Saint-Saens, with libretto by Ferdinand Lemaire. This opera depicts the relationship between Samson and Delilah as described in Chapter 16 of the Old Testament's Book of Judges.

sanctus (L., holy)   An important hymn of Christian liturgy, forming part of the Ordinary of the Mass. It is sung or prayed as a preface to the Eucharistic prayer.

Santana, Carlos (b. 1947)   A Mexican-born Grammy Award–winning rock musician and guitarist. His band (Santana) features blues-based guitar backed by Latin percussion grooves. Santana rose to prominence in the late 1960s.

sarabande   A slow dance in triple meter that originated in the Spanish colonies of Central America before traveling across the Atlantic to mainland Spain, where in 1583 it was banned for its provocative nature. Later, it became a standard movement of the Baroque Dance Suite (a type of instrumental baroque dance or dinner music with an A-A-B-B structure).

Satie, Erik (1866–1925)   A French composer and pianist who, with his first composition in 1884, signed his name Erik Satie. He was a colorful figure in the early twentieth-century Parisian avant-garde movement and was a precursor to other genres, such as minimalism, repetitive music, and theatre of the absurd.

Saul   English oratorio written by George Frideric Handel in 1738. The story closely follows the Biblical narrative of the relationship between David and Saul and was first produced in 1739.

saxophone   Also referred to as a sax, a saxophone is a keyed, single-reed, conical bore wind instrument that, although made of brass, is considered a member of the woodwind family. It was invented by and named after Belgian instrument maker Adolph Sax in 1841. Used extensively in jazz and commercial music, the saxophone is produced in several sizes from soprano (very small) to bass (very large).

scale   A series of ascending or descending pitches (usually stepwise) that forms the basis for all or part of a musical composition.

scale, blues   Several scales of varying numbers of pitches (five to nine) used extensively in improvised styles of music, such as jazz and blues.

scale degree   The distance between note intervals in a scale when used in harmonic analysis.

scaling   The ratio of diameter to length of an organ pipe.

scat singing   A means of vocal improvisation approximating sounds produced by wind instruments. Pioneered by jazz trumpeter Louis Armstrong and brought to fruition by Ella Fitzgerald, scat singing has found its way into other genres of commercial music.

Schenkerian Analysis   A system of analysis of tonal music based on the theories of Heinrich Schenker (1865–1935). The primary means of analyzing a musical passage employed by theorists is showing hierarchical relationships among the pitches of a passage through arrhythmic, symbolic reductions of the music.

scherzo (It., joke)   A lighthearted piece or movement of a larger work (for example, a symphony or string quartet). It developed from the minuet movement of a symphony and often serves to "cleanse the palate" before the final movement of a work.

Schmidt, Harvey (b. 1929)   A writer of American musical theater best known for composing the music for the longest-running musical in history, *The Fantasticks* (off-Broadway from 1960–2002). He and his lifelong creative partner, Tom Jones, met at the University of Texas–Austin.

Schoenberg, Arnold (1874–1951)   A self-taught composer of Austrian descent who was most noted for developing 12-tone composition, which—due to its lack of pitch hierarchy—has come to be known as atonal music. Schoenberg and his disciples established the Viennese School of composition, a group of composers who were proponents of atonal music.

Schönberg, Claude-Michel (b. 1944)   This singer, actor, songwriter, record producer, and musical theatre composer was born in Vannes, France, and is best known for his collaborations with lyricist

Alain Boublil. *Les Misérables* and *Miss Saigon* are among the most popular of their musicals.

Schubert, Franz (1797–1828)   Widely considered one of the greatest composers in the Western tradition. In his short lifetime, he composed 600 lieder (German songs), 9 symphonies, liturgical music, operas, and incidental music, as well as a large body of chamber and solo piano music. His music gained popularity only after his death, when it was championed by the likes of Felix Mendelssohn, Franz Liszt, and Robert Schumann.

Schumann, Clara (1819–1896)   A German musician and composer considered one of the most distinguished pianists of the romantic period. She and her husband Robert Schumann were very influential in the development of Johannes Brahms as a composer. Clara gave several of Brahms' piano pieces their first public performances.

Schumann, Robert (1810–1856)   A German pianist, influential music critic, and widely considered one of the most important romantic composers. A self-inflicted hand injury prevented him from pursuing his dream of becoming the foremost European concert pianist, so he turned to composition. Schumann wrote piano compositions, works for piano and orchestra, several lieder, and an opera, as well as chamber, orchestral, and choral pieces.

schwa vowel   An unstressed and neutral vowel sound in some languages, represented by "ə" in pronunciation guides and sounding like "uh."

Schwartz, Stephen (b. 1948)   An American theatre lyricist and composer. He has written hit Broadway musicals such as *Godspell* (1971), *Pippin* (1972), and *Wicked* (2003). He has contributed lyrics for several movies, including *Pocahontas* (1995), *The Hunchback of Norte Dame* (1996), and *Enchanted* (2007). Besides being nominated for six Tony Awards, Schwartz has won the Drama Desk Award for Outstanding Lyrics, three Grammy Awards, and three Oscars.

S

scoop   A vocal or instrumental inflection whereby the performer approaches a pitch from the underside and "scoops" up to the intended note, giving the musical passage a "bluesy" feeling.

score   The printed notation of a composition containing the individual instruments, organized one beneath another. This format allows the conductor to see the music to be played by each member of the orchestra.

score reading   When leading a group of musicians, conductors must be proficient at reading notes being played by all of the instruments in order to detect mistakes and to make certain that a representative performance of the score is achieved.

scratching   A technique employed by DJs whereby a portion of a track on an LP record is played forward and backward on a turntable by manually forcing the turntable. This technique is prevalent in rap and hip-hop.

sea shanty   *See* shanty.

Seasons, The Four (It., *La quattro staglioni*)   A set of four concerti for violin and string orchestra by Italian composer Antonio Vivaldi. Composed in 1723, *The Four Seasons* is one of the most famous works of the baroque era.

secco recitative (It., dry recitative)   A recitative that is accompanied only by bass continuo (such as harpsichord).

Second Viennese School   A group of composers who studied with Arnold Schoenberg between 1903–1925, using techniques such as expanded tonality, atonality, and serial 12-tone technique. Besides Schoenberg, Anton Weber and Alban Berg were the most visible members of this school.

secular music   Any nonreligious music.

Sedaka, Neil (b. 1939)   An American pop singer, songwriter, and pianist whose career has spanned more than 50 years. Three of his hit singles are "Love Will Keep Us Together," "Laughter in the Rain," and "Bad Blood."

segment   A short passage or section of a composition.

segno, dal (*D.S.*; It., sign)   A point in printed music to which musicians must return.

segue   To move seamlessly from one piece of music or movement to another.

semi   Half of something. In music, a quaver is an eighth note, and a semi-quaver is a sixteenth note.

semiquaver   *See* sixteenth note.

Semiramide   An Italian opera in two acts composed by Gioachino Rossini. The libretto by Gaetano Rossi is based on Voltaire's tragedy *Semaramis*. First performed in 1823, this was Rossini's last Italian opera and signaled a return to vocal traditions of his youth.

semitone   One half step in music (any two adjacent keys on the piano).

sempre   "In the same manner throughout"; for example, sempre staccato means "always separated." This is a means of musical shorthand. Rather than marking every note with a dot, a composer can write sempre under the staff and the performer(s) will know to always perform the notes in a separated manner.

sensations of vibration   The motion of any object creates vibration of air, which in turn stimulates the ear drum. This sensation of air vibration is commonly referred to as "sound."

senza   Italian term meaning "without." For example, senza vibrato means "without vibrato."

septuplet   A group of seven notes to be performed within a prescribed span of time.

sequence   The immediate repetition of a melodic or harmonic progression at a different pitch, usually step-wise.

S

serenade or **serenata**   A composition written or performed in somebody's honor. There are two other common usages of the term *serenade:* during the baroque period, some cantatas were entitled serenades; from the nineteenth century onward, a serenade is a multi-movement work for a large instrumental ensemble, related to the divertimento.

serialism   A means of composing music in which musical ideas are generated through a predetermined succession of pitches (tone row). This is the basis of 12-tone composition.

series   Also called a tone row, a series is a predetermined succession of pitches employed in serial music.

serpent   A bass wind instrument that's a descendent of the cornetto and a predecessor to the tuba. Though constructed of wood with finger holes and keys, the serpent employs a cup-shaped mouthpiece and the sound is produced by vibration of the lips. The body of the instrument is curved, thus its name.

Sessions, Roger (1896–1985)   American composer of serial music. A child prodigy, Sessions graduated from Harvard University at age 18. After further study at Yale University, he taught at Smith College. Upon his return to the United States in 1933, Sessions taught at Princeton and the University of California at Berkeley, returning to Princeton in 1954, where he remained until retiring in 1965, writing mostly in the serial style. He continued to teach on a part-time basis at the Juilliard School of Music. Myriad modern composers were influenced by Roger Sessions.

set   *See* series.

seventh chord   A chord consisting of a triad with an additional note on top (a seventh above the root or bottom note).

sextet   An ensemble of six instruments or voices.

sextuple meter   A meter in which measures are divided into six equal pulses. Sextuple meter is often thought of as compound duple, wherein the six pulses are grouped into two groups of three beats.

sforzando (*sfz*)   An indication to play a note with sudden emphasis.

sfz

shake—An older name for "trill." Also in jazz and popular music, a shake is a wide trill from one note to its minor third. When performed on brass instruments, it is the trill between the original tone and its overblown harmonic.

Shankar, Ravi (b. 1920)   A legendary Indian classical music artist and composer who was instrumental in bringing the music of India to the Western Hemisphere. Shankar is a virtuosic sitar performer who has traveled extensively throughout the world. He has forged close friendships with many popular music stars, including George Harrison of the Beatles. Shankar is also a jazz pianist.

shanty   From the French *chanter*, which means "to sing." These songs are usually referred to as "sea shanties" because they were sung onboard ships at sea. The rhythm allowed the oarsmen to stay in sync with one another. Some shanties are reputed to have dated from as early as the sixteenth century, and composers still write shanties for vocal and instrumental ensembles.

shape note   A notation used to facilitate music reading for nonmusicians in which the shape of the note refers to a specific pitch. Most often used in congregational singing, shape notes have been in use in the southern United States for more than two centuries.

fa   sol   la   fa   sol   la   mi   fa

sharp   When placed on the staff before a note, a sharp (♯) indicates that the pitch is to be raised a half step (a semitone).

Shaw, Artie (1910–2004)   American clarinetist, bandleader, composer, and writer. He was most noted for his use of unusual instrumentation and for having been the first white bandleader to have hired a full-time African American female vocalist: Billie Holiday. "Begin the Beguine," "Stardust," and "Moonglow" are three of his hit tunes.

Shaw, Robert (1916–1999)   American choral conductor most noted for his work with the Robert Shaw Chorale, the Cleveland Symphony Orchestra and Chorus, and the Atlanta Symphony Orchestra and Chorus. He was the recipient of 14 Grammy Awards.

shawm   A double-reed instrument used extensively in the medieval and renaissance periods. The body of the shawm is turned from a single piece of wood with finger holes and some keys; its bore is conical, and it comes in sizes ranging from sopranino (smallest) to the great bass (largest). Due to the loud, almost piercing sound, this instrument is played mainly outdoors.

Sheherazade A song cycle for voice and orchestra by Maurice Revel, to poems by Klingsor, inspired by *Arabian Nights*. In 1888, Nikolai Rimsky-Korsakov wrote a suite for orchestra inspired by *Arabian Nights* also titled *Sheherazade*.

shift To move one's hand up or down on the neck of a string instrument.

shimmy A dance move created in the 1950s whereby a person shakes his or her shoulders rapidly, in time with the music, while bending the knees.

shofar A horn (usually a ram's horn) that has been hollowed out and is used for Jewish ceremonies in synagogue on Rosh Hashanah and Yom Kippur.

Shorter, Wayne (b. 1933) Widely considered jazz's greatest living composer, Wayne Shorter has become a household name among jazz aficionados. He has won several Grammy Awards as both a leader and a sideman.

Sibelius Digital music-writing software named for Finnish composer Jan Sibelius.

Sibelius, Jean (1865–1957) A Finnish composer of the late romantic period whose music played an important role in the Finnish national identity. Chief among his compositions are seven

S

symphonies and several symphonic poems—one of which, *Finlandia*, although not the national anthem, is one of Finland's most important nationalistic hymns.

side drum   *See* snare drum.

Siegfried   The third of four operas by Richard Wagner that comprise *Das Ring des Nibelungen,* or The Ring Cycle. It premiered in 1876 as part of the first complete performance.

sight-reading   The ability to perform music the first time it is read. This is a skill that all musicians (instrumentalists and vocalists) strive to attain.

Signal Music   Established in 1992 to provide advertising agencies in Israel with jingles and music. Recently, Signal Music has expanded its offerings to productions for the Internet, and its services are available in the United States as well as in other countries.

signature   An indication of key and meter is placed by the composer at the beginning of a piece and wherever else needed. The signature is in two parts: key signature, which indicates the scale upon which a piece is based, and time signature, which indicates the pulse of the music (rate of strong and weak beats).

silence   In music, silence is indicated by symbols called rests. The shape of the symbol indicates the number of beats of silence desired by the composer.

Sills, Beverly (1929–2007)   American soprano who sang a wide range of operatic roles throughout her career. Upon her retirement from singing in 1980, Sills remained active in the arts as general manager of the New York Opera (until 1984), chairwoman of Lincoln Center (until 2002), and chairwoman of the Metropolitan Opera (until 2005).

Silver, Horace (b. 1928)   American jazz pianist known for his funky piano style and his compositional contributions to hard bop. Several of his compositions have become standards in the jazz repertoire.

simile marks   Notation instructing the performer to repeat the one measure or two measures preceding it.

Simon, Carly (b. 1945)   American musician, singer-songwriter, and children's author. She rose to fame in the 1970s and has won Grammy, Oscar, and Golden Globe (one each) awards. Simon is a former wife of James Taylor.

Simon, Paul (b. 1941)   American singer-songwriter. His early success was as a member of the duo Simon and Garfunkel. At the height of their success, the duo split and Simon continued to write and perform. In 1986, his album *Graceland*, which was a foray into African music, introduced much of the world to world music.

Simon Boccanegra   Italian opera composed in three acts (with a prelude) by Giuseppe Verdi, with libretto by Francesco Maria Pieve, based on the play of the same name by Antonio Garcia Gutiérrez. It premiered in 1857.

simple meter   A time signature in which each portion (or beat) is divisible into two equal parts.

Sinatra, Frank (1915–1998)   American singer and actor who got his start in the bands of Harry James and Tommy Dorsey. Nicknamed "Old Blue Eyes," he was not only an extremely popular singer but also won 11 Grammy Awards and an Academy Award for Best Supporting Actor in *From Here to Eternity*. Some of his hit songs include "You Make Me Feel So Young," "Witchcraft," and "New York, New York."

sine wave   Occurs when air is set in motion by a vibrating body. The human ear detects sine waves, which consist of amplitude (deviation from zero) and frequency (the number of times the body vibrates per second). Sine waves determine pitch (high or low).

sinfonia (It., symphony)   This term most commonly refers to a seventeenth- or eighteenth-century orchestral piece used as an introduction to an opera, cantata, oratorio, or suite.

singer-actor   A person who specializes in both singing and acting. In opera and musical theater, cast members are called upon to sing and act.

singer-songwriter   A person who composes and sings his or her own songs. Many popular musicians are singer-songwriters.

singer's formants   The peaks in the spectrum of a singer's sound. They determine the quality of the sound produced by a singer and can be measured on a spectrometer.

singing saw   In rural areas, people made music by striking a carpenter's saw with a hammer and flexing the blade to alter the pitch. When played with a violin bow, a player is able to approximate the sound of the human voice singing.

singspiel (G., song-play)   This term refers to an eighteenth-century comedic play interspersed with songs. It was a genre of opera used by Wolfgang Amadeus Mozart in *The Magic Flute*.

Sistine Chapel Choir   Based in Vatican City, one of the oldest choirs in history. When the church emerged from the catacombs (around the third century), there was a great need for music in the liturgy, thus beginning a long history of composers and musicians being employed by the church.

sitar A plucked string instrument used mainly in Hindustani classical music. Its unique timbre is the product of the vibration of sympathetic strings, a hollow neck, and a gourd-shaped body. Ravi Shankar (b. 1920) is the modern master of the sitar.

Six, Les (F., The Six) A name given to six French composers working in Montparnasse, France, whose music was seen as a reaction to the music of Richard Wagner as well as that of the Impressionists. The members of Les Six were: Georges Auric, Louis Durey, Arthur Honegger, Darius Milhaud, Francis Poulenc, and Germaine Tailleferre.

six-four chord A triad in second inversion (the fifth is in the bass), so called because the intervals between the upper pitches and the bottom are a sixth and a fourth, respectively.

sixteen-bar blues A variation of the standard twelve-bar blues in which four measures (two each, alternating between the dominant and subdominant triads) are inserted between the eighth and ninth measures.

S

sixteenth note   Also known as a semiquaver, it is one sixteenth of a whole note and is notated with a filled-in note head, a stem, and two flags.

sixteenth rest   A pause or rest equivalent to a sixteenth note, half of an eighth rest, or a sixteenth of a whole rest. A filled-in note with a stem and two flags.

sixth   The distance between the first and sixth pitches of a scale.

sixth chord   1. In classical music, a triad in first inversion (the third is in the bass and the root is a sixth above the bass note). 2. In jazz and popular music, a triad with an added pitch a sixth above the root.

sixty-fourth note   Musical note equivalent to one sixty-fourth of a whole note. Filled-in note with a stem and four flags.

ska   A genre of music that originated in Jamaica and is a precursor to rocksteady and reggae. It combined elements of Caribbean mento, calypso, American jazz, and R&B. It is characterized by a heavy accent on the upbeat and a syncopated, walking bass line.

skiffle   A style of music with jazz, blues, folk, and country influences that originated in the South early in the twentieth century that utilized homemade instruments. In the 1950s, it experienced a resurgence of popularity in England, mainly at the hands of Lonnie Donegan, and became a major influence on several bands such as the Beatles and the Rolling Stones.

skittle music   Sequenced music; an offshoot of techno.

slide   Pitches are altered on a trombone through the use of a slide, which consists of two sets of tubing, one inside the other. If the performer extends his or her arm, making the slide longer, the pitch will go down (and vice-versa).

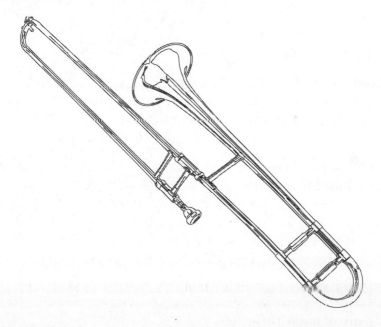

slide whistle   A wind instrument with a "fipple" like that of a recorder and an internal piston that is manipulated by the player. The slide whistle is often employed for comic effect in music.

slit drum   A hollow percussion instrument made of bamboo or wood that is made resonant by one or more slits cut into it.

sludge metal   A subgenre of heavy metal music that fuses doom metal and punk. It also gleans inspiration from industrial music and southern rock. Sludge metal is typically aggressive and abrasive, featuring shouted vocals, heavily distorted instruments, and sharply contrasting tempi. Many of its earliest pioneers were from Louisiana.

slur   A symbol in Western music represented by a curved line, indicating that the notes are to be played without articulation.

Smith, Bessie (1894–1937)   Known as "The Empress of the Blues," Bessie Smith was the most popular female blues singer of the 1920s and 1930s. She was a major influence on subsequent singers.

snare drum   Percussion instrument that has a body (shell) constructed of metal or wood with a top and bottom head. Its unique sound is due to the wires (snares) stretched across the bottom head, which vibrate when the batter (top) head is struck. Used in orchestras and all other bands using drums, it is an important part of a drum kit or trap set.

societies, musical   Organizations dedicated to promotion, preservation, and creation of certain ethnic musical genres, as well as music in general, which exist throughout the world. Some are scholarly associations, some focus on a particular instrument or area of musical emphasis, and some are purely social in nature.

sociology of music   The study of music's place in society. This includes society's influence on music and vice-versa.

soft palate   The velum or muscular palate; soft tissue at the back of the roof of the mouth. As opposed to the hard palate, it contains no bone and its position is very important to singers.

soft pedal   One of the standard pedals of the piano, placed leftmost, and when depressed shifts the action (keyboard) to the right so that the hammers strike only two of the three strings. This decreases the sound produced.

Soldier's Tale, The (F., *L' histoire du soldat*)   A 1918 theatrical work by Igor Stravinsky based on a Russian folk tale of a soldier who trades his fiddle to the devil for a book that predicts the economic future.

solfège—The practice of singing melodies utilizing prescribed syllables for each pitch (for example, "do, re, mi," and so on). A system used to teach sight-reading.

solid-body guitar   A guitar pioneered by Leo Fender in response to requests for electric instruments that would not produce feedback as easily as hollow bodied guitars. These instruments rely on pick-ups to transfer the sound of the vibrating strings to an amplifier.

solmization   *See* solfège.

solo   A piece performed by a single voice or instrument. This term is also affixed to a portion of a work for a large ensemble in which a single voice or instrument performs.

solo break   In jazz, a solo break occurs when the rhythm section stops playing for two or four measures at the start of a soloist's first chorus.

solo pitch   A means of tuning string instruments higher than usually prescribed, adding a greater degree of brilliance to an instrumental composition (also known as "solo tuning").

solo singing   To sing alone (one voice, not in a chorus or other ensemble) with or without accompaniment.

sonance   The sensation caused by vibrating air, which is perceived by hearing organs.

sonata   Italian term that literally means a piece which is "to be played," as opposed to a cantata, which is to be sung. Since the early nineteenth century, this term has been more closely associated with large, multi-movement works for solo piano or other instruments with piano accompaniment.

S

sonata form   Also sonata-allegro form; a standard musical form that has been in practical use since the classical period. It consists of three main sections: exposition, development, and recapitulation (with an optional coda). The thematic structure is: AABA (coda). The first movement of most symphonies is in sonata form, as is often the finale. Many solo pieces, overtures, and incidental music employ sonata form.

sonatina   Literally, a small sonata. Quite often, a sonatina is lighter in character than a sonata.

Sondheim, Stephen (b. 1930)   American composer and lyricist best known for writing the lyrics for *West Side Story*. He has won an Academy Award, nine Tony Awards, multiple Grammy Awards, and a Pulitzer Prize.

song   A simple piece written for the voice, stressing the text, as opposed to an aria, which is more elaborate. They are composed with or without accompaniment.

song cycle   A group of songs unified by a central theme, designed to be performed as a single entity. Often, singers will extract single pieces from a song cycle and perform them.

song form   A simple type of music for the voice, the most basic of which is AB. The ternary song form, ABA, is more prevalent in instrumental than vocal pieces.

song pluggers   Refers to singers in the early twentieth century (before the advent of the radio and phonograph) hired by Tin Pan Alley music publishers to perform new music for passersby in the lobbies of the publishing houses.

song recital   A program of pieces for solo voice (with or without accompaniment).

songwriters   People who write songs. Often, they are hired by music publishers and agents to write for particular artists.

sonograph   A device that makes sound visible. Sonographs in various permutations are used by musicians to evaluate the quality of their sound.

sonority   A term affixed to a group of pitches or to a group of timbres when played together. A major triad has a major sonority.

soprano   The highest female voice register; also, the highest instrument.

sostenuto (It., sustained)   The composer inserts this word to indicate the notes should be performed extremely legato.

sostenuto pedal   On a modern piano with three pedals, the sostenuto pedal is located in the middle. It causes only the keys that are played while it's depressed to be sustained.

sotto voce (It., under the voice)   Musical instruction to sing with normal volume. Often, this technique is employed to convey a certain degree of tenderness or as an "aside."

soubrette   Female role in an operatic or musical theater production that usually plays a stock character role like the young, flirtatious maid or coy girlfriend, such as Zerlina in Mozart's *Don Giovanni*.

soul   A style of African American music that combines elements of gospel and R&B music. Originated by artists such as Ray Charles and Sam Cooke and later dominated by Otis Redding, Aretha Franklin, and James Brown, soul music became prevalent in the mid-1960s and had a profound and continuing influence on popular music.

sound   Air molecules set in motion by a vibration or collision. Two types of sound are noise and tone. Sensations that receive this sound are relayed from the ear to the auditory nerve and then recognized by the brain.

sound collage   Sound that is "glued together"; a technique of putting together pieces of sound or music from different sources, such as digital samples or portions of recordings, to make a completely different composition.

sound hole   An opening in the upper soundboard of a string instrument.

S

sound ideal   Achieving the ideal sound according to performance practices specific to different periods of musical style.

Sound Imagination   A production company specializing in film scores, jingles for commercials, and sound effects.

sound post   A small dowel (cylindrical rod) spanning the space between the back and top of a string instrument. It is located under the treble foot of the bridge and is held in place by friction.

sound pressure level (SPL)   The intensity of sound that is measured by decibels (dB). These decibels of SPL are perceived by the listener as loudness.

sound system   An amplifier and speakers. Its main purpose is to reproduce sound and make it audible. It has several uses: a sound reinforcement PA (public address) system for amplification of live performances and a hi-fi (high fidelity) system for listening to recorded music.

Sound Tools   The first digital audio workstation released by Digidesign® in the late 1980s. Its successor, Pro Tools, is currently the industry standard for music production.

soundboard   The part of a string instrument that transmits vibrations into the air.

soundtrack   1. A recording (in various formats) of the music used in a movie. 2. The narrow strip on the side of a movie film that carries the sound.

Sousa, John Phillip (1854–1932)   An American composer and conductor who was most noted for writing American military and patriotic marches. Because of this notoriety, he became recognized as "The March King." The patriotic marches "Stars and Stripes Forever" and "El Capitan" are two of his finest marches.

sousaphone   A bass-voiced brass instrument designed by John Phillip Sousa. It features a forward-facing bell, and its wrap-around design allows its weight to be distributed on the player's shoulder. The sousaphone is best suited for outdoor performance, specifically in a marching band.

southern rock   A genre of country music and a subgenre of rock. As its name implies, southern rock originated in the southern United States and is a synthesis of rock and roll, country music, and the blues. It is generally focused on electric guitars and vocals. Southern rock artists include the Allman Brothers Band, Lynyrd Skynyrd, and the Marshall Tucker Band.

southern soul   Also known as "deep soul" or "country soul," it's a genre of soul music that originated in America's southern states—most associated with the music made at Muscle Shoals Sound in Alabama and the Stax studio in Memphis, Tennessee. Its roots are in gospel, country, blues, jump blues, early rock and roll, and R&B.

speaker key   Also known as a "register key" on a clarinet, it is depressed with the left thumb and moves the pitch up the interval of a fourth.

speaking stop   The pitch at which the voice or instrument ceases to "speak" or sound.

species   In musical theory and counterpoint, this term refers to various means of composing independent lines of music against a *cantus firmus* (an existing melody). The first species is 1:1, the second species is 2:1, the third species is 4:1, the fourth species employs suspensions, and the fifth species is florid and doesn't necessarily employ a cantus firmus.

Spector, Phil (b. 1939)   An American songwriter and record producer, he is most noted for having conceived the "Wall of Sound." Spector was closely associated with the girl groups of the 1960s, producing more than 25 Top-40 hits between 1960 and 1965. He produced the Beatles' Academy Award–winning *Let It Be* and the Grammy-winning *Concert for Bangladesh* soundtracks. Spector was inducted into the Rock and Roll Hall of Fame as a nonperformer in 1989. Long known for eccentricities that bordered on erratic and threatening behavior, at age 69 Spector was convicted of second-degree murder and is currently serving 19 years to life in prison. *See also* Wall of Sound.

S

spectrum   A visual representation of a sound. As with the spectrum of light (visual color), musicians refer to the range of tone in terms of color (usually plotted on a graph).

speed metal   A subgenre of heavy-metal music originating in the 1980s and rooted in the new wave of British heavy metal (NWOBM). Speed metal is a technically demanding, extremely fast, and abrasive music. When the tempos were toned down, it evolved into the subgenre "trash metal."

spinet   A small, inexpensive upright piano designed primarily for use in the home parlor.

spinto (It., pushed)   Refers to soprano and tenor voices residing between lyric and dramatic.

spiritual   A religious song originating in the slave culture of the American South. The spiritual (or Negro spiritual) is a mainstay in the southern black church. In recent decades, the spiritual has become a regular component of choral concerts around the world.

sprechgesang (G., spoken song)   An expressionist vocal technique between speaking and singing, meant to convey a particular emotion.

sprechstimme   *See* sprechgesang.

Springsteen, Bruce (b. 1949)   Nicknamed "The Boss," Springsteen is an American singer-songwriter who regularly tours the world with his E Street Band. His work has won 19 Grammy Awards, 2 Golden Globe awards, and an Academy Award.

"Stabat Mater"   A thirteenth-century Roman Catholic chant attributed to Pope Innocent III and Jacopone da Todi (a church friar). The title is actually an abbreviation of the first line of text: *Stabat Mater dolorosa* ("The sorrowful mother stood"). The hymn meditates on the sorrow experienced by the Blessed Virgin at Christ's crucifixion. Many composers have set this text to music.

staccato (It., to detach)   Notes played rapidly with distinct separation between them; indicated by the placement of a dot above or below a note.

staff   In modern music notation, the staff is a grid of five lines and four spaces upon which notes are written.

stage fright   The anxiety, fear, or persistent phobia of performing in front of an audience; also known as performance anxiety.

stanza   A term taken from poetry and commonly referred to as a "verse," a stanza usually alternates with the chorus or refrain. The stanza differs from the refrain in that the text is usually different for each stanza, whereas the text of the refrain is the same every time.

"Star-Spangled Banner, The"   The national anthem of the United States of America. During the Battle of Baltimore in the War of 1812, Francis Scott Key composed a poem commemorating the British bombardment of Fort McHenry. It was later set to a British drinking tune and became popular during World War I. It was made the national anthem by Congressional resolution on March 3, 1931.

Starr, Ringo (b. 1940)   Singer-songwriter, drummer, and actor famous for having replaced Pete Best as the drummer for the Beatles in 1962. During and after his time with the Beatles, Starr appeared in numerous films. He had success in the 1970s as a solo performer, and in 1988, along with his Beatles bandmates, he was inducted into the Rock and Roll Hall of Fame.

S

statement   The presentation of a motive, melody, or tune.

steel band   An ensemble of steel drums (steel pans or simply "pans": percussion instruments pitched chromatically) that originated in Trinidad. They are constructed from 55-gallon steel drums and are struck with mallets of varying hardness.

steel guitar   Also called the pedal-steel guitar, a type of guitar described not by the material from which it is made but by the steel that is used to fret the strings with the player's left hand. It is used extensively, although not exclusively, in country-western music.

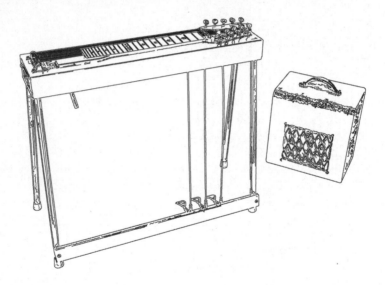

steg   German word for the bridge of a string instrument—a piece of wood or other material perpendicular to the body across which the strings are stretched.

stereoscopy   Any technique of recording three-dimensional visual information or creating the illusion of depth in an image. Stereoscopes are used in determining the shape of singers' throats while singing.

Sting (b. 1951)   Singer-songwriter and actor who received his nickname while playing bass in various jazz bands and wearing a yellow and black–striped shirt. Prior to starting his solo career, he was the principal songwriter, lead singer, and bassist of the rock band the Police. Sting has received 19 Grammy Awards and has been inducted into the Rock and Roll and Songwriters Halls of Fame. "Roxanne" and "Every Breath You Take" are two of his most famous pieces.

Stockhausen, Julius Karlheinz (1928–2007)   A German composer widely acknowledged by critics as one of the most important and controversial composers of the twentieth and early twenty-first centuries. He was known for his groundbreaking work in electronic music, aleatory music, serial composition, and spatialization in music.

Stomp   A nontraditional dance troupe originating in the United Kingdom, this ensemble utilizes body motion and traditional and nontraditional percussion instruments (5-gallon plastic buckets, paint cans, and so on) to make music.

stopped pipe   A pipe on an organ of uniform diameter in which one end is closed (stopped) and the other is open.

stopping   The act of depressing a string on a fingerboard at the precise point that produces a specific pitch.

straight four   Refers to common time (4/4) key signature in jazz.

straight organ   Constructed as a partially unified instrument. This means that not all its pipes are available to be played by all the manuals (keyboards) on the instrument. The pipes of a unified organ, on the other hand, can be played on any manual.

straight tone   A tone performed without any inflection, such as vibrato.

strain   A generic term for a section of vocal or instrumental music. In vocal music, a strain is a verse and a chorus. Instrumental marches are typically constructed of an introduction (4 to 8 measures in length) followed by two strains (usually 16 measures each) of music. The key signature changes at a point commonly referred to as the *trio*, and two more strains (also usually 16 measures each) close the piece.

S

Strauss, Richard (1864–1949)   A late romantic, early modern German composer who was also a prominent conductor. Best known for his tone poems, he also composed lieder and operas. Strauss was considered one of the greatest composers of his time.

Stravinsky, Igor (1882–1971)   Russian composer, conductor, and pianist widely considered one of the most important and influential composers of twentieth-century music. His early fame came from three ballets commissioned by Sergei Diaghilev (*The Firebird*, *Petrushka*, and *The Rite of Spring*). He later turned to neo-classicism and eventually, after immigrating to America, tried his hand at serial composition. Stravinsky is said to have had an everlasting influence on how composers view rhythm in music.

Strayhorn, Billy (1915–1967)   An American composer, pianist, and arranger best known for his nearly 30-year collaboration with bandleader Duke Ellington. Several of his compositions, including "Take the 'A' Train," "Lush Life," and "Chelsea Bridge," were first recorded by the Ellington band and are standards in the jazz repertoire.

street cries   The short, musical cries of merchants hawking their wares in busy marketplaces. Many of these have been recorded and subsequently incorporated in large-scale musical works.

street organ   A mechanical organ designed to be played in the street by turning a wheel that in turn operates the internal mechanism, creating music. The people who play street organs are commonly referred to as "organ grinders."

Streisand, Barbra (b. 1942)   An American singer and theater and film actress who has also achieved notice as a composer, political activist, film producer, and film director. By age 28, she had won 2 Academy Awards, 10 Grammy Awards, 4 Emmy Awards, a special Tony Award, and a Peabody. Streisand is one of only a few to have won at least one of each of these awards. She is the highest-ranking artist on the Recording Industry Association of America's (RIAA) Top Selling Artists List and the only woman in the top 10. Famous songs of hers include "Evergreen" and "People."

Strouse, Charles (b. 1928)   An American composer and lyricist. He is a three-time Tony Award winner and is most noted for having written *Bye Bye Birdie* and *Annie,* the latter of which garnered him his third Tony Award and two Grammy Awards.

studio engineering   Also called audio engineering, part of the science of recording and reproducing sound, either mechanically or electronically.

sturm und drang   The conventional translation of this term is "storm and stress," and it's defined as the name of a movement in German literature and music during the late eighteenth century. The hallmarks of this movement were an emphasis on individual subjectivity, and extremes of emotion were given free expression in response to the confines of the Enlightenment and associated esthetic movements. Ludwig van Beethoven used this effect in his music.

style   Refers to traits of music created during a particular time in music history that distinguish it from that of other time periods.

Sub Pop   A record label founded in 1986. Sub Pop achieved its fame for having been the first to sign Nirvana, Soundgarden, Mudhoney, and many other bands in the Seattle area closely associated with the grunge rock movement.

subdominant chord   The term associated with the fourth scale degree and the chord built upon that scale degree, so named because it resides two semitones below the dominant.

subito (It., suddenly)   This term is used in reference to dynamic and/or tempo. It is most commonly abbreviated *sub* or *subito p*, meaning "suddenly soft."

$$subito\ \boldsymbol{p}$$

subject   The first melodic statement in a fugue.

successive counterpoint   *See* species.

stretto   In a fugue, stretto is an imitative device whereby a ment of the subject is interrupted (but not silenced) by anot statement of the same material in another voice. These two ments partially overlap, thus ending at different points in ti

stride   A jazz piano technique that developed from ragtin Its name comes from the left hand "striding" up and down keyboard. Great stride players include Fats Waller and Jell Morton.

string instruments   Musical instruments that produce s by plucking, bowing, or hammering one or more strings, stretched over a bridge and tuned to specific pitches.

string quartet   A chamber ensemble comprised of two one viola, and one cello. This term is also given to pieces written for this instrumentation.

string quintet   With the addition of a contrabass viol, quartet becomes a quintet. As with the quartet, this tern given to pieces of music written for this instrumentatior notable is *The Trout Quintet* by Franz Schubert.

string trio   A chamber ensemble comprised of a violir and a piano. As with the quartet and quintet, the term also given to pieces of music written for this instrumen

stringendo (It., squeezing)   To increase the tempo lit as a climax is approached.

strophic   A type of composition that has verses. Mos songs are strophic.

strophic bass   The method of using the same bass li verses of a song.

strophic form   Also called "chorus form," it is a sec tive way of structuring a piece based on the repetitio mal section of music. The accompaniment of each st can be varied slightly to add a degree of interest.

suite An ordered set of instrumental or orchestral pieces intended to be played in a concert and not as accompaniment to or incidental music for anything else. From the Renaissance forward, composers have written suites of combinations of various dances. Additionally, certain movements have been extracted from ballets, operas, and films to form suites (for example, Tchaikovsky's *Nutcracker Suite*).

Summer, Donna (b. 1948) An American singer-songwriter who gained prominence during the disco era of the 1970s, earning her the title "Queen of Disco." Although known primarily for her disco hits, she has also recorded contemporary R&B, gospel, rock, and pop. Summer is one of the most successful artists of the 1970s and was the first to have three consecutive double albums hit number one on the Billboard Chart. Although never a winner, she has been nominated for 12 Grammy Awards.

supertitles Also called surtitles, these provide translations of opera text into the vernacular and are projected on the teaser above the stage or a screen that is prominently placed near the stage.

Supremes, The A female singing group that was the premier act of Motown in the 1960s. Their repertoire included doo-wop, pop, soul, Broadway show tunes, psychedelic soul, and disco. The Supremes are, to date, America's most successful group, with 12 number-one singles on the Billboard Chart. Some of these hits include "Baby Love," "Where Did Our Love Go," and "Love Child."

surf music A genre of music popular from 1961–1965 that was centered in Southern California (in particular Orange County). There are two main types of surf music: instrumental, pioneered by Dick Dale and the Del-tones, and vocal, performed by groups such as the Beach Boys.

Susannah An American opera composed in two acts by Carlisle Floyd, who wrote the libretto and music while serving on the piano faculty at Florida State University. In 1956, it was awarded the New York Music Critics Circle Award for Best New Opera. The music is largely characterized by Appalachian folk music.

S

suspension   A way of creating tension in music in which one or more notes are held before resolving to chord tones.

sustain or **sustaining pedal**   The most commonly used piano pedal, the rightmost pedal on two- or three-pedal pianos. When depressed, it removes the dampers from all strings, allowing them to vibrate freely.

sweet music   A name given to highly arranged "society" music played for social functions.

swell   A section of pipes on an organ, the volume of which may be manually controlled by the player by means of a "swell pedal."

swing   Also known as "swing music" or "swing jazz," a style of jazz music that started in America in the 1930s and solidified as a distinctive style by 1935. It is characterized by a rhythm section (piano, bass, and drum set) with saxophones, trumpets, and trombones and occasionally a vocalist. These groups specialized in up-tempo music with a lilting spirit, making it easy for people to dance.

swing band   An ensemble specializing in performing swing music.

symphonic band   A concert band comprised of woodwinds, brass, and percussion instruments that performs transcriptions of orchestral music as well as pieces written exclusively for this combination of instruments.

symphonic jazz   A combination of a jazz band and string orchestra. The New York Symphonic Jazz Orchestra specializes in blurring the lines between symphonic, jazz, world, and popular music.

symphonic poem   Also called a tone poem, a piece of music for symphony orchestra that tells a story. Richard Strauss was a master of the symphonic poem.

Symphonie Fantastique   A five-movement symphony of program music for large orchestra written in 1830 by French composer Hector Berlioz. It is representative of the music of the early romantic period. The protagonist in the music's story has an opium-induced dream wherein he witnesses his own death.

symphony   A large-scale work (usually four movements long) composed nearly exclusively for orchestra. It is based on the "sonata principle" and dates from the eighteenth century. During the twentieth century, composers wrote symphonies for concert band as well as for orchestra.

syncopation   Includes a variety of unexpected rhythms that stress different beats or portions of the beat within a prescribed meter.

synopsis   A brief story outline of an opera printed in the program, which allows concertgoers to better understand the action onstage. This is particularly helpful when an opera is in a foreign language.

synth-pop   A subgenre of popular music in which the synthesizer is the dominant musical instrument. It originated during the new wave era of the late 1970s and early '80s and has continued to develop.

synth-punk   Also known as electropunk, synth-punk is a music genre combining elements of electronic rock and punk (1977–1984). The term was invented in 1999 by Damian Ramsey to retroactively name a small subgenre of punk in which the musicians used synthesizers instead of guitars.

synthesizer   An electronic keyboard instrument capable of producing a variety of sounds by generating and combining signals of different frequencies. Rather than acoustic sounds, synthesizers create electrical signals that are played through an amplifier or headphones.

system   A generic term for a line of music consisting of one or more staves on a page. This term also refers to specific ways of playing instruments—specifically, the fingering system.

tablature   A type of musical notation indicating fingering positions instead of musical notes.

tacet (L., silent)   Instruction in a musical score that indicates to the performer that he or she has no part to play for quite some time. *Tacet al fine* indicates that the performer is done playing.

tag   A jazz term for a passage or section added to the end of a composition to emphasize or confirm the feeling of finality; also known as a coda.

tailpiece   Used on members of the violin family to anchor the strings to the bottom front of the instrument; usually made of ebony or some other wood.

Tales of Hoffman, The (F., *Contes d'Hoffmann, Les*)   French opera composed in a prologue, three acts, and epilogue, with libretto by Jules Barbier; first produced in Paris in 1881.

talking drum   A drum (percussion instrument) from West Africa whose head can be tightened while playing to change the pitch. This instrument is hit with a stick or mallet.

tam-tam   A flat, saucer-shaped gong that has no pitch when struck.

tambour   A drum or drum player.

tambourine   Percussion instrument with a plastic or wooden frame.

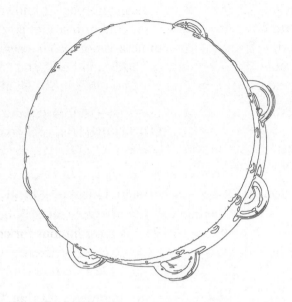

tampon   A drumstick with two heads used to make a roll on the head of a bass drum by holding it in the middle and shaking the wrist.

tango   A type of musical genre and dance influenced by African and Spanish culture that came from the low-class suburbs of Buenos Aires in the 1890s. A tango uses a syncopated pattern in a 2/4 time signature.

Tannhäuser   German opera composed in three acts by Richard Wagner to his own text. First produced in Dresden, Germany, in 1845, the story is based on two German legends.

tape recorder   An audio storage and playback machine that plays magnetic tape on a reel-to-reel tape or cassette deck. Magnetic tape was used in a steel tape recorder for the first time in 1931.

tarantella Traditional Italian music in a fast 6/8 meter and accompanied by tambourines.

tasty Jazz slang describing the well-executed or interesting way a song or passage is played.

Tatum, Art (1909–1956) An American jazz pianist known for his virtuosic improvisational skills, making him one of jazz's most respected all-time greats. Although he was not a composer, his renditions of popular songs such as "Body and Soul" and "Makin' Whoopee" were unique. He performed on more than 60 albums.

Taylor, James (b. 1948) American singer-songwriter and guitarist. Winner of five Grammy Awards, Taylor's folk, rock, country, and blues-rock songs were huge hits in the 1970s, starting with his hit "Fire and Rain."

Tchaikovsky, Pyotr (Peter) (1840–1893) Russian romantic-period composer whose ballets, symphonies, and operas are still being played in the current repertoire. He was most famous for compositions such as the opera *Eugene Onegin*; ballets *The Sleeping Beauty*, *Swan Lake*, and *The Nutcracker*; and the *1812 Overture*.

"Te Deum" An early Catholic hymn of praise meaning "We Praise You, God."

technique A particular way of accomplishing a desired aim. In music, the way the performer plays his or her instrument.

techno An electronic dance music that developed in Detroit, Michigan, in the 1980s. Instrumentation includes a synthesizer, keyboards, a sampler, a drum machine, and a sequencer. Techno uses elements of electric jazz, funk, Chicago house, and other African American styles.

Tejano A mixture of folk and popular music from Mexico and central and southern Texas that was transformed and made popular worldwide by artists such as Selena Quintanilla, Mazz, and La Mafia.

Telecaster   A type of solid-body electric guitar made by the Fender company and known for its rich cutting sound. The Telecaster has been played by guitarists such as Jeff Beck, Merle Haggard, George Harrison, and Bruce Springsteen.

Telephone, The   American opera composed in one act by Gian Carlo Menotti as a companion piece to another of his operas, *The Medium*; produced in New York City in 1947.

temperament   Musical systems of tuning. Different types include Pythagorean tuning (used before the renaissance), meantone (used in the renaissance), well, equal, regular, and just tone temperament.

tempo   How fast a composition is; the speed at which a musical work should be played.

tempo marks   Tempo is indicated in the music by metronome markings, either by the composer or the publisher. (For example, q=120 means 120 quarter notes or beats per minute.) Also, the tempo may be indicated in general terms, such as *largo:* broad, *lento:* slow, *adagio:* slow, *andante:* walking speed, *moderato:* moderate, *allegretto* or *allegro:* fast, *presto:* very fast, and *prestissimo:* as fast as possible.

Adagio   ♩ = 40

Tender Land, The   An American opera composed in two acts by Aaron Copland, with libretto by Horace Everett. Originally meant to be presented on television, it was rejected and produced for the first time at the New York City Opera House in April 1954. The setting is a farm in the United States Midwest.

tenor   1. The highest natural singing male voice. 2. The part that carries the *cantus firmus* (the melody used in Gregorian chant) in early polyphony (composition that uses more than two independent melodic lines) between 1200–1500 C.E.

tenor clef   A C-clef positioned on the fourth line of the music staff to make it easier for the high ranges of the cello, double bass, bassoon, trombone, and euphonium to be played.

tenuto (It., to hold)   Musical term that instructs the performer to hold or sustain a note or chord to the next note or chord as if in *legato* (smooth, with no breaks).

ternary form   A musical form indicating there are three sections (A-B-A) in the composition. The third section is often identical to the first section (as in da capo arias) but with extra ornamentation and may be indicated as A1 or A'. The contrasting B section is often called a trio and is often in another key.

tessitura (It., texture)   The part of the vocal range that the majority of the notes in the composition are centered around. May also indicate the area of the voice where the singer is most comfortable.

tetrachord   A four-note segment in a tone row (12 notes that make up a chromatic scale) or scale.

text, music   The words or lyrics used in vocal music.

texture   The overall quality of a composition and how its individual ingredients, such as rhythm, voicing, tempos, and harmonies, interact with each other.

thematic transformation   A type of musical composition invented by the Hungarian composer and pianist Franz Liszt (c. 1859–1865) that takes the theme of the song and makes several variations of it throughout the piece. It can be disguised with different harmonies, rhythms, or augmentations.

theme   The main melody of the composition. The theme is the subject or principal musical idea that is the starting point for further development in an extended piece.

theme and variations   When the main musical idea (theme) is used over and over with changes in its rhythm, dynamics, melody, harmony, or tone color. An example is Aaron Copland's theme and variations on the song "Simple Gifts" from his ballet score *Appalachian Spring* (1944).

theorbo   Another name for a bass lute, a plucked string instrument from the renaissance and baroque periods.

theory, musical   Includes the study of musical harmony (harmonic analysis), counterpoint, music composition, orchestration and arranging, solfège, and melody.

theremin   One of the first electronic musical instruments, named after Léon Theremin, a Russian inventor, in 1928. Known for its eerie sound, it can be heard in movies such as *The Lost Weekend*, *Spellbound*, and *The Day the Earth Stood Still*.

third   The interval between two notes that are whole steps (for example, C and E).

third-stream music   Term signifying a merger of classical and jazz music.

thirty-second note   A musical notation equal to one thirty-second of a whole note; a filled-in black note with a stem and three flags.

thoroughbass   The same as "figured bass." In musical notation, a stenographic system of writing out the bass part with numbers above indicating chords, nonchord tones, and intervals in the attached harmony.

thrash metal A heavy-metal subgenre recognized for its aggression, fast tempo, and shredding (fast) guitar licks. Four bands famous for thrash metal are Slayer, Metallica, Anthrax, and Megadeth.

thrashcore A much faster subgenre of hardcore punk music that developed in the early 1980s. Its songs are short with lyrics that are either rebellious or anti-militaristic. Bands that play thrashcore music are Das Oath and Limp Wrist.

Threepenny Opera, The A musical theater piece composed by Kurt Weill with Bertolt Brecht and adapted from John Gay's eighteenth-century English opera *The Beggar's Opera*. This piece was produced for the first time in Berlin, Germany, in 1928.

through-composed A song that is composed using new musical material in each stanza; the opposite of "strophic." "Der Erlkönig," a through-composed lied (German song) by Franz Schubert (1797–1828), is a fine example of this type of music.

through-imitation When an entire composition is based on the principle of imitation.

thumb piano A plucked idiophone (instrument that vibrates without the use of a membrane or strings) used in sub-Saharan Africa.

thumb-brush style A guitar style made famous by early country music (then called old-time music) performer Maybelle Carter (1909–1978), where the melody is played on the low strings while the chords of the piece are interpolated on the upper strings.

thunder machine A rotating drum containing large, hard balls used to imitate the sound of thunder. First used by Richard Strauss in his composition *Alpensinfonie, op. 64*, in 1915.

Thus Spake Zarathustra A tone poem composed by Richard Strauss in 1896 based on the "prose poem" by the famous German philosopher Friedrich Nietzsche. It is the theme song for the movie *2001: A Space Odyssey*.

tie   Musical marking used to "bind" notes together that are separated by a bar line or to combine a number of notes together to create a longer note value.

timbales   A shallow, high-pitched, and single-headed metal drum that is struck with a stick. Invented in Cuba, it is used in many different styles of music, especially Latin music and the "Bounce Beat" of a Washington, D.C.–based funk subgenre style, Go-Go.

timbre   The "color" or quality of a sound.

time   Musical term used to indicate tempo, meter, or a note's duration.

time signature   Meter indication using two numbers at the beginning of a composition that specify the unit of measurement (quarter note, half note, and so on) and the number of those units comprised in a measure.

timing   The length or duration of a composition; important in planning a recital, concert, television, or radio performance. Also refers to how notes are subtly adjusted when being performed in different styles such as "swing" or "laidback" or "rushing."

timpani   Also known as a "kettle drum," a large, bowl-shaped drum with a skin membrane (head) stretched across the top. Made of copper or fiberglass, it is struck with a timpani mallet or drumstick to produce a pitch. This instrument evolved from the military drum and is now used in classical orchestras.

Tin Pan Alley   Historical name for the U.S. music industry.
Tin Pan Alley was the original area (West 28th between 5th and
6th avenues) in New York City that housed many of the country's
music publishers and songwriters between 1885 and 1930.

toasting   A precursor to rapping; Jamaican music from the 1960s
and early '70s in which DJs would perform commentaries, rhythmic chants, screams, squeals, and storytelling over the top of the
latest hit ska, reggae, rocksteady, or dancehall songs or "riddims."

toccata (It., to touch)   A virtuosic keyboard (or plucked string
instrument) composition written to emphasize the performer's finger agility and technique. First appearing in the later renaissance
period, Johann Sebastian Bach (1685–1750) was a major composer
of toccatas—most famously, his Toccata and Fugue in D Minor,
BMV 565, for organ.

tom-tom   A high-pitched, tunable drum used in jazz, rock, and
other popular music genres.

tonality   When the pitch relationships in music are centered around the tonic or "key" center.

tone   In music, tone can represent a number of different aspects, including pitch, timbre (color), the name of a note, or the distance between two notes (for example, whole tone scale).

tone cluster   Any musical chord consisting of three consecutive tones or more. Usually based on the chromatic scale, the tone cluster has been used since the early twentieth century by ragtime composers Scott Joplin and Jelly Roll Morton, avant-garde composer Henry Cowell, and others such as Béla Bártok and Charles Ives.

tone color   *See* timbre.

tone deafness   A hearing impairment, not a lack of training, rendering a person incapable of telling the difference between different musical notes.

tone poem   Also called a "symphonic poem," a total movement in a symphony that musically represents a painting, poem, novel, or any other nonmusical source with the intent of evoking an emotional response from the audience.

tone production   The way a performer produces a certain tone; the manner in which the vocal or instrumental technique is used.

tone row   In serial music, it is a 12-tone system using all 12 tones of the chromatic scale where the composer cannot repeat a note until all 11 of the other notes have appeared. Arnold Schoenberg devised serial music as a composition technique around 1910.

tonguing   The use of the tongue by the performer to articulate a passage being played on a brass or woodwind instrument. There are four types of tonguing: single tonguing (used by all instruments), double and triple tonguing (used mostly for brass instruments), and flutter tonguing (a special effect introduced by the German composer Richard Strauss).

tonic   The main note of a key, such as C in the key of C Major or minor; the first note or keynote of the scale.

tonic chord   A triad built on the tonic (first) note of the scale; usually used as the first and last chord of a song or movement.

topical songs   A popular song or folk song that comments on current social or political events. They are often protest songs. A topical song that reached number one in 1966 was Staff Sergeant Barry Sadler's "Ballad of the Green Berets."

Tosca   Italian opera composed in three acts by Giacomo Puccini, with libretto by Luigi Illica. First produced in Rome in 1900, it is currently one of the most loved and performed operas in the operatic repertoire, being number eight in Opera America's 2008 list of the most-performed operas in North America.

Toscanini, Arturo (1867–1957)   Italian conductor who was one of the most famous and respected of all classical artists in the twentieth century. His intensity, perfectionism, and attention to detail was renowned, and his interpretation of the greatest composers' works was legendary. He was most famous for being the NBC Symphony Orchestra's first music director in 1937.

touch   The dexterity and sensitivity to pressure used by the player of the instrument in relation to the dynamics needed in the interpretative performance of a composition. When used in music, it is the approach and feel the performer has when fingering the piano, playing the keys or valves on a wind instrument, or hitting a mallet or stick on a percussion instrument.

Townshend, Pete (b. 1945)   Songwriter, guitarist, and vocalist for the English rock group the Who. His 40-year career has earned him Grammy and Tony awards, and he has performed on 35 albums for which he wrote more than 100 songs. Some of his most famous solo recordings include "Rough Boys," "Slit Skirts," and "Let My Love Open the Door."

tracker action   The mechanical key action used in organs made before 1900. A wooden rod in the windchest connects the key to the organ's pipe valve.

transcription   1. The notation of music from a sound source such as an improvised jazz solo, indigenous folk music (see Béla Bartók), or nature sounds such as bird calls. 2. The rewriting of a composition for an instrument it was not originally intended for, such as an ensemble into a solo or a solo into an ensemble.

transformation   When a performer, composer, or analyst transforms a piece of music into something else. Some types of transformations include inversions, transpositions, rotation, multiplication, and permutation.

transistor radio   A radio receiver that uses transistors instead of vacuum tubes. First demonstrated to the public in 1947, it was more portable and much lighter than radios using heavy vacuum tubes.

transition   Also called a bridge, a passage that connects two sections of a composition.

transposing instruments   A method used with wind instruments where the music is written in a key or octave other than what is actually sounded. For example, the B♭ clarinet playing a C-Major scale would sound one step lower in B♭ Major.

transposition   Changing the key of a composition by moving all the notes to another key. The two different methods are scalar and chromatic transposition. *See also* modulation.

transverse flute   Another name for the modern flute, compared to the recorder.

trap drums   Set of drums used in jazz, rock, and popular music bands; includes a bass drum (with foot pedal), snare drum, tenor drums cymbals, and so on.

traps   Special-effect instruments usually used in the percussion section. Examples of these include the cowbell, whistle, whip crack, thunder machine, and so on.

Traviata, La   Italian opera composed in three acts by Giuseppi Verdi, with libretto by Francesco Maria Piave, based on Alexandre Dumas' novel *La dame aux Camélias*. First produced in Venice in 1853, it was first considered a failure. It is now the third most popular opera performed according to Opera America's list of the 20 most-performed operas in North America.

treble clef The top half of a grand staff. The right hand of the piano plays in this clef as well as most high voices and instruments (as opposed to the bass clef, which is used for the left hand and most lower voices and instruments).

tremolo (It., tremulous) Effect created when a single note of a string instrument is played by repetitive up-and-down strokes of the bow.

triad A chord consisting of the root, third, and fifth notes of a scale. The four different triads are the major, minor, diminished, and augmented triads.

triangle A percussion instrument (idiophone) made from a metal bar and bent in the shape of a triangle. It is held by a string or wire and is struck with a metal beater, producing a high-pitched ringing sound.

trill A musical ornamentation indicating the rapid alternation between two notes a whole or half step apart; originated in the sixteenth century.

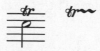

trio 1. A composition played by three performers. 2. The second part of a *scherzo* or minuet movement of a sonata. 3. The three parts of a contrapuntal (piece using counterpoint) composition, such as Johann Sebastian Bach's six Trio Sonatas for the organ.

triphongs   The vocalized unification of three vowels in one sound.

triple concerto   A musical composition written for orchestra and three solo instruments, such as Ludwig van Beethoven's Concerto for Violin, Cello, and Piano, op. 56.

triple meter   Three musical beats to a bar or measure. The time signatures of 3/4 and 9/8 are the most common.

triple stop   A string technique where the bow is drawn across three of the strings at the same time, creating a chord. *See also* double and single stops.

triple time   *See* triple meter.

triplet   Three notes grouped together, noted with a slur and a 3, and performed in place of or in the same time allotted for two of the same kind of notes.

Tristan und Isolde   German opera composed in three acts by Richard Wagner to his own libretto; first produced in Munich in 1865.

tritone   The same as an augmented fourth or diminished fifth, such as C to F♯.

Trittico, Il   A collection of three short operas by Giacomo Puccini. These operas are *Il tabarro*, *Suor Angelica*, and *Gianni Schicchi*. They were first produced together in New York City in 1918.

trombone   Moderately low brass instrument used in symphonic orchestras, jazz, and big-band ensembles. The trombone uses an elongated tube and a telescopic slide, which changes the pitches. The tenor and the bass trombones are the most common, and both are pitched in B♭. There is also a valve trombone, which is more popular in Europe, India, and South America.

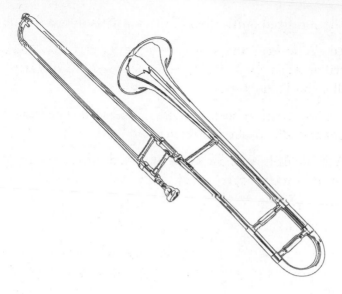

troubadours　Also called minstrels, troubadours were poets and performers of songs that came from Occitania (southern France and parts of Spain and Italy) around 1100 to 1350 C.E. Their songs and storytelling usually dealt with courtly love and chivalry, and they often entertained at weddings and fairs. Called *trouvères* in northern France and *meistersingers* in Germany.

trouvères　*See* troubadours.

trumpet　The highest brass instrument, pitched in B♭, which is oblong in shape and produces a bright, piercing sound with three rotary or piston valves. One of the oldest musical instruments, it dates back to before 1500 B.C.E. Used in classical, jazz, and other forms of music, the trumpet evolved from the natural trumpet, which had no valves. These were used in the military (bugle) and for hunting.

tuba The lowest and largest of the brass instruments, the tuba first appeared in modern symphony orchestras in the mid-nineteenth century, replacing the ophicleide. It's used in orchestras, polka, Dixieland jazz, and other bands.

tubular bells   Also known as chimes, tubular bells are part of the percussion family of musical instruments. The song "Carol of the Bells" and, of course, "Tubular Bells," the opening theme to the movie *The Exorcist*, are examples of tubular bells being played.

tune   1. A melody or song. 2. To adjust a musical instrument to the proper tone frequency using a fixed reference, such as A = 440 Hz (440 vibrations per second). "Out of tune" indicates when the tone is on either the high or low side of a fixed reference.

tunefulness   If a sound has the property of music; melodious.

tuning   In ear training, the voice technique of matching pitches is used for tuning. To tune a wind instrument, shortening or lengthening the tube will lower or raise the pitch. With string instruments, turning the tuning peg will tighten or loosen the string and raise or lower the pitch.

tuning fork   A device used to tune a musical instrument. Made from steel with two prongs, new tuning forks are usually made at the international pitch of A, which has a tuning of 440 vibrations per second.

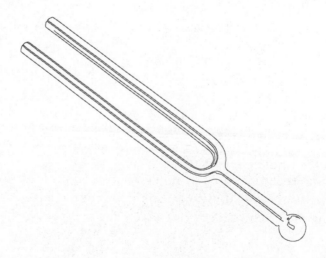

Turandot Italian opera in three acts (unfinished) composed by Giacomo Puccini, with libretto based on a play by Carlo Gozzi. This opera was finished by Franco Alfani; produced in Milan, Italy, in 1926; and conducted by Arturo Toscanini.

turn A short musical ornamentation that starts on the note above the indicated pitch, the pitch itself, the note below the pitch, and back to the designated pitch. It's designated by an S lying on its side above the staff.

Turn of the Screw, The English opera composed in two acts (and prologue) by Benjamin Britten, with libretto by Myfanwy Piper based on the novella by Henry James. It was first produced in Venice in 1954.

Turner, Tina (b. 1939) American singer and actress whose nickname "The Queen of Rock 'n' Roll" comes from five decades of singing in rock bands. She is "one of the greatest singers of all time," according to *Rolling Stone* magazine, and has sold around 200 million records. Three of her most famous songs are "Private Dancer," "Proud Mary," and "What's Love Got to Do with It?"

tutti (It., all together) Musical instruction asking for the entire orchestra and/or chorus to play at the same time.

tutti

twelve-bar blues A popular progression of chords used in popular, blues, and jazz music that are based on a key's I-IV-V chords. Songs with twelve-bar blues chord progressions include "Shake, Rattle and Roll," "In the Mood," and "Why Don't We Do It in the Road."

twelve-tone technique System of composition invented by Arnold Schoenberg around 1920. Also called "serial" music, it is derived from using the 12 chromatic tones of a scale in a special order. *See* tone row.

twentieth-century music   The different styles of music invented between 1900 and 2000. Some of these styles include serial music, atonality, expressionism, neoclassicism, musique concrète, and aleatory and electronic music. This term usually does not refer to popular forms such as jazz, musical theater, rock, and so on.

T

U

Un ballo in maschera (It., *A Masked Ball*) Italian opera composed by Giuseppe Verdi in three acts, with libretto written by Antonio Somma. First produced in Rome in 1859, the story involves the murder of an English count in Boston and is based on the real-life assassination of King Gustav III of Sweden.

una corda (*u.c.*; It., one string) A musical direction for the pianist to play with the soft pedal (leftmost pedal) depressed.

underscore A type of background music used to enhance the mood of, for example, a soap opera or news bulletin. Atmosphere-enhancing music that does not use a strong melody or orchestration to distract from the main focus.

unequal voices The mixing of different voice types in a choral work.

"unfinished" symphony An incomplete symphony work usually lacking one or more movements. The most famous work to use this title is Franz Schubert's Symphony No. 8 in B Minor, which he began writing in 1822 but abandoned after finishing only two movements. It is considered one of the composer's greatest orchestral works.

unison The playing of the same note by various instruments or voices, either on the exact same pitch or at the octave.

up-tempo   A fast and exciting song with active rhythms found in blues, R&B, and soul music. James Brown and Marvin Gaye are two artists who performed up-tempo songs.

upbeat   The first notes of a melody that occur before the first measure. It is also the last beat of a musical measure that sets up the following measure.

urban music   A radio format used in large cities that plays mostly contemporary R&B, hip hop, and rap. Stations playing "urban contemporary" focus this type of music and marketing on 18- to 34-year-old African Americans.

utility music   Music composed for a specific practical purpose, such as a political rally, military function, wedding ceremony, or for a student or amateur musician to play.

Valkyrie, The (G., *Die Walküre*)   Second of the four German operas that make up the opera cycle *Der Ring des Nibelungen.* Composed by Richard Wagner with his own libretto taken from Norse mythology. First produced in Munich, Germany, in 1870.

valve   Invented in 1815, the mechanism on a brass instrument that allows the player to produce all the tones of the chromatic scale by increasing or decreasing the length of the tube in which the air passes. Most brass instruments use three valves (sometimes four) and can have one of two types: the piston valve or the rotary valve.

valve instruments   Any instrument that uses piston or rotary valves. This includes most brass instruments except the slide trombone.

vamp   The continued repetition of a section or musical figure (usually simple chords), used mostly in jazz, musical theater, blues, and rock. In hip-hop, it is called a "loop"; in classical music, it is called "ostinato."

vamp till cue   A term used in jazz or musical theater referring to a music passage of one or a few bars that is repeated until the performer or conductor is ready to begin or move to the next part of the song.

Van Halen   Hard-rock band formed in the United States in 1972. They have sold more than 90 million albums and were one of the leading hard-rock touring bands. Members have included Eddie Van Halen, David Lee Roth, and Sammy Hagar. "Runnin' with the Devil," "Dance the Night Away," and "Jump" are some of their biggest hits.

variation   Musical material that is first altered then repeated. This change in orchestration can involve harmonic, melodic, rhythm, or timbre variations. This technique has been used in various forms such as the *chaconne, passacaglia*, and theme and variations. Famous examples of variations include Johann Sebastian Bach's (1685–1750) *Goldberg Variations* and Johannes Brahms' (1833–1897) *Variations on a Theme by Haydn.*

vaudeville   A favorite theatrical style in Canada and the United States from the 1880s to the 1930s. A variety show developed from minstrel shows, burlesque, freak shows, concert saloons, and other types of popular entertainments, vaudeville presented all types of different acts and entertainment. Musicians, acrobats, magicians, trained animals, and so on could all be used in one vaudeville show.

Vaughan, Sarah (1924–1990)   American jazz singer famous for her renditions of songs such as "Tenderly," "Misty," and "Whatever Lola Wants." Her voice was known for its rich and beautiful contralto (low female voice range) tone. She was considered jazz royalty, earning the nicknames "The Divine One" and "Sassy."

Vaughan, Stevie Ray (1954–1990)   American guitarist, songwriter, and singer. He was one of music history's most influential blues guitar players, ranked 7 in *Rolling Stone* magazine's 100 Greatest Guitarists of All Time.

veejays   Television personalities made famous in the early 1980s by the MTV (Music Television) network. These personalities introduce and comment on music videos made to market the music of individual musical groups.

Venetian school   Composed of Flemish and Italian sixteenth-century composers working in Venice, this school was known for its affinity for innovative thinking, the use of chromaticism, progressive use of instruments and echo effects, and freer use of modulation. Adrian Willaert (1490–1562), Giovanni Gabrieli (1555–1612), and German composer Michael Praetorius (1571–1621) were some of the important composers from this school.

Verdi, Giuseppi (1813–1901)   Italian opera composer of the romantic period whose 28 operas were a great influence on other composers of the nineteenth century. Many of his operas are still performed today, with *La Traviata*, *Rigoletto*, *Il trovatore*, *Aida*, *Otello*, and *Falstaff* being his most popular.

verismo opera   A post–romantic period (late-1900) Italian opera style meaning "realism." Verismo's main function is to convey the character's feelings, the scenery, and the action and can be found in the operas *Cavalleria Rusticana* (1890) by Pietro Mascagni, *Pagliacci* (1892) by Ruggero Leoncavallo, and *Tosca* (1900) by Giacomo Puccini.

verse   In popular music, the verse is a poetic stanza when two parts of the music have identical music but different words. Often used in verse-chorus form, the verse is also a strophic (repeating) form used in religious hymns.

vespers   An evening prayer service of Catholic and Protestant churches that have interested many prominent composers to write music for it. Seasonal hymns and sacred holiday music are sung at the popular vesper services held around the world during the Christmas season.

vibraphone   Also called "vibes," a member of the percussion family of musical instruments related to the marimba and xylophone. It is made of aluminum bars instead of wood, uses resonator tubes (with motor-driven butterfly valves for vibrato), and is connected to a sustain pedal. Vibraphones are used mostly in jazz. Milt Jackson and Lionel Hampton were the two most famous jazz vibes players.

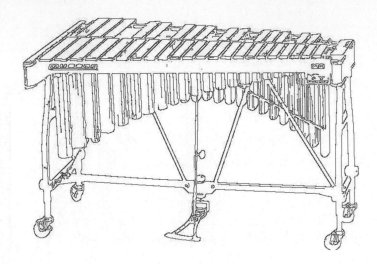

vibration   A reaction a rigid surface has to something touching it (forced vibration), such as the body of a violin vibrating when bowing the strings. Also, a vibration is a sympathetic reaction to natural frequencies where the resonator and vibrator have identical sympathetic vibrations.

vibrato   Oscillation of sound molecules between two tones or pitches, which gives buoyancy, vitality, and richness of tone to a given instrument or voice.

vide (L., to see)   A musical direction often used in operatic music scores, indicating an omission of music between two locations in the composition. An example is, "go immediately from *Vi—* to the place marked *—de*."

Viennese classical school   Composers who worked and were active in Vienna, Austria, from about 1770 to about 1825. This school included composers such as Haydn, Beethoven, and Mozart.

viol   Abbreviation of "viola da gamba." Shaped much like today's cello, it was the biggest of the violin family. The name *viola* was a generic name for most of the string instruments in the baroque and renaissance periods but was later identified as the viola da gamba (bass violin) and later the cello.

viola The second or alto member of the violin family of instruments. One seventh larger and tuned a fifth lower than a violin, it plays the inner parts of the ensemble and is not often used as a solo instrument. The name *viola* was a generic name for most of the string instruments in the baroque and renaissance periods but became known as the viola da braccio (alto violin) and later just viola.

violin The most important member of the string family, it is an essential part of the orchestra and chamber ensemble as well as a solo instrument. Its extreme dynamic range and sensitive timbre lends itself to a variety of musical genres, including jazz, classical, bluegrass, rock, country, and more. Not until Antonio Stradivari (1644–1737) started making violins around 1700 did it assume its current shape.

violoncello   A member of the string family similar in appearance to the violin but approximately twice as large and tuned an octave and a fourth lower. It is tuned in fifths like its smaller family member, the viola, and is typically made of spruce and other woods.

virginal A small harpsichord with a rectangle shape and no legs, popular in Italy and northern Europe in the renaissance and medieval periods.

virtuoso An excellent or brilliant performer with superior technical ability on his or her instrument.

vivace (It., vivacious) A brisk, lively tempo that is a little faster than allegro.

Vivaldi, Antonio (1678–1741) Italian baroque composer, violinist, and priest (called "The Red Priest" because of his red hair) who was a prolific composer of opera and orchestral works. His most famous was a series of four violin concerti called *The Four Seasons*.

vocal chords A muscular valve located in the larynx (voice box) which, when activated by air passing through the glottis (space between the folds), causes phonation (sound vibration caused by the vocal folds). Also called vocal folds.

vocal disorder Any physical, medical, or neurological dysfunction of the singing or speaking apparatus that affects pitch, intensity (loudness), or quality (resonance). These include laryngitis (caused by fatigue and inflammation of the vocal folds), vocal lesions, hemorrhage or paralysis, cancer, a virus, nodules, polyps, sores, acid reflux, and sinusitis. Other vocal disorders include stuttering, a lisp, cleft palate, or stage fright.

vocal endurance The ability to sing for a set length of time without fatigue or poor after-effects; a reflection of correct vocal technique and coordinated vocal muscles.

vocal faults Flaws in the voice caused by poor physical coordination, bad physical and vocal habits, and wrongly applied concepts.

vocal folds *See* vocal chords.

vocal music Music composed specifically for the solo or choral voice.

vocal range How high or low a particular voice can phonate; also called a "voice register." There are three female voice ranges, from highest to lowest: soprano, mezzo-soprano, and contralto; and three male voices: tenor, baritone, and bass.

vocalist A person who sings or augments regular speech to produce musical sound; a singer.

vocalization The act of "warming up" or exercising the voice.

vocalize Also called a "vocal exercise," they help to strengthen and coordinate the voice by repetitive use of all the muscles used for singing. Effective vocalizes are designed to develop specific vocal skills, such as vocalizing a scale up and down on the vowel "ah."

voice A result of rapidly contracting and expanding air particles. The process starts when the vocal folds or musical instrument's vibrator (reed or mouthpiece) allows air to pass through it. The end product of the voice is a result of this mechanical process of phonation.

voice box   Slang for the larynx—the place in the throat that holds the vocal folds.

voice exchange   The exchange of a melody from one instrument or voice to another; for example, when sopranos sing the melody in the first verse and tenors sing the melody in the second verse.

voice-leading   A decision the arranger makes when deciding which instrument plays which melody or harmony in its progression from one chord to the next.

voicing   In piano tuning, voicing refers to the adjustment of the hammer felts to produce the best sound. With an organ, it is the adjustment of the pitch and timbre of an organ's pipes.

volta brackets   Notation placed over the last measures of a repeated section of music indicating a first or second ending to that section.

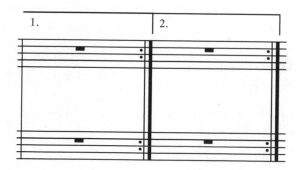

volume   The quantity of sound produced relative to one's hearing ability. In music, it is a measure of intensity and instrumental acoustics. Electronic amplification produces much louder volume than natural acoustics.

voluntary   An English organ composition played at a church service. It's most often performed between the psalm reading and the first lesson.

Wagner, Richard (1813–1883)   German composer and conductor known for his use of chromaticism, leitmotifs (short musical themes depicting a certain character, emotion, plot element, or location), and orchestration in his many operas, especially his four-opera cycle *Der Ring des Nibelungen*. He produced most of his operas in the opera house he built, the Bayreuth Festspielhaus. He was a major influence on all composers who followed him.

Wagner tuba   Brass instrument invented by Richard Wagner that combines the elements of both the tuba and the horn. Invented to meet the needs of Wagner's four operas in the cycle *Der Ring des Nibelungen*, this instrument uses rotary valves and is pitched in the keys of B♭ and F.

wah-wah pedal   Invented in 1966, a guitar special-effects pedal that makes the instrument mimic the sound of the human voice. The up and down frequency sweep, called a "spectral glide," happens when the pedal is pushed to cause "the wah effect."

walking bass   A style of double bass or electric bass accompaniment most common in jazz. The player "walks" a series of quarter notes in straight, unsyncopated time up and down scales, arpeggios, and chromatic runs to help outline the song's chord progression.

Walkman   A personal audio cassette stereo invented in 1978 by the Sony Corporation that changed people's listening habits by allowing them to carry their music around with them and listen to it without other people hearing. In 2007, Sony introduced the video Walkman, an all-digital video player called the A800 series.

Wall of Sound   A 1960s recording technique developed by record producer Phil Spector that records more than one instrument on a part, or a big orchestration, all while running everything through an echo chamber.

Waller, Thomas "Fats" (1904–1943)   American jazz pianist and composer who was one of the most popular performers of his time. Famous in both the United States and Europe, he wrote hit songs such as "Ain't Misbehavin'," "Honeysuckle Rose," and "The Joint Is Jumpin'."

waltz   An Austrian dance developed from a peasant dance around 1800. It is set in a moderate 3/4 time and has been the inspiration for many composers. Frédéric Chopin (1810–1849) and especially Johann Strauss (1804–1849) were famous for their waltzes.

warming up   Flexing of the muscles needed to sing or play an instrument; meant to help ease the muscles into movement so they will be able to perform at a higher level.

Water Music   Orchestral suites composed by George Frideric Handel in 1717, performed on boats on the Thames River for a party put together by King George I.

Waters, Muddy (1913–1983)   Born McKinley Morganfield, an American blues musician known as "the Father of Chicago Blues." He was an important inspiration in the 1960s blues explosion in England. *Rolling Stone* magazine ranked him number 17 in its 100 Greatest Artists of All Time, and he was awarded six Grammy Awards (all in the folk genre). Three of his most famous songs include "Hoochie Coochie Man," "Got My Mojo Working," and "Rollin' Stone."

wavelength   Related to both velocity of sound and frequency of pitch. It's the distance it takes for a sound wave's shape to repeat.

Webber, Andrew Lloyd (b. 1948)   English composer of musical theater. He has written 13 musicals and been awarded 7 Tony Awards, 3 Grammy Awards, and an Oscar. Three of his most famous musicals are *The Phantom of the Opera, Jesus Christ Superstar,* and *Cats.*

Weber, Carl Maria von (1786–1826)   German composer known for his innovative composition and orchestral techniques that influenced many of the romantic period's composers, including Felix Mendelssohn, Franz Liszt, and Frédéric Chopin. He wrote the opera *Der Freischütz* and the concerto Konzerstück (Concert Piece) in F Minor.

Webern, Anton (1883–1945)   Austrian composer of the 12-tone technique influential in forming the musical technique of total serialism. He was a student of Arnold Schoenberg and a member of the Second Viennese School.

Weill, Kurt (1900–1950)   German American composer of stage and concert works. He was the composer of the musicals *Street Scene* and *Lost in the Stars* and many famous songs, including "Mack the Knife" and "September Song."

Welk, Lawrence (1903–1992)   American bandleader, accordian player, and television personality, he was the host of *The Lawrence Welk Show* from 1955 to 1982. His orchestra, singers, and dancers performed arrangements of popular tunes, polkas, and novelty songs. His conservative style was family-oriented easy listening.

Well-Tempered Clavier, The   A collection of keyboard music composed by Johann Sebastian Bach (1685–1750). There are two books, each with fugues and preludes written in 24 major and minor keys. It is one of the most influential works written in music history.

whisper   A breathy, toneless vocal quality where vocal fold tension is at a minimum.

whistle   1. When sound is created by blowing air through shaped lips. 2. Instrument (aerophone) that makes sound when air is forced into it. Different types include dog whistles, train whistles, sports whistles, and steam whistles.

whistle flute   Another name for a "fipple" flute with a stopper in the upper end of the pipe. The recorder is a whistle flute.

whistle register   The "altissimo" or highest pitches possible in a human voice. Mariah Carey and Minnie Riperton ("Loving You") are famous for their whistle registers.

white noise   A hissing sound much like the sound of a waterfall or a blank television channel. It can be found in the production of electronic music and a cymbal's crash, which has similar noise content in its frequency range.

whole note   A length a pitch is held, equal to four quarter notes and notated as an open oval note.

whole rest   Pause or space equivalent to the length of one whole note, two half notes, or four quarter notes.

whole tone   The distance between two pitches on a scale. A whole tone equals 2 semitones (half steps), 4 microtones (quarter step), or 100 cents (extremely small tuning intervals).

whole-tone scale   A musical scale with notes that are separated by an interval of a whole step.

Williams, Andy (b. 1927)   American pop singer and television personality whose solo career started in 1952. He is famous for the beauty of his warm baritone voice and has 3 platinum records and 18 gold records. Some of his most famous hits include "Moon River," "Can't Get Used to Losing You," and "Butterfly."

Williams, John (b. 1932)   American composer and conductor famous for his many successful film scores over a 50-year period. His most famous films include *Star Wars, Superman, Raiders of the Lost Ark, Schindler's List, Jurassic Park, E.T. the Extra-Terrestrial*, and *Harry Potter*. He's the winner of 5 Oscars and 21 Grammy Awards.

Wilson, Meredith (1902–1984)   American composer, conductor, and playwright famous for his Broadway musicals *The Music Man* and *The Unsinkable Molly Brown*.

wind band   Also called a "wind ensemble," it consists of brass, woodwind, and percussion and has evolved over the years from military bands and minor roles in the orchestra to large ensembles whose composers, such as John Philip Sousa (1854–1932), started composing just for them. This has brought a need for better instruments and more advanced compositions. Many compositions have been arranged for wind ensemble from orchestral scores, such as *Carmina Burana* by Carl Orff (1895–1982).

wind chest   An airtight box on an organ that controls the air sent to the pipes from the bellows.

wind instruments   Also known as an aerophone, wind instruments are musical instruments with an enclosed column of air that makes a sound when set into vibration. These include both the brass and woodwind families.

wind machine   Machine that imitates the sound of wind; sometimes used in descriptive orchestral pieces, such as Richard Strauss' *Don Quixote*.

Winterreise   A set of 24 German lieder (songs) composed by Franz Schubert in 1827. They are romantic songs about a man rejected by his lover and feeling lonely in wintertime.

wirbel   1. A rapid succession of notes or drum roll. 2. The peg or pegbox on a violin.

wobble   A result of poor muscular coordination during phonation (making a sound), causing erratic tonal movement.

wolf   A disagreeable effect that results from an instrument's imperfect tuning. The difference in intensity and pitch (the wolf-note) between two different instruments (such as violin and cello) or two pipes of an organ. A wolf is caused by an inherent defect in an instrument's design.

W

Wonder, Stevie (b. 1950)   American songwriter, keyboardist, and singer who has recorded with Motown Records since he was 11. He has won 22 Grammy Awards and recorded more than 30 top-10 hit singles. Three of those hits include "You Are the Sunshine of My Life," "Signed, Sealed, Delivered, I'm Yours," and "Ebony and Ivory."

woodshedding   Rehearsing or practicing in private to gain technical mastery of an instrument before a performance or jam session.

woodwinds   One of the musical families of instruments in an orchestra. They include single-reed instruments (saxes and clarinets), double-reed instruments (oboes and bassoons), and flutes. These instruments can be made from wood, metal, or plastic and sound when air is blown in the opening (mouthpiece) and vibrates the resonator.

word painting   Also called text painting, used especially in baroque music compositions where the words are expressed in the music. The two types of word painting include songs that imitate natural sounds, such as birds or laughing, and songs that imitate physical movements, such as running or descending a hill.

work songs   Songs connected to certain kinds of work. For example, workers on a railroad would sing to coordinate the timing of laying track. African American slaves picking cotton would sing to alleviate boredom and pass the day faster. Work songs include sea shanties and street cries.

world beat   Beginning in the mid-1980s with musicians such as Paul Simon and Peter Gabriel, world beat fuses folk music from around the world with rock and pop influences.

world music   Music from different countries from all over the world. World music is traditional music using ethnic or folk styles and indigenous musicians. This term was invented in the 1980s as a way to market and sell non-Western music.

Wozzeck   German opera composed in three acts by Alban Berg to his own libretto. Produced in Berlin in 1925, the opera's setting is 1830s Germany. *Wozzeck* was written in an atonal style.

Xerxes An Italian opera composed in three acts by George Frideric Handel, with libretto by Silvio Stampiglia. First performed in 1738 in London, the story takes place in Persia (Iran) in 480 B.C.E. and was originally written for a castrato (male soprano singer castrated at a young age to retain his high voice) but is now sung by either a counter-tenor (male falsetto singer) or mezzo-soprano (female with a lower voice).

xylophone A percussion instrument made of wooden blocks of different sizes and shapes that are set in such a way as to form a musical scale, much like a keyboard, and struck with a mallet or stick to produce a musical tone. The xylophone is used in symphony, musical theater, and jazz music.

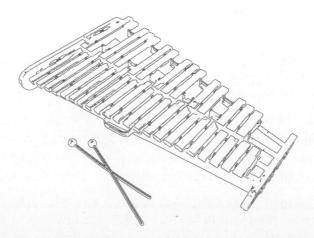

Y

"Yankee Doodle"   A patriotic song of the American Revolutionary War that originated in the Seven Years War (1754–1763) in Europe. The song is currently Connecticut's state anthem.

yodeling   A singing technique that rapidly switches back and forth from the chest voice to the falsetto range. This technique most likely originated in the Swiss Alps as a means of communication and was later incorporated into their folk music. Famous examples are the "yodel-ay-HEE-hoo" Alpine call and the movie character Tarzan's "aaaaah-AH-ah-AH-aaaaah-AH-ah-AH-aaaaaah" jungle call.

Young, Lester (1909–1959)   American jazz legend who played tenor saxophone and, less frequently, clarinet. Also known by the nickname "Prez," he was a member of Count Basie's Orchestra and one of the most influential performers of the early jazz era. With his porkpie hats, eccentric manner, and unique lingo, Young epitomized for some the "hipster" life—the jazz performer's cool lifestyle of the 1940s.

Young, Neil (b. 1945)   Canadian singer and songwriter famous for his guitar playing and falsetto voice. Later named the "Godfather of Grunge," he often changed his musical styles from folk, acoustic, and hard rock to jazz, electronic, and blues. Formerly a member of the rock groups Buffalo

Springfield and Crosby, Stills, Nash and Young, his solo albums *Harvest* and *After the Gold Rush* were hits in the early 1970s.

Young Person's Guide to the Orchestra, The   A popular orchestral work by Benjamin Britten written in 1946 and often accompanied by a narrator. Based on a melody by Henry Purcell (1659–1695), the work highlights the characteristics of each instrument in the orchestra.

Z

Zaide   An unfinished opera by Wolfgang Amadeus Mozart, with libretto by Johann Andreas Schachtner. Mozart began the opera in 1779 but abandoned it to work on another opera, *Idomeneo*. *Zaide* includes spoken dialogue, which technically makes it a singspiel, or "singing play." The opera is set in Turkey, and despite lacking an overture and third act, is performed today as a complete opera by adding other Mozart operatic music.

Zappa, Frank (1940–1993)   American guitarist, composer, and producer whose experimental and eclectic style was a combination of electronic, rock, jazz, and classical genres. He led his band, the Mothers of Invention, from 1964 to 1975.

zarzuela   A Spanish form of musical drama that differs from opera in that the music alternates with spoken dialogue. Developed in the early seventeenth century, the genre was named after the Palace of La Zarzuela, a royal estate outside Madrid. The form had a revival in the mid-nineteenth century and remains popular throughout the Spanish-speaking world.

Zauberflöte, Die   *See Magic Flute, The.*

Zawinul, Joe (1932–2007)   Austrian jazz composer and keyboardist who was instrumental in developing jazz fusion (a mixture of jazz, rock, and world music). He revolutionized the use of the synthesizer in jazz, had important collaborations with Miles Davis, and co-founded the renowned fusion group Weather Report.

zero audibility The lowest level of sound that can be heard by human ears, equal to 0 decibels.

zils Small metal jingles on the side of a tambourine (percussion instrument) or finger cymbals used by belly dancers.

zither A stringed musical instrument used in Austria, Hungary, Slovenia, Germany, and China. A zither is a member of the "citre" family of string instruments, whose strings do not extend past the frame of the sounding box (such as the autoharp, harpsichord, and piano).

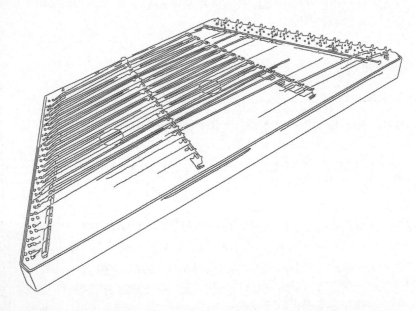

ZZ Top American blues-rock group formed in Texas in 1969 consisting of Billy Gibbons (lead guitar and lead vocals), Dusty Hill (bass, keyboards, and vocals), and Frank Beard (drums). In their four decades of performing, they have made 20 albums and had their biggest commercial success in the 1970s and 1980s. Their trademark sunglasses and long beards make ZZ Top one of the most recognizable bands in the music business. "Tush" and "Sharp-Dressed Man" are two of their big hits.

Appendix A

Resources

A compilation of recommended books and websites for your ongoing exploration of music.

Country

For country enthusiasts, a who's who of country music.

Carlin, Richard. *Country Music: A Biographical Dictionary*. New York: Routledge, 2002.

Guitar

Start building your guitar library here and check out some helpful Internet sites.

Burrows, Terry. *Play Rock Guitar: The Complete Guide to Playing, Recording and Performing All Styles of Rock*. London: Carlton Books, 2002.

Cutchin, Rusty, and Paco Pena. *The Definitive Guitar Handbook: Comprehensive—Amateur and Pro—Acoustic and Electric—Rock, Blues, Jazz, Country, Folk* (Handbook Series). London: Flame Tree, 2009.

Denyer, Ralph. *The Guitar Handbook*. New York: Knopf, 1992.

Chord Master: Application for iPhone & iPod Touch
Learn guitar chords on your iPhone.
www.planetwaves.com/PWChordMaster.Page

Guitar Tricks: On-Line Guitar Lessons
www.guitartricks.com/

Guitar Tuner
www.gieson.com/Library/projects/utilities/tuner/

Jazz

In-depth resources for jazzers.

Tomaro, Mike. *Instrumental Jazz Arranging: A Comprehensive and Practical Guide.* New York: Hal Leonard, 2009.

Tirro, Frank. *Jazz: A History, Second Edition.* New York: W.W. Norton, 1993.

Your Guide to Jazz Guitar
www.jazzguitar.be/

Performance and Practicing

Suggested reading for all-around advice and inspiration.

Bruser, Madeline. *The Art of Practicing: A Guide to Making Music from the Heart.* New York: Bell Tower, 1997.

Elson, Margret. *Passionate Practice: The Musician's Guide to Learning, Memorizing, and Performing.* Oakland, CA: Regent Press, 2002.

Green, Barry. *The Inner Game of Music.* Garden City, NY: Doubleday, 1986.

———. *The Mastery of Music: Ten Pathways to True Artistry.* New York: Broadway Books, 2003.

Greene, Don. *Performance Success: Performing Your Best Under Pressure.* New York: Routledge, 2002.

Klickstein, Gerald. *The Musician's Way: A Guide to Practice, Performance, and Wellness.* New York: Oxford University Press, 2009.

Werner, Kenny. *Effortless Mastery: Liberating the Master Musician Within.* New Albany, IN: Jamey Aebersold Jazz, 1996.

Westney, William. *The Perfect Wrong Note: Learning to Trust Your Musical Self.* Pompton Plains, NJ: Amadeus Press, 2003.

Piano

A short list of interesting resources for piano students of all ages.

Cooke, James Francis. *Great Pianists on Piano Playing.* Whitefish, MT: Kessinger Publishing, 2008.

Gerig, Reginald R. *Famous Pianists and Their Technique, New Edition.* Bloomington, IN: Indiana University Press, 2007.

Hinson, Maurice. *Guide to the Pianist's Repertoire, Third Edition.* Bloomington, IN: Indiana University Press, 2001.

———. *The Pianist's Dictionary.* Bloomington, IN: Indiana University Press, 2004.

Rosen, Charles. *Piano Notes: The World of the Pianist.* New York: Free Press, 2004.

Free On-Line Piano Lessons
www.gopiano.com

Virtual Piano
www.cmagics.com/beta/piano/

Religious

Reference works for the church musician's bookshelf.

Capuchin, Edward, Mark Bangert, Melva Costen, and Mark Kligman. *Worship Music: A Concise Dictionary* (Reference Works), Collegeville, MN: Liturgical Press, 2000.

Swain, Joseph P. *Historical Dictionary of Sacred Music (Historical Dictionaries of Literature and the Arts)*. Lanham, MD: Scarecrow Press, 2006

Rock

Suggested reading for detailed information about rock 'n' roll.

Phillips, William, and Brian Cogan. *Encyclopedia of Heavy Metal Music*. Santa Barbara, CA: Greenwood, 2009.

Campbell, Michael. *Rock and Roll: An Introduction, Second Edition*. Belmont, CA: Thomson-Schirmer, 2008.

Tech

A handy reference book for music techies.

Gallagher, Mitch. *The Music Tech Dictionary: A Glossary of Audio-Related Terms and Technologies*. Florence, KY: Course Technology PTR, 2008.

Theory

A sampling of reference books and websites about theory, the nuts and bolts of music.

Black, Dave, and Tom Gerou. *Essential Dictionary of Orchestration* (The Essential Dictionary Series). Van Nuys, CA: Alfred, 1998.

Gerou, Tom, and Linda Lusk. *Essential Dictionary of Music Notation: The Most Practical and Concise Source for Music Notation* (The Essential Dictionary Series). Van Nuys, CA: Alfred, 1996.

Harnsberger, L. C. *Essential Dictionary of Music Theory: Handy Guide* (Essential Dictionary Series). Van Nuys, CA: Alfred, 1996.

Wyatt, Keith, and Carl Schroeder. *Hal Leonard Pocket Music Theory: A Comprehensive and Convenient Source for All Musicians.* New York: Hal Leonard, 2002.

———. *Harmony and Theory: A Comprehensive Source for All Musicians* (Essential Concepts-Musicians Institute). New York: Hal Leonard, 1998.

The Lesson Room: An interactive resource library with videos, sheet music, and articles. Excellent reference.
www.emusictheory.com

Music Theory and History Online (Dr. Brian Blood)
www.dolmetsch.com/theoryintro.htm

Music Theory Online: An interactive college preparatory distance-learning theory course.
http://music-theory.com

Ricci Adams' Musictheory.net: An excellent interactive reference for everything you want to know about music theory.
www.musictheory.net

Vocal

Insightful reading and detailed reference books for singers and singing teachers.

Brennan, Richard. *The Alexander Technique: A Step-by-Step Guide to Improve Breathing, Posture and Well-Being.* Boston: Journey Editions, 1996.

Emmons, Shirlee. *Power Performance for Singers: Transcending the Barriers.* New York: Oxford University Press, 1998.

Emmons, Shirlee, and Stanley Sonntag. *The Art of the Song Recital.* New York: Waveland Press, 2002.

Fleming, Renée. *The Inner Voice: The Making of a Singer.* New York: Penguin, 2005.

Hines, Jerome. *Great Singers on Great Singing.* New York, NY: Limelight Editions, 1984.

Kimball, Carol. *Song: A Guide to Art Song Style and Literature.* Milwaukee, WI: Hal Leonard, 2006.

Lamperti, Giovanni. *Vocal Wisdom: Maxims of Giovanni Battista Lamperti.* New York: Taplinger, 1957.

Reid, Cornelius. *A Dictionary of Vocal Terminology: An Analysis.* New York: Joseph Petelson, 1983.

Ristad, Eloise. *A Soprano on Her Head.* Moab, UT: Real People Press, 1982.

Sheil, Richard F. *A Singer's Manual of Foreign Language Diction.* New York: YBK Publishers, 2004.

Ware, Clifton. *Basics of Vocal Pedagogy: The Foundations and Process of Singing.* New York: McGraw Hill, 1998.

Other Dictionaries

Some big, some small, some specialty, and all helpful.

Ammer, Christine. *The Facts on File Dictionary of Music.* New York: Facts on File, 2004.

Apel, Wili, and Ralph T. Daniel. *The Harvard Brief Dictionary of Music.* New York: MJF Books, 1997.

Brooke-Hall, Peter. *Concise Dictionary of Music* (Pocket Reference). Perivale, UK: Tiger Books International, 1993.

Chambers Dictionary of Music. Edinburgh, UK: Chambers, 2007.

Cirone, Anthony J. *Cirone's Pocket Dictionary of Foreign Musical Terms.* Galesville, MD: Meredith Music Publishing, 2008.

Cummings, David, ed. *Random House Encyclopedic Dictionary of Classical Music.* New York: Random House Reference, 1997.

DeVito, Albert. *Dictionary of Music Terms and Chords*, Milwaukee, WI: Kenyon, 1995.

Elson, Louis Charles. *The New Elson's Pocket Music Dictionary.* King of Prussia, PA: Theodore Presser, 2009.

Ely, Mark C., and Amy E. Rashkin. *Dictionary of Music Education: A Handbook of Terminology.* Chicago: GIA Publications, 2004.

Feldstein, Sandy. *Alfred's Pocket Dictionary of Music.* Van Nuys, CA: Alfred, 1986.

Gallagher, Mitch. *The Music Tech Dictionary: A Glossary of Audio-Related Terms and Technologies.* Boston: Course Technology PTR, 2008.

Gilder, Eric. *Dictionary of Composers and Their Music.* Avenel, NJ: Wings Books, 1993.

Griffiths, Paul. *The New Penguin Dictionary of Music.* London: Penguin Books, 2006.

Hal Leonard Pocket Music Dictionary. New York: Hal Leonard, 1993.

Harnesberger, L. C. *Essential Dictionary of Music.* Van Nuys, CA: Alfred, 1996.

Hickman, James. *Official Contact Pages: The Music Industry Dictionary.* Atlanta: Bullet Entertainment Group, 2006.

Hitchcock, H. Wiley, and Stanley Sadie, eds. *The New Grove Dictionary of American Music.* (4 vols.) New York: Oxford University Press 2002).

Hixon, Donald L. *Music Abbreviations: A Reverse Dictionary.* Lanham, MD: Scarecrow Press, 2005.

Hubbard, W. L. *The American History and Encyclopedia of Music Dictionary*. Whitefish, MT: Kessinger Publishing, 2005.

Kennedy, Michael, and Joyce Bourne. *The Oxford Dictionary of Music*. New York: Oxford University Press, 2006.

Latham, Alison. *The Oxford Companion to Music*. New York: Oxford University Press, 2002.

———. *The Oxford Dictionary of Musical Terms*. New York: Oxford University Press, 2005.

Music Dictionary: A Pocket Reference Guide for All Musicians (Paperback Lessons). Milwaukee, WI: Hal Leonard, 2008.

Randel, Don Michael. *The Harvard Biographical Dictionary of Music*. Cambridge, MA: Harvard University Press, 1996.

———. *The Harvard Concise Dictionary of Music and Musicians*. Cambridge, MA: Harvard University Press, 2002.

Room, Adrian. *A Dictionary of Music Titles: The Origins of the Names and Titles of 3,500 Musical Compositions*. Jefferson, NC: McFarland Publishers, 2000.

Roychaudhuri, Bimalakanta. *The Dictionary of Hindustani Classical Music*. Delhi, India: Motilal Banarsidaas Publishers, 2007.

Santorella, Tony. *Santorella's Dictionary of Music Terms*. Danvers, MA: Santorella Publications, 2000.

Slonimsky, Nicolas. *Baker's Dictionary of Music*. New York: Schirmer, 1997.

———. *Webster's New World Dictionary of Music*. New York: Wiley, 1998.

Stainer, John, and William Barrett. *A Dictionary of Musical Terms*. Cambridge: Cambridge University Press, 2009.

Upshall, Michael, ed. *Hutchinson Dictionary of Classical Music (NTC Pocket Reference Series)*. Lincolnwood, IL: NTC Publishing Group, 1997.

Wadhams, Wayne. *Dictionary of Music Production and Engineering Terminology*. New York, NY: Schirmer, 1988.

Whitsett, Tim. *The Dictionary of Music Business Terms*. Vallejo, CA: ArtistPro, 1998.

Appendix B

Visual Index

Notes

Rests, Breaks

	Sixteenth rest	236
	Multi-measure rest	158
,	Breath mark	35
//	General pause (railroad tracks)	96
⌢	Fermata (pause)	85

Staff

		Page #
	Staff	245
	Bar line	20
	Double bar line	70
	Final bar	87

𝄢	*Bass clef (F clef)*	22
𝄡	*Alto clef*	8
𝄡	*Tenor clef*	259
𝄡	*Baritone clef*	21
𝄞	*Octave clef (octave below)*	172
𝄞	*Octave clef (octave above)*	172
𝄦 𝄦	*Neutral clef*	166
	Bracket	34

Articulation Marks

Ornaments

		Page #
	Trill	267
	Mordent (turn)	156
	Half mordent	105
	Appoggiatura	11
	Acciaccatura	3

Note Relationships

		Page #
	Tie	262
	Glissando	98

Repeats, Codas

D.C. al Fine	*D.C. al fine (repeat to end)*	64
Fine	*Fine (end)*	87

Tempo Marks

		Page #
Adagio ♩ = 40	*Tempo mark (metronome mark)*	258
	Time signature	262
	Common time	53
	Cut time (alla breve)	60
rall.	*Rallantando*	206
rit.	*Ritenuto, ritard (ritardando)*	215
A	*Rehearsal letter*	210

	Ossia	176

Dynamics

s*fz*	*Sforzando*	229
fp	*Fortepiano*	90
subito *p*	*Subito*	250
	Crescendo	59
	Diminuendo (decrescendo)	67

Miscellaneous

Page #

	Tacet	255
tutti	*Tutti*	272

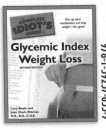
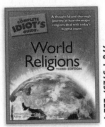

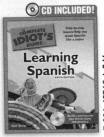

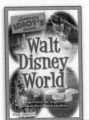